You honor me when you read my book.

Best wishes,
June Wandrey
The Bedpan Commando

BEDPAN COMMANDO

The Story of a Combat Nurse during World War II

June Wandrey

It wasn't merry

This wasn't merry either

Elmore Publishing Company

><><><><><><><><><><><><><><><><><><><><><><><><><><><><><><><><><><><><><><><><><><><><><><><

To my husband King, the diplomatic critic.

To my children Paul, Geoffrey, and Gail, who had no
comprehension of the misery and suffering of war and
thought mothers only baked banana doughnuts, mitered bed
sheets, and demanded "soldiers' shoulders".

To Jennifer and Jessica, who dressed up in Grammy's
uniforms and thought war was a game
with exciting props.

><><><><><><><><><><><><><><><><><><><><><><><><><><><><><><><><><><><><><><><><><><><><><><><

Decades after the war ended, the army sent us our 8th battle star for Anzio!

Elmore Publishing - Franklin, TN 37064
419-862-3472

Printed in the United States of America

Third Edition

ISBN 0-9625555-0-9

Contents

About
The Author

June Wandrey was born in Wautoma, Wisconsin, June 25, 1920, the daughter of Herman and Alvina Wandrey. Although she was raised by strict Methodist parents who believed that dancing, card playing and alcohol were sinful, June had a wonderful and occasionally bawdy sense of humor.

Although she stood only five feet two, June had a lifelong love for sports, particularly baseball and tennis. In a letter home she boasts of "finely honed muscles that were dynamite ready."

You can tell from her letters that she had a keen intelligence so it's not surprising to learn that she was class valedictorian of the class of 1937 at Wautoma High School. She went on to study nursing at the Kahler School of Nursing, an affiliate of the Mayo Clinic, in Rochester, Minnesota, graduating on December 1, 1941. Although she enlisted shortly after Pearl Harbor, her unit was not activated until late 1941. From 1942 to 1946 she served in the Army Nurse Corps and attained the rank of First Lieutenant and eight battle stars for campaigns in North Africa and Europe.

Battling not only the Nazis, but also hunger, exhaustion, weather, and malaria, Lieutenant Wandrey soldiered on -- working steady 18 hour days caring for the sick, the wounded, and the dying -- from theaters in North Africa, Italy, Belgium, France and Germany. Her compassion and commitment to the American soldiers dying and wounded everyday on behalf of their country, helped many of them to make it through their pain and fear.

Later she received a Bachelors of Science from the University of Wisconsin where she met Kingsley Mann who was teaching at Urbana, Illinois. Three months later they were married in her mother's home in Wautoma.

Fiercely independent, outspoken and staunchly partisan in her politics she referred to Roosevelt as, "our horrid, war-loving president" and called Truman, "Harry Ass Truman").

June said of her married years, "I was not really the domestic type. I resented giving up my maiden name. Suddenly I became the second signature on an income tax form. But we've had and are still having a happy life."

Well into her seventies, June could be seen power walking 3 miles every day, shoveling snow, or "helping" the roofers put on a new roof with a rope tied around her waist and the chimney.

It's somewhat ironic that despite her partiality for Republican politics, it was a Democratic President who paid her the honor she so deserved. She met with President Bill Clinton in Nettuno, Italy, on June 2, 1994, in commemoration of the 50th anniversary of the Anzio beachhead invasion, and again at the groundbreaking ceremony for the Women in Military Service for America at Arlington National Cemetery on June 22, 1995.

Maureen Dowd, writing for the New York Times described June as, "a 73 year old pint-sized former nurse who fought death in Sicily, Cassino, Anzio, Naples and Dachau."

"Proud that she could fit into her 51-year-old wool uniform, with eight battle stars bespeaking her heroism, June greeted the President with a saucy smile and the crisp salute of a professional."

In 1995 at Arlington, President Clinton recognized her "courage and caring" and asked her to stand up to be recognized. After doing so, Clinton couldn't help himself from adding, "And might I add, you look terrific in your uniform."

Although she died at the age of 85 in Northwood, Ohio on November 27, 2005, it was Wautoma where she belonged "I was always glad I grew up in Wautoma. My roots are there even though my feet have traveled thousands of miles."

ONE

After You Volunteer

Fort Custer was swarming with 94th Division recruits, stern-faced MPs, fly-boys from Kellogg Field, plus "Hello Girls" who usually wore white angora sweaters, which shed alluringly on the olive drab of the officers' dress uniforms.

The hospital barracks were new, with lots of fine pine knot-holes. They came in handy when the Major was doing a psychiatric examination of a patient. He'd send me into the linen closet behind my office from where I could hear the interview and understand my patients problems better.

I was assigned three wards, each holding approximately thirty GIs and a few private rooms for the sick officers. One ward was full of fellows suffering from pilonidal cysts, affectionately called Jeep Seats. It was the most cheerful ward. Each AM, when the Major and I walked in to change their dressings and check their surgery, I'd call out, "Bottoms up, fellows." Thirty plump pairs of smiling buns would turn skyward.

We had frequent inspections by people who didn't have anything better to do, but had lots of brass on their shoulders. I was told that my ward always got top honors and they wanted to keep it that way. One of the patients -- a sergeant -- was in charge of policing the kitchen. I stopped in to check on his progress and found him spitting on the drinking glasses and polishing them with a hand towel. He said it got the water spots off. It sure did.

My move towards the latrine was greeted with agonized shouts, "You can't go in there, Lieutenant, men only." But of course I did, unannounced. How else do you find out where they have been hiding the liquor they weren't permitted to have? The lineup at the urinals stopped in full stream as they stood at attention. The liquor cringed in the bottom of the waste basket, neatly covered with a folded towel. While they zippered in unison, the door opened and the room filled with GIs crowding in to see what was going to happen to their two quarts of liquor. In horror, they watched me pour the cheap rot-gut down the sink, following Army instructions and mother's WCTU training. Anguished groans accompanied the gurgling liquor on its final journey, while I opened the window to dissipate the fumes. Thirty healthy young men my age didn't dare attack a 5'2", 110 pound nurse with finely honed muscles that were dynamite ready. I marched smartly out of the room, back to my office, just in time to meet the arriving inspectors. The liquored latrine flap was never mentioned. We took top honors.

One of the male officers from the 94th Infantry refused to bare his anatomy to have his surgery checked unless I left the room. The Major, a Southern gentleman, was quite annoyed with him and ordered him to take off his pajama bottoms PDQ. After we finished the dressing and started for the door, a plaintive voice from the bed asked, "Doc, how can a guy ask a gal out to dinner if she has done his pelvic dressings?" The Major smiled, winked at me, and said, "Do you want to make a bet?"

Johnny and Fritz were my special wardmen. They were plugging for my promotion and went around collecting silver bars from any officer patient who had just made Captain. Eventually, they sent me a whole box full. I covered the bars with clear fingernail polish to keep the metal from tarnishing; I knew my hair would turn silver in this man's Army before my bars did.

They used to say that the Army signed up any enlistee for the infantry, if his body was warm to the touch. Such a new recruit in his thirties was promptly hospitalized on one of my wards. At morning inspection, his bed was wet and I ordered him to change his sheets. Turning back, I saw him exchanging his soiled bottom sheet for his top sheet. To him, that was changing it. The Army sent him back home immediately.

Back at the nurses' barracks 3172, some hospital officers asked me to make a recording at the Red Cross Club of a parody they had written about a much disliked fellow officer. It was to be sung to the tune of an Irving Berlin song. It started out," I'm a Son of Heaven .... and I throw smiles where ere I go. I've got the rank but plenty.....so what....etc." As fast as I made the recordings, they were passed around the post. Shortly after, I was ordered to report for overseas duty.

But before I left, my Air Force friend, the General's pilot, took me flying over Lake Michigan and let me take over the controls. I'd swoop down to the shipping on the lake, looking for the Wm. A. Reiss -- the ship my brother was working on for the season. Never did find it. Chiefy met us at the barrack's door in her nighty, hair all done up in braids, to inform us it was illegal for nurses to fly. I agreed not to fly anymore.

Grounded, we went to the Officer's Club, my three-inch-heel, non-regulation dancing shoes in my date's overcoat pocket. He was very tall and I was very short. The Infantry officers weren't very happy to see the Air Force in their domain so they started cutting in. Irritated, my friend went to the phone and called the motor pool, "General....... is ready for his car." When it arrived, the sergeant driver looked at us, with a twinkle in his eye, and said "Good evening, General, and where would you and your lady like to go?"

2-2-43 Battle Creek, Mich.
Dearest family,

By the time you get this I will be well on my way overseas. You'll be getting a huge package of clothes by freight. Please dry clean them and pack them away. Give the shoes, hunting boots, sweaters, and riding breeches to Ruth. Put the rest in my cedar chest 'til I come home.

I'm okay and happy that at last I'm leaving. I was so tired of explaining to venomous people that I enlisted shortly after Pearl Harbor and was in the Mayo unit, which had not activated yet. Besides that I was too young to be in the Army Nurse Corps; you had to be 22 years old. They need surgical nurses so badly. Congratulations on your wedding anniversary March 8th. Some day I'll get you a nice gift, but at present I need all the money I have kept here. I make less than half the money I earned in Rochester. As of January 1, we get $171.00 a month and $21.00 of that is subsistence. I can't believe that where I'm going that I'll have much to eat or that it's fit to eat. Keep my leaving a secret until you hear from me again. If you'd buy some

V-mail stationery to write to me, I'd get my mail faster as it doesn't run the risk of being sunk by torpedoes. I'll write often if I can find some paper. Be sure and have a new innerspring mattress on granddad's antique bed when I get back. Could we have chop suey with bean sprouts for supper?

Tell Ruth to behave, get good marks, be valedictorian, and to write to the soldiers from her class. Hope Bud makes the grade as a pilot. 'Til I see you all again, all my love. Your littlest tomboy, June

On February 20, 1943, I'd fought my last battle at Fort Custer and with four cohorts started on the nightmarish trek to Camp Kilmer. Uncle Sam's orders had said "Be at Kilmer, February 21, 1943" and we planned to obey. For endless hours, we chugged through this barren snow-swept field and around the next, cementing foreign relations with the Canadians.

One of my cohorts, a gorgeous blonde nurse and a dead-ringer for Marlene Dietrich, refused to check her mammoth piece of luggage, just purchased at the Custer PX, because it contained a beautiful mirror she wanted to take intact to Africa. Whether she planned on frightening the spear-carrying natives with it or if she planned to join the Signal Corps, I never found out. Because of it, our progress was cut to a snail's pace.

We scurried for the powder room to change into pajamas before the midnight rush came. Our reservations had called for all lowers, but somehow two of the nurses had to take uppers. Our Kate Smith duplicate with the big Eddie Cantor eyes fell lot to an upper. Not all black porters will go to heaven, but the one in our car will because chubby got caught beam-side-to and he had to hoist and shove. Soon sleep pulled its mantle over the car as it rumbled eastward.

With the break of dawn, there lay New Joisey in her bed of mud. We struggled aboard the trolley for New Brunswick and a future into which we couldn't peek because God was holding all the strings. Looking like frowsy, frumpy quintuplets, we wobbled into the local post office and asked a Bronx-type MP to tell Kilmer we had arrived. Every time we questioned the MP, he assured us they'd call for us in half-an-hour. For hours plus, we sat propped on our makeup kits, watching people mail their letters. We began to think perhaps President Roosevelt was personally coming to see us off or that if they ignored us long enough we'd go away because we looked so bedraggled.

Finally, a multi-seated, olive-drab contraption drove up and a cocky little sergeant unlimbered himself from behind the wheel and gave us the once over. "My Gawd," he said, "no wonder they send them overseas." We ignored his questionable greeting and clambered into his vehicle, trusting to his sense of duty to take us to the proper place. En route, he gave us a thumbnail sketch of hell-in-mud and regulations called Kilmer. Through the mud-spattered windows, rows of weirdly camouflaged buildings separated by ankle-deep, wet, red clay greeted us. I think that the song "Show Me the Way to go Home" was written for just such a moment.

Our room, if that's what you could call it, had a number -- 1169, just like prison -- two occupants, a floor, a roof, two army cots, a window, and no door. What more could I possibly want? The latrine was only one mile down the corridor left-hand side and last door. I'd get my turn at latrine detail. Best to sign up on the bulletin board and pick Saturday if I wanted Sunday off for something special. I secretly thought of trying to evade the issue. Who wanted latrine hands?

The rain God was kind. He sent his blessing every day to lubricate the mud. The PX with its Nestlé bars and malteds was worth the slippery trip. No passes were permitted, so the bright lights of New York were only a myth. I could go to the PX and to the Officer's Club and dance to the jukebox and drink Coca-Cola. Kilmer reeked with secrecy. Some days, you were permitted to call your love long distance, while the operator sat and sighed with her ear glued to the receiver ready to cut you off if you gave out any sailing information or the name of your present station. Meals were an event. The mess line, four persons wide, extended down the street a block from the mess door. In zero weather with my feet firmly anchored in cold mud, I stood and waited and waited -- sometimes three-quarters of an hour. Everything went on one dish. My first meal was a plate of peach sauce with a big glob of creamed spinach on top. Eating this awful mess with only a knife was a real problem, apparently forks had been left out of the requisition.

The day I met our male officers for the first time is burned on my brain. I was shell-shocked before I left the States. The Mayo Clinic was never like this, I thought. Here was this mixture of alphabetical soup: DDSs, MDs, MACs, National Guardites, WWI retreads, and Army Reserve grab-baggers, and one jovial, recently graduated MD-- all jockeying for promotions. They had been feuding and drinking in the southwest for months, waiting for the overseas call and had just completed ten-day furloughs at home. Though also officers, the nurses had no furloughs and were discriminated against in treatment

10

and in salary. Our Chief nurse had generously supplied them with our personal description: age, height, weight, college education and photograph. Too bad she didn't give us forewarning and their dossier. Fair is fair.

Eighteen nurses were assigned to our unit from different army posts. We were not assigned according to any special fitness for combat duty or for nursing specialties. Most had been in the Army a very short time, had no training in Army discipline, rules, and regulations nor been trained for combat nursing. We had to purchase men's heavy underwear, fatigues and raincoats. When issued my huge heavy bedroll, I filled it with large-sized bars of Wrisley's pine soap from the PX, Kotex, plus three dozen Birdseye baby diapers for when the Kotex ran out. With 55,000 volunteer nurses in the military and subject to overseas duty at any time, the required purchase of the three dozen diapers created a shortage in USA. The usual soldier's issue of combat equipment and clothing, impregnated against gas, was also issued to me in men's sizes. One year later, I was issued the proper women's clothing in this category.

Some of us made recordings at the Red Cross to send to our boy friends so that long after we were gone they could listen to our cheerful patter. Despite the inconveniences, we continued to live unto that day for which we had come so far.

New York postmark on letter 3-2-43
Dear family:
I had a bad accident at Camp Kilmer. One of our new male officers called me for a date after apparently going over the nurse's photographs. I didn't know who he was and told him that he should bring another officer and I would bring my roommate. We just went for a walk. It was very icy and the ground was frozen in mud spikes. The other couple was walking ahead of us and I wanted to talk to them, but he didn't want me to talk to anyone but to him. Weird. So I started to run to get away from him, but he caught the buckle to my coat belt that was flying out behind me as I ran. He yanked on it so hard that I fell to the ground landing on my left hip on a spear of ice. In the morning my hip to my knee was one pitch-black-and-blue hematoma. I never spoke to him again. The Chief Nurse looked at it and said "It looks like it hurts." Actually it's throbbing forty per.

Did you get my letters and my telegram and the cedar chest key? I haven't heard from you for weeks. Is someone on a writer's strike around there? If I should wire any money home, put it in bonds for me. What's the home-town scandal? Do write soon. Much love, June

TWO

On the Way to War

In my Mainbocher-designed blue dress uniform and winter coat, my pistol belt around my waist carrying a canteen of fresh water, gas mask slung under my left arm, musette bag loaded with feminine essentials resting on my bosom, musette bag strapped on my back filled with impregnated clothing, in my left hand my blanket roll and pup tent secured in a neat little bundle, in my right hand a suitcase, and on my head a steel helmet......I marched slowly down the road to the troop train. Hut-two-three-four! Hut-two-three-four! Thousands of tense GIs with full packs were marching from every direction to the same train. From somewhere a loud speaker poured out stirring march music. God bless Sousa. It brought tears to my eyes, a catch to my throat, and somehow my packs all of a sudden didn't feel so heavy. The March 4th breezes played havoc with the Stars and Stripes, but it held its head high and so did I. My future looked grim for the tasks ahead. I was a volunteer.

I munched candy bars while the train took me to my destination. Now and then, someone would break out into song. The enlisted men played poker, and small fortunes were won and lost.

The ferry stood waiting, tugging at its mooring. I marched on and found a seat by the window. Next stop Staten Island. Everyone off. The ships were being loaded. White soldiers and black soldiers went up the gang plank in a steady stream, shouting out their first names as they passed the officer holding the passenger list. The cold was unmerciful. It bit through the innumerable layers of clothing I wore. My pack cut into my shoulders. There was no place to sit down. High-ranking army officials ran here and there in a dither. Hurry -- hurry -- hurry! Finally, my turn came to load. It was an effort to walk with my heavy pack. I'd had it on for six hours. Did they expect me to walk up that slanting gang plank loaded to the hilt? Yes, they did and I did.

The day of chivalry had passed. No one offered to help me with my luggage. C'est la guerre! The 19th amendment to the Constitution had given me the right to vote, but not to be pampered. Okay ...lady carry your load, you're on your way to war.

Four to a stateroom meant two upper bunks and two lowers. Prewar they accommodated only two people. The old Santa Elena had once been a luxury liner carrying movie kings and queens on peaceful, pleasure-filled cruises to South America.

More nurses and doctors had joined our unit, some had been placed on the Shawnee to operate the hospital en route. Twelve nurses to approximately three thousand men were on our ship. If Cleopatra could have known the odds she would have crawled out of her tomb and joined us. The poor GIs were in the hold of the ship, packed in like sardines.

3-4-43

Dearest family:

I got your most welcome letter just before we started our march to the train. We were loaded to the gills with equipment and we marched to music. It was all very thrilling. My past went through my mind's eye in a flash. Before I knew it, I was on a ferry, then up a ship's gangplank without a backward glance. If I would have looked back I would have lost my balance and fallen in the dirty harbor water. As the Statue of Liberty faded from view I traded my gas mask, pistol belt and musette bags for a life jacket, which then became my security blanket. Four of us share a stateroom, like bugs in a rug. I'll try to write you a line each day. Good night, June

At 5 AM the following morning, the starting of the engines awakened me. Huge battleships and assorted destroyers escorted our convoy out into the awesome Atlantic. The ship began to rock and roll. We were off, no turning back now. I wore a tunnel between my bunk and the latrine the first twenty four hours. Mostly bloody retching. The only consolation I had was that I was not alone in my misery. The ship's surgeon recommended a turn about the deck to overcome my seasickness. Some MP offered to help me navigate. We got to the rail. I took one look at the rest of the convoy spread out as far as the eye could see, about ninety ships, and tried to concentrate on our smoke stack and forget that it was jitter-bugging. Matter triumphed over mind and I just made the latrine in time. Someone slipped me a sedative and when I came out of it I had my sea legs...sorta.

Romances flourished and were no respecter of rank. 2nd Lieutenants, also called Shavetails, are more popular socially. Russian Bank, hearts, poker and bridge were worked out to a science. Impromptu skits put on by the enlisted men kept us in stitches. The nurses set up emergency supplies and rotated working in surgery on the ship. We cared for surgical and medical patients. Moth-eaten and time-mellowed movies played several times a week. Mostly we saw "Casablanca" and took the hint. Abandon ship drills, fire drills and air raid alerts at any time of the day or night kept us very attentive. Our life belts were a must -- like a puppies tail they were always with us.

Webster hasn't thought of a word to adequately describe the meals and the service. Each delicious meal lingers in my memory. My lifeboat mate, a connoisseur of good food, rolled her eyes and said "Something must be up, such good food, is it our last meal before the killing?" At that very instant, the blackout signal pierced the silence, forgetting that it wasn't abandon ship, she grabbed the huge steak from her plate, and started crawling into her life jacket dripping gravy. She also kept lipstick, mascara, red Revlon nail polish, and large chocolate bars in the crevices. Life in a small lifeboat couldn't be too bad with a steak tucked in the pocket of your jacket.

Our life boat crew could have stepped from the pages of "Mutiny on the Bounty." We shivered every time we thought of spending time with them in the same life boat, being tossed about for days. The Merchant Marine in charge of our boat would shout out names and the crewmen would call out their particular duty. When the Merchant Marine finished the list, crewmen all repeated after him in broken English "Remember, women and children first."

3-5-43 At sea and sick.

Terribly seasick; in bed all day; vomited repeatedly. Don't care if we get torpedoed, would almost welcome it.

3-6-43 Feeling 100% better this AM. Explored the ship. Looked over the rest of the convoy through field glasses and got acquainted with some war correspondents, men from the Office of War Information, Lend Lease officials, P-38 pilots, and Infantry officers. The ocean is beautiful, the waves are terrific. We're having a movie tonight.

All the decks were crowded with kibitzers, sunbathers and the ones with chronic seasickness during the day and far into the night. Sun up and sun down, moon up and moon down were never to be forgotten sights. Once a school of flying fish went through their paces for our amusement. Dolphins kept racing us. A daily scandal sheet was put out by the war correspondents aboard. OWI officials and dark-skinned Lend Lease men attempted to look important and nonchalant during the trip.

Three men approached me on deck looking for a fourth to play bridge. One was a society doctor from out East. One was a professional gambler from Las Vegas, now with the infantry. One was an OWI official. I told them I had never played cards, my parents considered it a sin. Laughing uproariously they said that was okay. They would teach me, and then we would play for a penny a point. You learn fast that way. I asked Mr. OWI how come he was so sharp at bridge. He said he had spent twenty years with a government agency in Paris and played bridge most of the time. I told him that I thought that was why we were going to war, because they had been playing bridge instead of eaves-dropping.

Sometimes we zigged and sometimes we zagged, that way it took us longer to reach our destination. Apparently it was the safest way to go. They'd drop ash-cans whenever submarines were in our area and the whole ship would shudder. It's frightening and I never get used to it. We had our first burial at sea, a member of the crew died of heart failure. They draped him with a flag and slipped his body down the plank into the ocean.

3-7-43 We had religious services in shifts on deck this morning to accommodate all the soldiers. I also had my first bath in hot water-- one helmet-full of hot fresh water. What a luxury. Then you do your laundry in it before you throw it out. We wear our life belts at all times, except when sleeping, and then we have them loosely attached to our bunks. We wear slacks and shirts.

3-8-43 Today I worked in the dispensary, giving shots. So many interesting things happen, but I can't write about them. I'll just tuck them away in my elephant memory.

3-16-43 Sorry I skipped a few days in between, the days vary little. I dreamed about home and fresh raspberry pie. Just as I was about to take a bite of it, someone woke me up to go on duty. I'm still wondering what it tasted like. I'd love to get my feet on land again.

3-17-43 This wasn't like any other St. Patrick's day in my lifetime. Destination unknown. Subs had chased us and ash-cans had plagued us. Tonight's menu: grilled filet mignon, roast stuffed Vermont turkey, cranberries, poached halibut with hollandaise sauce, relishes, French onion soup, garden peas, fresh asparagus, French fried and mashed potatoes, hearts of lettuce, ice cream, French pastry, fresh fruit, cheese crackers and coffee. Chief Steward Joseph Fiorello made a permanent taste impression on me.

After this fabulous meal, I returned to sick bay, down in the bowels of the ship, to be with a crew member dying of meningitis and pneumonia. The abandon ship signal sounded. I started to prepare him to be evacuated. He and I waited for what seemed an eternity. No one came down to check on us. I couldn't leave my post and my dying patient. My heart nearly stopped. I kept praying it was only another drill as I felt I was too young to go down with the ship. Before the all-clear finally sounded, I had aged decades.

As the first streaks of dawn cut the sky, the morning of the 17th, the convoy split. Part of it went to Casablanca. It was like seeing your best friend leave as the destroyers and mighty battleships dipped over the horizon. Several spunky little English corvettes popped up and proudly said, "We are your escort through the Straits of Gibraltar".

It was getting dusk as we sighted land for the first time. We could see faint lights glistening like fireflies along the rugged shore line. I think everyone even the atheists said a prayer of thanks. Gibraltar held out her hand in welcome as we silently slid through her portals. All the next day we searched the shoreline with powerful field glasses. Arabs in turbans and droopy drawers slouched along the coast on their aimless way. Rocks and sand and an occasional disabled Allied ship cluttered the land-seascape. The Mediterranean was awash with orange peelings, floating fruit crates, and other litter. We'd been told that "A Slip of the Lip Can Sink a Ship"...but this flagrant floating garbage certainly heralded our coming.

3-18-43 Four o'clock and chow time found us weaving our way into the beautiful harbor at Oran. To the right, a mountain rose majestically above the deep blue of the Mediterranean. Perched on the side was an ancient monastery, which had been used as a fortress in the invasion. Below it, jutting out so it could see and be seen, was the beautiful Belvedere Hotel. A huge Singer sewing machine sign loomed over on the right, in sharp contrast to the drab surroundings. The big city at the foot of the mountain was quiet. Piles of supplies waiting to be moved to the troops dwarfed the bevy of little beggar children looking for chewing gum and chocolate. Many of the children were crippled, some blind, and all swathed in dirty rags.

As our ship scraped against the wharf, we hung over the railings and waved to the American and French soldiers who were there to greet us. Shouts floated up to us, "Fresh from the States? What do Cokes and ice cream taste like? Do you have any chocolate bars?" Outstretched arms came up to catch the boxes of candy we threw to them. Disappointment crossed every face as the order came that we couldn't disembark 'til the morrow. We spent the evening and until the wee hours saying goodbye to the many friends we had made in crossing. What was our future? How long would any of us live?

Hurried farewells the next morning and then I found myself gingerly touching African soil with my toe, the other nurses impatiently waiting behind me. We piled into ambulances and were whisked through the ancient streets. A French officer hopped off his bicycle and urinated. A few dogs and chickens blocked our path, and several screaming dirty little Arabs dashed in our way. Persistent honking cleared the roughly paved streets, and we were on our way out of the odor-filled city. Someone had opened the pages of history, and we were back in the Dark Ages. Did people actually live in such filth, squalor, and ignorance? Begging was a science here. The children ate out of the garbage pails in the cities, and the French policemen beat a tattoo on their heads when they caught them. Pathetic cripples dragged themselves about shining shoes. The minute a vehicle stops, these tragic beggars clamber over it and you, grasping for anything in sight to eat or wear. Allez-vite! at the top of your voice is supposed to clear the area, but they come back in hordes. Their ragged filth tears at your heart.

The country air was sweet and clean. We turned into a muddy

very rutty road at high speed. One minute you were sitting on the seat, the next minute you were on the ambulance floor. Vineyards abounded on either side of the road. There, between two vineyards, was our bare rocky home called Lizard Ledge by the nurses and Vinc Hill by the men. It was here we began our gypsy-like existence. North Africa wasn't exactly fun-country for camping in 1942-43, but that's all the T.O. called for our heal-and-move-on field hospital. The mer weren't too clever when pitching our original tent-city, but they were eager and willing.

Eighteen trip-weary nurses huddled into one large ward tent with cot-to-cot carpeting. Bivouacking they called it. Our enlisted mer put up their pup tent city on the far side of the hill. Other medica units were already here and more kept coming as the older groups moved out and up to the front lines.

We were promptly told what prices we should pay for such services as laundry or produce and not to exceed that limit. Americans always wrecked the local economy by over paying for everything. The Arabs offered you $20.00 for a sheet or a barracks bag, $10.00 for an old pair of shoes.

I'd called a strike against a soldier in the 13th Armored while I was umpiring a softball game between his outfit and our wee field hospital. He shouted at me, "You're nothing but a BEDPAN COM-MANDO like all Army nurses." How wrong he was, how misinformed Maybe he said this because my call was in favor of the humble, mis-understood, soon to be over-worked medics. His words are burned on my brain.

3-18-43 *Somewhere in North Africa*
Dearest family,
    When you write, make your letters yeah long so it takes me a week to read them. Perhaps you read about us landing. I was the first person off the ship. Love, June

June 3-22-43 Somewhere in North Africa
Dear family,
    I just finished transplanting a beautiful wild flower garden in front of my tent. The plants came from the hillside, daisies, poppies, crocus, ferns, gorgeous maroon violets, and other nameless beauties.
    My ancient French, taught to me at the University of Wisconsin by a Polish Professor with a thick accent, comes in handy when talking to the

18

Arabs and French natives. They come out around the camp selling oranges and lemons. We wondered if they'd been stolen. I trade my cigarette ration for fresh fruit. Combat troops get a free pack a week. Otherwise they cost five cents a package if you could find some. The doctors are annoyed that I don't give my ration to them. You've never dreamed of such poverty and filth in all your life. I worked in the slums of Chicago and the stockyards clinic area and that was bad, but this is 100% worse.

Our newest beggar today was a little six- year-old girl with a baby strapped to her back. They were covered with lice. I itch thinking about them.

My size 4 1/2 shoes are wearing out. All I can get are men's size five, with constant standing, I can feel my feet spreading out to fill them. The smallest men's fatigues are size 36. Heaven help this little shrimp. With a small needle from my Red Cross kit, I laboriously took 12 inches out of the waist and put in a 'drop' seat. It's like sewing on leather with a fine embroidery needle. At least the seat is up now where it belongs. It used to hit me in my popliteal space and, if your fatigues were wet, it felt like you were a toddler with a soggy diaper. I was tired of toileting myself along the roadside without the luxury of a drop seat. With fatigues down, you were as good as nude. It never failed, some jeep would come along and a happy extrovert GI would call out "Hi Lieutenant, how you-all doin' honey?" Time was always a factor, it took me a while to check for land mines first or booby traps. The engineers always put up signs that said MINES SWEPT TO DITCHES.

My Red Cross sewing kit is 9 1/4" long x 4 3/4" wide made of some olive drab plastic kind of material. It has three folds in it. On the middle fold is a small piece of olive drab felt, in that are some needles and a few safety pins. There are two pockets in it. On the cover it says GIFT OF AMERICAN RED CROSS and under that Pat. US Army and a number. Why clutter up the patent office with that one?

We eat out of our mess kits, outside, sitting or standing, whichever you prefer. We have something like a marinade called ALLEY SLOP, that's the actual commercial name. If you pour it on anything that you are lucky enough to get to eat, I think it kills the wild life that might be in it. What I wouldn't do for a case of ice cold Coca-Cola.

The nurses easily talked me into foraging for some grapes in the vineyards as they hadn't seen any natives working there and thought the grapes were going to rot. We were really hungry. I took my galvanized laundry pail and bandage scissors and headed for the vineyard. Being so short was an advantage I thought, as no one would observe me. Just when I had my pail full of grapes a sheet-clothed very angry Arab materialized out of nowhere.

He had a knife and started shouting at me. He ran, I ran, but I ran faster a
I was wearing pants. Never dropping a grape I managed to reach the safet
of our compound. I felt like I was stealing a base in a ball game back home
But this was real stealing. The Arab was so mad, I was afraid to give th
grapes back. Whether they believe in forgiving and forgetting I don't know
Please, say an extra prayer for me tonight. A scared, June

March 27, 1943 Our first air raid alarm today.
          Whenever I complained to the Quartermaster corps about th•
fit of clothing for small nurses, they'd laugh and say, "A few mor•
weeks of daily C rations and you'll fill out the pleats." "Sammy, yot
made the pants too long" is one of my favorite songs.

Ration C

Ye sons of Epicurus,
Who in worldly joys delight
Come, gather around the mess tent,
We've a special treat tonight;
And ere we've licked our mess kits clean
In mirthful revelry,
We'll drink a dehydrated toast
To the ration men call "C",

Oh, there are those who turn their nose
And call it hardly fare;
They murmur of the dishes
Their mothers would prepare.

Don't point accusing fingers
At our subject's ancestry,
Nor call it in less kindly words
A "hybrid potpourri."
Graven there upon the can
For everyone to see
In letters black on field of gold
Is writ the pedigree.
A glorious list of forebears
Sired the ration men call "C".

T-4 *Ira H. Stein (Stars & Stripes)*
Ira, the nurses had another name for that ration. A medical dictionary refused to list our description.

3-28-43 One hour air raid tonight. My raincoat got liberated or lost. Now all it does is rain so I wear a shelter-half commuting to and from the mess tent and latrine.

3-30-43 Africa...had our pictures taken today in our tents for Mediteranean Base Section. However, we have no proof.

Dear Betty,

Twice in one week we crawled out of our mannish garb into wrinkled dress uniforms and were herded like cattle into a two and half ton truck for the dances at the Red Cross in Oran.

Fortunately, on one of these soirees, I met a high ranking British naval officer who had been cruising in the Pacific for many months. He greeted me with open arms and great enthusiasm. Not a typical British welcome. I thought perhaps it was because I was white, young, had had a bath, didn't chew gum, and spoke fluent English. Actually, he was carrying a large cargo of Kotex, but had never met any young women who might want it. I offered to exchange the Birdseye diapers for them as they should come in handy for polishing brass on a ship, but he was just happy to get them out of the hold. Not all of my conversations at dances were as practical as this one was. The whole episode was delightfully funny.

Sometimes, you could dance as many as three steps with the same officer before the stag line moved in like turbulent surf. The music was good, the company very entertaining. And don't think for a minute it wasn't charmin'-- cause it was. The men were either on their way to the front or had just returned.

I keep bumping into many old friends from the States like our milk-man's son. He was in the Navy and had been in the Pacific for ages. This was his first shore leave. I was the first American woman he saw. Now that's sweet-cream.

Our one luxury is the open air shower. The Air Corps would buzz the area daily. We had difficulty in changing the shower hour often enough to avoid those peeping playboys. I often wondered if one of our GIs sold that information to the Air Corps.

We had one redheaded character from Brooklyn who brought his jeweler's eyeglass and was constantly stopping the natives to buy their

rings off from their hands or out of their ears. I often thought he might ask
for the gold from their teeth. He disappeared from the ranks of our enlisted
men shortly after that. Was he done in by a client? Another possibility is
that the CO shipped him off to the ranks of a litter bearer at the front. Their
life expectancy was limited.

One day we decided not to shower in the jerry-rigged shower, instead
we would all stay in the ward tent and take a PTA--bath from our helmets.
PTA is short for Privates, Tits and Axillae. One of our jolly nurses made
that one up so the men wouldn't know what we were talking about. Water
was a very precious commodity. You could really milk the usefulness out of
a helmetful of water. First you brushed your teeth, then you washed your
hair, your body, and gave your underwear a soak. Depending on the density
of the water by then you could throw it out or use it to wash the mud off from
your boots.

Visualize eighteen nude, unacquainted women, assorted sizes, shapes,
and varying from twenty plus years in age, all sitting cross-legged on a 100%
scratchy wool horse-blanket on top of a tippy-narrow-army-cot with four
rocks holding a round-bottomed helmetful of cold water between their legs.
It's dark in the tent, it's Africa-hot --- you soap the body beautiful lightly.

Suddenly there is the sound of the shower-spy-plane flying very,
very low toward the tent. Apparently the spy-pilot found we were not in the
shower and in his angry-fly-away inadvertently clipped off the top of the tent
pole and the whole shebang collapsed on all these heavenly bodies. The GIs
screamed and came running to help us. We nurses screamed and grabbed
our tiny bath towels. Love, June.

4-2-43 We're assigned to 5th Army with General Mark Clark.

4-12-43 Somewhere in North Africa
Dear family,

I'm propped on an old tin can outside the tent, sleeves rolled past my
elbows, trying to answer thirty, month-old letters that just arrived. I shared
them with everyone as many didn't get any. Mother, the fellows think you
have beautiful penmanship. As long as your daughter was born with verbal
diarrhea, expect many letters when I have the time and paper. It's nice I don't
have to pay postage.

Got a letter from my first-grade teacher, the one who had all those
ugly pugs of hair. Because I talked so much, remember how she used to make
me sit with Emma in the bench seat. Emma always wet her pants, and that
seat was like a trough. It's debatable whether I answer her letter she was so

mean to me.

When I catch some more rainwater I'm going to wash my dress uniform. Today I bought some handmade goatskin purses from the Arabs. If I find some paper and string, I'll send them to you. You'll be the only woman at the WCTU and Red Cross with a goatskin purse. We're so desperate for something to read that we read the labels on cans. What I wouldn't do for a subscription to the Argus; at least it is written in English. Thinking in French is difficult.

Sunday afternoon and evening a few of us went to the city to a mammoth cathedral to hear "La Passion" the Easter story. Hundreds of people jammed the seats. Gorgeous stained glass windows let the sun stream through and paint prisms everywhere. Many refugees were dressed in the last of their Parisian finery. Their jewelry is about all they salvaged in their frightened dash across the country.

There were four adult soloists and a large choir of small boys with high soprano voices, all robed in black garments with huge white collars. I wanted to get up and sing with them. All the while the sacred concert was in progress, a quaint, elderly bearded priest, swathed in robes of many colors, baptized innumerable little babies. The whole family would follow the mother down the aisle. They have huge families. The concert lasted three hours. I had dead-enditis from sitting still that long. In the middle of the program, a priest preached a sermon in French. I understood about every fifth word. If they didn't talk so fast, I could comprehend most everything.

En route to the concert, we stopped for pictures in a poppy sprinkled field. Although Camp Kilmer ordered everyone to send cameras home our Chief Nurse and Colonel brought theirs.

Everywhere you turn, you see small, badly crippled children with congenital defects. They hop around on one leg and a stick.

They tried to teach us how to march this week. Why would a nurse have to know how to march? It just wears out your shoe soles. Mine are shot already and for sometime I've been wearing my Daniel Green bedroom slippers. On these rocks and in a constant blackout it is really dangerous.

Today, my Italian wardman asked me to cut his hair. He figures I'm real handy with bandage scissors. Lucky Dad let me watch him cut the hoboes' hair when they came for a meal and some clothing during the Depression. One of our nurses asked me to cut her hair too as her old dye-jobs were growing out and looked horrid. She sat outside on a wooden box. The wind came in gusts and each time I started to cut the hair blew in all directions. She looked like the shady lady from Shinglesville. I don't permit any kibitzing while I cut hair. Laughing by the audience is okay. Love, June

4-14-43 A new convoy of 90 ships arrived today via Bermuda.

The nights are bitter cold and I slept in my woolen uniform, boots and all. I had three woolen blankets, which I made into an envelope-fold around me. Still, lizards found their way in and frequently run up the inside of my pants leg. The first time it happened, I was almost hysterical -- couldn't find my flashlight to investigate.

A GI from the lst Armored told me that he and his buddy drove a truck to keep vehicles gassed. One day when they were driving down the road, they spied a clothesline filled with nurse's lingerie. His buddy stopped the truck, ran out and sniffed the whole row of underwear. He was so preoccupied he failed to notice that standing at the end of the line was a Major ready to have a bloody fit. He beat a very hasty retreat.

4-19-43

Dear Family,

No mail for ages, the postal department sent it to a hospital hundreds of miles from here. We got a GI Victrola and six records. It's our only entertainment. Could you buy me a popular swing record? Wrap it well, be sure it doesn't weigh over eight ounces. Anything over that you need special permission from the Colonel to present to your postal office. The Colonel's mustache matches his personality--it's just like Hitler's. If there's space, tuck in a small silk head scarf. Riding in the back of a 2 1/2 ton truck wrecks your hair, with too much sun, wind, rain, and dirt.

Our mail is so strictly censored, at least twice a week they impose a new restriction on what we can write about. As it is for our own protection I don't mind, but it sure makes my letters dull. In my bedroll I will try and save dates, names and places of events so that I can tell you about it after the war.

This afternoon it started to pour. I ran out to let the tent sides down and loosen the ropes. Then some of us stripped and put on raincoats and ran out to wash our hair. We just got nicely soaped when the rain stopped. Water is very scarce here. It is so heavily chlorinated it makes me ill to drink it. Most everyone got diarrhea from it. Love, June

4-19-43 Ate dinner aboard a battleship in Oran as guest of Lt. James Lindeman Jr. and Lt. Commander Harris. They gave me a new water can filled with fresh water to keep. For me it was a gift of life. The GIs call me the two canteen kid.

4-20-43 North Africa
Dearest Family,

You've never seen such queer weather. One minute it rains while the sun shines through it all. Then it turns cloudy, and it doesn't rain. The soldiers took one of the dirty little Arab boys that comes here to beg for food, unwound the sheets and rags from around him, stuck him under the shower and scrubbed him 'til he shone. The poor kid looked so confused. Too bad they didn't have something clean to put back on him.

We got an old Methodist hymnal today. The older nurses are reading the marriage ceremony over and getting a good laugh. Aging rapidly, Love, June

4-22-43 Somewhere in North Africa
The following is an Army-prepared letter for us to send to our Mothers.
Dearest Mother:

Although a vast distance separates us on this Mother's Day, somehow or other we seem very close together. It is impossible to go to the corner drugstore and buy a card or a box of candy, or go to the florist and have a beautiful bouquet of flowers sent to you, yet I want to let you know that you are uppermost in my thoughts on this Mother's Day. Thus far we have been fortunate and have reached this land safely. Some of us are learning to trust God as we have not done before. As we work and serve here, it is with confidence that in time we shall again be at home with our loved ones. May God bless you and keep you in his love and care.

A Prayer for Mother
O Lord, when meting out Thy blessings
Day by Day,
Forget not her, whose earthly tasks
Within her own four walls, must lay,
Whose workworn hands, so willing yet
　　To serve,
Can never rest, nor from a duty swerve;
Whose calm and steadfast heart,
Through countless years
Must stifle all life's hurts and bitter tears,
Whose thoughts and dreams, which on occasion
　　Yearn
Toward other paths, will ever
To her home return.
Whose spirit, filled with her abiding love

Can ev'n in time of trial, rise above,
To her, whose footsteps tread the humble way,
O Lord, accord Thy Blessings day by day.

- Le Cigne

Devotedly, June

En route to front in Algiers, 8 day convoy

THREE

The Road to Bizerte

4-25-43

Dearest Family,

While the Easter parade did Fifth Avenue, we picked our creaking bones up from the hard earth, splashed water in our faces and decked ourselves out in fatigues and little Abners. Leaving Assi-Ameur, we were ready to start by truck and ambulance convoy across North Africa to the fighting front.

Our Colonel said it would take many days and women would make a few complications in a military convoy such as ours, but we'd iron the problems out as they arose. The latrine screen came first on the list. Fate put this major detail in the hands of an old bachelor doctor who is always slightly tipsy. The convoy took a ten-minute break every two hours. The Captain was supposed to bustle about and find a logical, isolated spot for the screen. But our first stop found us without a screen on a barren plain. Some things just can't wait. The men were ordered to turn their backs while we went. Then we turned our backs while they went. Modesty flew farther away with each passing mile. Necessity took precedence.

At lunch time today my thoughts turned frequently to you. We had cold meat and beans out of a C ration can at the roadside. I cannot recognize the flavor and texture of the meat. Perhaps it was left over from WWI, like the cases of adhesive tape that didn't have any stickum on the back. We have tried heating the tape gently but it doesn't work. Some crooked wholesaler made a killing on that sale. Writing in a bobbing ambulance isn't exactly easy. Easter bonnets and such are far from our minds.

We saw our first wire fence today. Otherwise they plant trees or cactus for fences. Olives, figs, oranges are all along the way. There is always a screaming horde of dirty, starving children running alongside begging for food and candy. Half of them are nude. The scraps of food we leave behind, they fight over, pick it up from the filthy earth, and eat it. Hungrily, they run their tiny fingers around the inside of our near-empty C ration cans. I can't bear to eat in front of starving children. But we must. Today we rode for 13 hours and, believe me, the hard ground felt mighty good when we camped for the night. We bivouacked at Afreville in the village park, Oran Province. American women are a great curiosity. The moment we stop the crowd thickens. Some day, we may start charging admission just to look. Then it's up and away again at the break of dawn after a piping hot breakfast.

My neck got disjointed trying to see out of the ambulance window. Nine nurses and their luggage in an ambulance is impossible, inhumane. To keep us amused, I started everyone singing and the only songs we knew in common were Protestant hymns. Rock of Ages, Blest Be the Tie That Binds, and Onward Christian Soldiers were our favorites. I call our song fests HYMNS and HERS Along The Tunisian Trail. And blest be the tie that binds us together today, June

4-26-43 L'Arba, Algeria Province, and its radio station loomed into sight. That night we bivouacked in an orange grove on the outskirts of the village. The usual horde of Arabs clustered about begging and trying to sell vino. Early the next morning all the natives cheered us on our way giving the V-for-victory sign.

4-26-43 North Africa
Dearest family,
Today, we are riding above the magnificent clouds, past mines high in the mountains. The scenery is breathtaking. The Arabs run behind the vehicles and try to grab hold. There are villages all along the way. Lots of vegetation high in the mountains. We got some dates from the natives. They were delicious, but the fresh figs I didn't like and they didn't like me.

We passed through a village that had a large market square. All the Arabs sitting on their jackasses were selling carrots, onions and oranges. They sit on the very rear end of the jackass. That's why I have this little ditty *to describe it. Sketch a jackass first, please.*

As I sit on MY ASS on the ass of my ass,
A paradox comes to my mind.
Two-thirds of my ass is in front of MY ASS,
And the rest of my ass is behind.

I think Dad and Doc Ogilvie will love it. Hugs and kisses, June

4-27-43 North Africa
Dear Ones,
    We bivouacked at Setif, Algeria Province in a fragrant sheep field.
Multitudes of Arabs penetrated the camp selling Abbi-dabbi stoves and dag-
gers made out of German bayonets. The blades were eight inches long and
decorated on both sides with crude designs. The steel part of the handle was
wound with 44 turns of heavy wire neatly fastened on both ends. The bottom
part of the handle is made of tapered wood. The sheath is 9 1/4" long made
of tapered wood and covered with goat skin laced together with string. It's
a good vicious weapon. Francs were useless, but a package of gum or some
cigarettes could complete a big business deal.
    Breakfasts and suppers were the only hot meals during the day, un-
less we put our C ration cans on the motor and melted the grease. We were
allowed 30 minutes each meal to choke on the usual cold, greasy concoction.
Beans taste more like beans every time I eat them.
    I turned into a beggar myself. Every passing Army vehicle was a
potential source of food. If a lone jeep got caught in the convoy behind our
ambulance I made a series of hurriedly written placards. Placed in the window
they got results. DO YOU HAVE ANY FOOD, I'M STARVED, ONLY
C RATIONS TO EAT, SEND BREAD. The jeep or weapons carrier would
follow slowly along until we had our latrine break and then they would share
whatever they had with me. The Air Corps had the best food. Even dry bread
secured this way was super delicious. Love, June

4-28-43 A barren hillside at Ammlila provided sleeping space that
night. The GIs pitched their pup tents by the numbers, much to the
amusement of the veteran 3rd Auxiliary Surgical nearby. For a minute,
the place looked like basic training camp. We'd lost track of time by
now, and our one suit of clothing felt like armor plate. There were no
laundries or dry cleaning establishments along the way.

4-29-43 We were guests of the 77th Evacuation hospital near Morris, in the Constantine Province. Lt. Col. John Snyder from Mayo's was in command and they gave us army cots and clean white sheets. We sat at a table and ate out of enamelware. Civilization felt good, but it was our last.

4-30-43 Last stop about twelve kilometers from Tabarka, Tunisia province. I couldn't believe my eyes. There were cork trees, a few blades of grass and a tiny stream that trickled across the rocks. The trucks were unloaded. Up went the tents. The laundry pails came out of storage. Everyone started to clean up. What a luxury.

We sit out under the cork trees, chat, and listen to the Jerries flying along the coast. The nurses are like a family of sisters who love and respect each other. Never have I heard a cross word.

4-30-43 *Somewhere in North Africa*
Dear Mom and Dad,

Late today I got word that a P-38 pilot friend of mine who came over with us on the Santa Elena was killed dive-bombing in Tunis. I was very sad. He had given me a pair of wings and asked me to wear them and think of him everyday and I promised I would. I took a thoughtful walk along this pretty little mountain stream, and cried for him. When I returned I was restricted to my tent that night. The Army is running a nursery school. If you don't tell Gruesome and Chewsome (he chewed his mustache) where you are going you're a naughty, naughty girl. As you know, I've been on my own since I was sixteen. These old grumps tried to make me go to Quartermaster Corps dances in Oran so we'd get more and better hospital supplies. When I told them to fill out forms to get their stuff through channels, a chill descended on North Africa and me. Since I kicked the Colonel's shin for touching me aboard ship, plus my unsolicited QM advice, I have headed every work list and I'm sure I will end every leave list. Sticks and stones may break your bones, but words will never harm you. The guy who wrote that had never met Gruesome and Chewsome. I'll never out-rank them, but I will outlive them. Hopefully, June

5-1-43 *Somewhere in North Africa*
Dear Family,

It's the first of May and we're still on the move. The wind is terribly strong. It seemed like our tents would blow away last evening. Everyone was sick most of the night from the anti-malarial drug we are taking. Vomiting over a slit-trench is a horrible experience in this heat. All urped out, June

At this time, no nurses were ever allowed out of the hospital area without one of our male officers to accompany them as a chaperone. Actually, they came along as far as I could see just to get some free liquor in case our date was a Britisher. They also liked the British licorice candy. We weren't permitted the luxury of complaining. When your escort is old, short, fat, bald and boring it's better to stay in camp.

After the unit equipment arrived, the hospital was divided into three platoons six nurses in each one. Five nurses took care of the wards and one nurse (usually me) was on 24-hour call in the shock ward and operating tent. Everything was subject to change at a moment's notice. Laparotomy sheets were made and cuffs sewn on surgeon's gowns. These things should have been done before they were sent to us.

Stuka Road ran in front of our camp. Twenty four hours a day munitions, supplies, and men went in a steady stream to the front at Beja. In the still of the night, Jerry would fly over. The engine sounded like a washing machine on the fritz. Sometimes he dropped flares, perhaps to check for our RED CROSSES.

Ball games with the neighboring camps were the highlights of the day. Soldiers who had managed to store their guitars and ukuleles in the motor pool equipment now brought them out into the open.

One of our GIs called himself "Luke Warm and his Hot Towels." He'd bring out his Gibson guitar and beat out the Nashville sound. Some of the men imitated the Ink Spots. We all sang along on-key or off-key. All the old familiar songs were worn to a frazzle, but it helped to pass the time. The air force shot down a Messerschmitt in the next field. Many of us ran over and got a piece of aluminum and started to make a ring to send home.

5-3-43 North Africa   It was a scorching hot day and our platoon decided to go swimming in the Mediterranean, our CO was not in camp at the time. Most of us had never been swimming in such a large body of water. Bathing suits were something we didn't have. Some of the improvised models that appeared on the beach, along with all of the birthday suits, created quite a sensation.

I took my old blue, cotton seersucker dress that was no longer official clothing, cut the skirt hip-length and sewed some GI undies underneath. Prayers kept my hand stitching intact. From a distance we could see that a stretch of beach was crowded with British enlisted men and officers, so our outfit moved down further. Our nurses lay down to sunbathe. Not too long after that along came a scrawny, scrappy, cadaverous, middle-aged British officer, wearing only a monocle while sprinting sprightly along the beach. He nearly stepped on my feet. "Watch it", I shouted. He stopped, stared blankly in the direction of my voice, fumbled for his monocle--put it in place, made a disgusting "Bloody" sound, rattled his nude bones into high gear and made a sandy getaway.

Our men, mostly mid-westerners or from the southern hills, had all plunged in to swim not knowing anything about the terrific undertow. Their screams alerted everyone on the beach, but no one had a rope or preserver to throw to them. Nothing. One of our men had been on the Harvard swimming team and was a powerful swimmer. He saved about seven men and was awarded a medal. When we returned to camp, one of our GIs was missing. He had drowned. One of our doctors had tried to resuscitate him, but couldn't. We were so new to each other that we didn't recognize who belonged to our unit. What a tragic day. Our Colonel forbade any of us to ever go swimming again in that area.

5-8-43 We barged into the thistle patch at Souk-el-Arba at the edge of the A-20 Bomber airfield. Here we operated a convalescent hospital. Seven ambulance loads of patients were already waiting for us. The hospital went up so rapidly that one thought someone had waved a wand or rubbed Aladdin's Lamp.

Everyone helped set up cots and tents. In half-an-hour the first patients were being comfortably settled on cots. The soldiers in the mess had prepared a delicious meal for the wounded. Briefly, there were nurses to spare, and the wounded men couldn't talk fast enough to us to make up for lost time. Five months or more since they'd seen or talked to an American woman. They wanted to know if we had any red fingernail polish and, if so, to please go and put it on.

Patients poured in from the front and stayed with us until the hospital planes came and flew them back to Oran or Casablanca. Our hospital registry looked like a roster of the Foreign Legion--Poles, Arabs, Germans, Italians and Americans. Atabrine day came along, as it does all too frequently and the patients take it too. Because of the language problem, I decided to demonstrate how to take the medication by swallowing it with water. One of the Arabs chewed his instead. It's as bitter as gall. He must have thought he had been poisoned. He came flying off his cot straight for my throat. The stronger patients who could get up, tackled him and held him until I gave him a sedative.

Patients who had to be evacuated by air were kept only long enough for emergency treatment. The demand for sterile supplies and instruments was unending. The sterilizer is so high that I have difficulty reaching into it and have to stand on a tippy old box. Many times I have slipped and burned my arm. The pattern of burns is like a ladder.

The men made ward boxes so that packing each platoon's equipment was more efficient. Our nurses were now on twelve-hour duty as there were so few of us and so many wounded.

One of the pilots gave me a pail of airplane gas and showed me how to dry-clean my dress uniforms in it. I shared the wealth with my grateful tent-mates.

5-11-43 *Somewhere in North Africa*
Dear Ruth,

Just a short note in between shipments of patients. The enclosed check is for you. It's a refund on part of my Pullman ticket from Ft. Custer to Brooklyn that we never got as we had to ride in coaches. I'm bee-busy. The only piece of clothing I have that fits me is my little olive drab hat. It says GYPSY across the top.

I bargained with some natives for oranges. They fight with each other over their customers. Little boys come around on donkeys with huge hand woven baskets hanging on each side full of oranges and lemons. They sell eight of them for twenty francs, which is five cents apiece. The oranges are red on the inside and very, very sweet. Some are very large. One I bought today was rotten and I made him give me another one. He crossed himself he was so mad. I just laugh watching them perform.

An orange juicy kiss, June

Bizerte and Tunis fell to the Allies. For days, thousands of prisoners standing in the back of large trucks rode by on their way to prisoner-of-war camps in the USA. Many GI drivers stopped to chat with us en route. Frequently a prisoner who spoke English would call out to us. An Italian officer gave me his curved, polarized sun glasses that snugly fit his head. He said he thought I would need them more than he would. How right he was. While he was handing the glasses to me, one of our doctors kept trying to grab them, so the Italian whipped them out of his reach. He was very annoyed, and so was I

One of the favorite songs going the rounds is ..."Have you heard of Dirty Gerty from the City of Bizerte, where the women are ooh-la-la? Now the cigarettes are ranka down in old Casablanca where the women are ooh-la-la. And the coffee isn't Sanka down in old Casablanca where the women are ooh-la-la. In Port Lyautey they give it away. The Sultan's got it all in old Rabat. But give me fifty francas down in old Casablanca where the women are ooh-la-la."

5-15-43 I sang for a British troop show.

5-17-43 We packed up our tent hospital, left Souk-El-Arba, and passed through all the recent battlefields on the way to Ferryville. We're living in a German hospital on a hillside. The building is doorless, windowless and its large shell holes make it well ventilated. It's nice to have a roof in spots. Gun emplacements and tunnels undermined the area behind the hospital, but for fear of booby traps we didn't investigate. It is the first time we have lived in a building. We scrubbed the black and white tiled floors that were left and washed the Swastikas from the walls. German troops had lived in it before we arrived. Some of our men were cartoonists and they filled the small patches of standing walls with humor--not hate.

My off-duty hours I spent viewing the modern ruins of Bizerta and Tunis and the ancient ruins at Carthage, while our troops rested in bivouac. All the natives were selling ancient counterfeit Carthaginian coins. There were movies almost every night in some neighboring field, mostly, Victor Mature in "Moon over Miami". Sometimes they were cut short by an air raid on the harbor, which was filled with ships preparing for another invasion. When the flak began to fall, we crawled under trucks or whatever we could find for shelter. Huge barrage balloons floated over the invasion fleet.

Again we moved to a dry barren valley, still near Ferryville. Huge cracks in the dry earth made it difficult to walk, even in the daylight. Nights were most dangerous; flashlights and lighted cigarettes were only permitted in the tents with the flaps tightly closed. We sweltered in the 130 degree heat by day and froze at night.

Sometimes, one of our Jewish doctors and I would walk over to a French graveyard and sit on the stones and I would teach him

Protestant hymns. The natives would gather around us and just stare. The beadwork in floral patterns on their graves was so beautiful.

My friends from the AAA left for Cape Bon. I will miss them as their battery commander was a baker in civilian life. He would whip up some doughnuts in the afternoon and some ice cream made out of powdered milk, powdered eggs (ugh), and vanilla tablets. If we had time in the evenings, we'd eat it while one of his men played a piano accordion. Our cook couldn't cook, he was bogged down in serving greasy-spoon cuisine. I thought he might be a reject from an oil salvage station.

5-31-43 Somewhere in North Africa
Dear Ruth,

V-mail is safer as it is flown over and doesn't run the risk of being sunk. I celebrated Memorial day by going swimming at Ferryville. The beach isn't bad, but not as nice as the one at Bizerte, which is really sandy. I cut my foot on some stones. The sun is very, very hot.

My friend from the AAA took me to Tunis last Saturday. We had dinner at a beautiful French home. Our host owns a brewery. Tell mother not to worry; I don't drink liquor. I've always been happy drinking tap water. We had fried hominy, some sort of meat, perhaps lamb, heavily seasoned with garlic, dark French bread, garlic-onion-ripe-olive salad with paprika and olive oil dressing. You could smell yourself coming for days after. We had iced pears and some grapefruit juice and white bread that we brought with us. They were so thrilled to have the white bread and we were so desperate to have the dark bread. Their bathrooms are the funniest things. We are afraid to ask what the one gadget is for. I know the fellows who live in buildings tell us that they soak their socks in it.

I planned to buy you a silver bracelet but we had jeep trouble on the way up so we didn't get to Tunis until closing time for the shops. Our male officers are the only ones who can use our hospital transportation. The nurses never go anywhere unless they walk, hitchhike, or have a friend who has a jeep.

My friend gave me a bracelet made out of elephant's hair braided, varnished and then wrapped with gold. It is rather pretty, at least it is different. The enclosed pieces of money are worthless. It is money the Germans used to pay off their troops here in Africa. It should be worth two dollars. The money that we use looks almost like that.

Once we were stationed next to an airfield. They had the niftiest little bombers. They promised to give me a ride in one some day. You would have to lie up behind the pilot's head. It's a very small space. They let us clean our clothes in aviation gas. The dirt just fell out of our uniforms. Neat.

Surprising how one becomes used to an air raid. It's about the most spectacular thing one could possibly see. You are so fascinated watching the anti-aircraft fire and the light from the bursting bombs that you forget about your own personal danger. No one panics. They are so well trained. There isn't any confusion, no one makes an outcry. On a pitch-dark night, an air raid looks like a big Fourth of July celebration. You can hear the enemy planes overhead, and when they get in the beam of the large searchlights, you can see the planes, if they are low enough, even the pilots. But then it is too bad for them. The enemy planes usually drop flares so that they can see where they want to bomb. It's eerie watching the flares float to earth. It's then that I wish our huge Red Crosses were as big as the Empire State building.

By the time you get this, you will be out of school for a nice long vacation. In a way I envy you, but just for a minute. While this war is on, I just couldn't be back in the States, despite the inconveniences we experience. They are so desperately in need of surgical nurses. The newspapers and magazines that we get to read are months old. We've sung and resung all the old songs that we can remember the words to and the other songs we just hum the melody. Could you please send me the words to "Star Dust, Make Believe, You'd Be So Nice to Come Home To" and a package of phonograph needles.

Saturday I went through the most beautiful cathedral in Carthage. The ceilings were all done in mosaic; the stained glass windows and statues were gorgeous. It was mammoth, sitting high up on a hilltop overlooking the brilliant blue waters of the Mediterranean. You have never seen anything quite so beautiful as the blue of the sea with the purple mountains in the distance. It is difficult to get any developing done over here as the Germans cleaned house when they passed this way.

Dad, I heard that some of my favorite baseball players are also in the armed services. A Lieutenant in the Navy picked the following teams to play in a World Series when the war ends. It will never happen....but here they are...Greenberg and Mize 1st base; Crespi and Reese 2nd base; Shortstop... Travis and Rizzuto; 3rd base...Lewis and Pesky; Left field...Reiser and Williams; Center field...Joe DiMaggio and Dom DiMaggio; Right field...Terry Moore and Max Marshall; Catcher...Danning and Pytlak; Pitchers (Army) Beazley, Ruffing, Hughes, Mulcahy; Pitchers (Navy) Feller, Lyons, French, Olson.

When I was a student nurse I had Bob Feller's dad for a patient.

Bob would just sit in a chair by the door. He didn't talk to anyone. I always wanted to ask him to come out to Soldier's Field and play with our Fellow's team on Saturdays. I would love to have been a big league ball player, but I didn't chew tobacco and I was the wrong sex. Wide-eyed as always, June

5-8-43 Somewhere in North Africa
Dear Family,

Three weeks since I've gotten any mail. It's extremely hot, dry and very dusty. You eat your lifetime quota of dirt in one day. I haven't felt truly well for a long, longtime, maybe it's just a combination of lousy food, heat, work and constant uncertainty. You no doubt know more about what the troops are doing and what we are expected to do than we do. No radio, no newspapers, just silence. Wonder where I'll be spending my birthday? A QM truck lost a case of dried yeast several days ago and some soldiers picked it up and gave us a pound of it. We had the cook make some scrumptious doughnuts. You'd be amused and surprised how we manage to get food, other than that horrible GI stuff. Top secret--will tell you later.

Several of us were invited to a very modest, very poor French home for dinner. The place was off-limits because of typhoid, and typhus. The meal and its preparation lasted for hours. The whole evening was unreal. There wasn't one semi-modern convenience. The Arab woman, who was married to a French legionnaire, cooked the whole, flavorful, five-course meal for eight of us over a number 10 can, with holes poked in the sides using a bit of charcoal and great ingenuity. She washed the few dishes between servings. The ladies sat on a plank, the fellows on the ground. We ate by lantern and candlelight. Col. Deifenbach, infantry combat veteran, furnished the food and arranged the whole thing as a surprise for us. The first course was lentil soup. A few days later my friend was killed in combat.

I hurt my left knee badly in a jeep accident. The driver hit a deep rut and I was thrown over the front seat into the windshield. Lean and hungry, June

North Africa
Dear Family,

At a movie last night held in the adjacent field, I tripped over some soldiers long legs in the dark. He turned out to be a classmate of Elizabeth. We never did see the end of the film, with Victor Mature. Kept being inter-rupted by air raids. We got tired of crawling under trucks (they are dubious protection), so they finally postponed it. Probably never will see the end of it.

Time drags here, I've the feeling that I have never lived any place but Africa. I bumped into an officer who used to be stationed with me at Fort

Custer. He'd been here six months and of those six hadn't seen a white woman in four months. He said sometimes he'd get so tired of seeing men that he half wished he had a pair of his sister's silk hose or her skirt in his bedroll so that he could take them out and just look at them for awhile. He was in the Battles of Mateur, El Guettar and Bizerte, so he's more than willing to go home. And a short sheet to all of you from the Arabs, June

6-13-43 North Africa
Dear Ruth,

After days in my lumpy cot with some sort of tropical fever -- so far undiagnosed -- I'm beginning to feel like I might like to go on living. I vomit constantly and have terrible diarrhea. Of course, all we have is a slit trench for a toilet. The men who dig them have long legs, and mine are so short, one takes one's life in one's hands to straddle the trench. I'm too weak to manage this alone and two of the kind nurses hold me, one on either side of the trench--while I'm stripped naked. The stench and the view is awful. Because I produce from both ends at the same time, I have wished frequently that I could die. I tried praying but I'm apparently not on the right wave-length or my petition isn't strong enough to penetrate canvas.

The hot sirocco winds that are coming off from the desert are strong and laden with prickly sand that cuts into one's eyes and skin like large hypo needles.

One night when I quit vomiting for a bit, my concerned tent mate, went to the mess tent to get a piece of dry bread for me. She thought I might be able to keep that down. Unfortunately, just as she was walking out with the bread, our mean old Colonel walked in to get some food for himself no doubt. He asked her where she was taking the bread and she told him it was for me. He snatched it out of her hand and said I didn't need it as I'd vomit it up anyway, so why waste it.

Do you know that miserable old man has a massive mustache that he chews frequently. He and the Chief nurse have never even been to my tent to see me. After my Mayo Clinic training, I thought all doctors were next to God and about that smart, but not some I've met recently.

One clodhopper, oversexed and underprivileged, who looks like a bald-headed wrinkle on an Ichabod Crane body, did what he called a hemorrhoidectomy on a poor soldier. The nurse who scrubbed for the operation told me he put on a pair of rubber gloves, stuck his two index fingers into the poor guy's raw rectum, and then pulled in opposite directions, stretching all the way around the anus. She didn't know where he got his surgical training, but I think he just ordered his degree from Tears & Roebuck.

Days later: One of our kind doctors, who sort of assigned himself to take care of me, finally got some fresh eggs from the French people last night. He poached one for my breakfast on a tank stove I have. It's the first thing I've eaten in days and kept down. The French also sent me a tiny fresh tomato. It looked like red gold to me. I'll bet Doc traded his cigarette ration for the food for me. How he loves to smoke. He keeps an old Raleigh pack, but refills it with Camels. When he offers them to some one, no one takes any. People can't stand Raleighs.

Still later: Jaundice acute catarrhal is my final diagnosis. Mom, my liver hangs down about five finger widths below my rib cage and is it ever tender. My green eyes are rimmed with yellow and my skin is pure Chinese. I look like a refuge from a morgue. I'm weak as a kitten and feel just about as hairy. You'd think they'd send me to the rear to a hospital where I could get some long-term care and at least be in a bed with a mattress and pillow, toilet and running water. I fold over my field jacket for a pillow. When I do get to sleep, I wake up with zipper prints on my cheek.

I've been living on those colored candy wafers that come in a roll. We get about one-a-week as a ration, but everyone from far and wide has sent their ration to me. The son of a neurosurgeon I knew in Rochester is an infantry officer here, he hitchhiked over 90 miles with all of the candy ration he could scrounge from his buddies to give to me. My tears of gratitude are real. All that sugar is helping me to keep going.

You know how much I love water -- fresh well-water. This stuff is so heavily chlorinated I can't stand to drink it. They've tried putting coffee in it, but I still can't take it. As you know I'm not used to coffee. This wonderful nurse from Chicago helps the Doc care for me. She has the most beautiful blond hair I have ever seen and lovely features. The nurses who have long hair keep it clean by rubbing small strands of it with a towel. Until next time, Your Yellow Menace, June.

Much, much later:

A Piper Cub flew very low and very slow over my tent today. I ran out to see what was going on and the pilot dropped several small homemade parachutes. As they fluttered earthward I caught them and read the messages. IF YOU WILL COME TO OUR DANCE TONIGHT, WAVE YOUR ARMS WILDLY. HOW MANY CAN COME? WE'LL PICK YOU UP AT DUSK, PLEASE. PLEASE---WAVE! It was signed by Lt. Berlin. He flew in circles over our tents until five of us, who weren't scheduled for night duty, waved and waved and waved the answer he wanted to see. He flew off smiling. That evening several jeeps arrived on schedule to take us to their dance.

We moved again to another new bivouac area near Ferryville. We're on a small hill with our cook stoves sitting out in the open. It was late in the day and most everyone took off to see the local sights before the invasion. I still don't feel too well, so I stayed in camp with a handful of GIs, whose names I don't know. Suddenly, at the base of the hill we heard the horrible noises of a donkey, bellowing in pain, being beaten to death by an irate native using a huge piece of wood. The animal was on its knees and bloody, still attached to a tiny cart carrying a large barrel on it. The enlisted men, mostly ranchers or farmers in civilian life, ran down the hill, drove the man off and released the donkey. Then they brought the wine barrel up the hill and proceeded to dump the wine into all available water cans and personal canteens. The small amount that was left over they brought to me and asked me if I could bake a cake using it. They didn't want to waste a drop. I told them I'd never baked a cake. That didn't discourage them; they said they would help. With that, one of them fired up the stove, someone got two big cake sheets. We found the powdered eggs, powdered milk, and other powdered things and I threw them all together, laced them with the rest of the wine, and tossed it into the oven. By then it was totally dark. When the cake was done we started to eat it. It wasn't bad, sort of unleavened in spots. We had just put the excess cake in the oven for safe keeping when we saw flashlights down on the road. With a French gendarme was the cruel native, shouting and pointing in our direction. The men scattered in the darkness. The gendarme climbed the hill, flashed the light in my face and asked if I'd seen a barrel of wine. I shrugged my shoulders and gave my best mime performance of the word "NO". He left. I didn't even offer him a piece of cake.

6-28-43 Saw General Eisenhower in Ferryville.

Got word that Bill -- the young man who brought me his unit's candy ration -- was killed in combat.

7-2-43 Some AAA friends of mine were loaded aboard an LST in the harbor ready for the invasion. It looked like that was to be the end of a very good friendship. Four nights later, however, there they were, hiking across the field toward our tents. They'd ship-hiked in from the ship and then hitchhiked over from Bizerte.

Nothing is impossible. Several nights later, four of us were

40

dinner guests of theirs aboard the LST. They met us at the docks in a small naval boat and took us out to the ship. The sailors lent us their slickers to keep off the salt spray. On the way out we dodged many sunken German and Italian ships. On arrival at LST 157 the railings were loaded with grinning sailors and soldiers watching us as we pulled up. Two big derrick-like hooks dropped from above, fastened on each end of our craft and pulled us to the upper deck. If I never remember another thing about the pleasant evening, the ice cream will be sufficient. They stuffed us with it.

7-6-43 4AM another air raid over Bizerte. Falling bombs and anti-aircraft fire woke me. I dumped the wash water out of my steel helmet that hung on my cot and pajama-clad dashed outside. The sky was ablaze with anti-aircraft barrages. The beams from a score of powerful searchlights crisscrossed the heavens.

Jerry bombers were trying to hit the ships in the harbor. Plane after plane went hurtling to the earth, smoke streaming behind them. Suddenly, in the brilliant glare of the weaving lights there appeared a twin engine bomber. It seemed impossible that it could escape the avalanche of shells that were sent skyward. This way and that way it went, climbing higher but always in the center of light. It started our way, getting bigger and flying lower. You could hear the whine of the bullets as they whizzed by. The bomber came so low over our tents one could see the black insignia on the wing and the pilot. It seemed that if you stretched a bit you could touch it. Everyone was screaming "Get him boys!" But by then he was out of range and heading toward Mateur.

7-7-43 The 817 Aviation Engineers invited me to a dance in Tunis and I sang with their band.

The Tunisian campaign was more than a victory over the Axis: it was also a medical triumph over disease and battle wounds. Major General Cowell, director of Allied Medical Services in this theater noted that the mortality rate of the injured was reduced to far less than one percent, from the nearly ten percent mortality of World War I. In that war, there were only five surgeons for every 70,000 men. In today's British 1st Army, there is a complete surgical team for each 2,000 men.

7-8-43 Nurses from our unit were segregated in a small camp in Bizerte, in preparation for the invasion of Sicily with the 3rd Division. As part of "Joss Force", we would act originally as an evacuation hospital.

Barbed wire fences to control our movements wove their way around us. Or was the fence to protect us? Three times a day, we were fed C rations and coffee to cover up the horrible taste of the water. Bread was something we craved.

7-9-43 Somewhere in North Africa
Dear Family,

Just a note to tell you I'm wide-eyed and curious as ever. They've isolated us and tried to feed us C rations. I wouldn't give the stuff to a garbage plant. It might kill it. We were trucked to a delousing unit for a bath, by then I was so hungry I felt I could smell food even if it was in a tin can. On our way back to barbed-wire-camp, I sniffed out a ration dump and single-handedly raided the place and liberated canned chicken, turkey, pork sausage, fruit, candy, gum, and K rations. I wondered why our hospital had never seen rations like that. Probably the rear echelon sells it in the black market. Because we were a field hospital, I guess they thought we should live off from the land. We're living in an olive grove and sleeping on the ground. No lizards here though. I was so sick of those little devils crawling up my pants leg while I slept.

Never turn a beggar away from the door. If you could have seen me begging for just a loaf of dry bread yesterday -- not even asking for jam -- would you have been ashamed of me? My tummy was so empty.

One of our nurses had a brother in the Navy, whose ship just docked in the harbor. He immediately started looking for us, but it took him four hours to find us behind barbed wire. We shooed him away with orders not to return unless he brought food to share. Hours later, he staggered back with his freshly baked raisin cookies, spice cake, bread, and a gallon of peanut butter. Even the breezes carried messages of our search for food, and soon the Air Corp dropped in with fresh vegetables and some vino. We couldn't invade Sicily on an empty stomach.

Take $10.00 out of my account and buy Ruthie something unexpected for her birthday. Much love, June

7-10-43 We left our Texas staging area and went up another gangplank on a dinky craft the Navy called Landing Craft Infantry (LCI). It's a highly specialized craft, designed to land ground troops on enemy beaches. They also are used as a dispatch craft, escort vessel and for transportation of wounded or prisoners from the embattled beaches.

This time our accommodations were terrible. There were twenty four nurses in one compartment; three bunks to a tier. Alphabetically or age-wise I rated the last bunk the top one, right next to the vents from the "head". It smelled like it hadn't been cleaned since the time of Christ. Adjacent to our quarters was the hot, noisy engine room. When it was chow time, the Navy placed a huge vat of beans in the middle of the deck. As hungry as we were, we didn't touch it.

All of our gear, including our wrist watches and gas masks, had been waterproofed as they told us we might have to wade ashore in Sicily. The skipper circled the harbor so many times trying to get into convoy formation that my stomach objected.

I sat on the deck, hung my legs over the edge, and looked off into the distance as we silently sailed to another battle area. Being very far-sighted and having excellent night vision, I spied a large round object floating to the left of our convoy, not far from our LCI. Thinking it might be a mine I reported it to the sailors. It was. Fortunately the rest of the convoy managed to miss it. By then, I was all keyed up. At 10:30 PM they announced general quarters. I hurried to my prison-like hold. We had all been issued May Wests when we boarded and were told to wear them constantly. As I climbed up into the narrow spot between my bunk and the low ceiling, the cord that releases the CO_2 cartridge caught on the bunk rail and inflated the life preserver. I lay there wedged in. Trapped. Destination...Licata, Sicily. Arrival time--D 2.

Sicily 1943

FOUR

Ashore in Sicily

During the night, a violent storm tossed our little craft around like a cork, even the pack mules aboard got seasick too. By six AM the next morning, we were within view of the harbor at Licata. For ever so many miles, I could see our ships guarding the shoreline. The D-Day forces covered a 69 mile beach front. It was D-2 and the harbor bristled with anti-aircraft guns. A number of sunken vessels were cluttering up the harbor. Some fishing boats were blown out of the water and were sitting upright on land. One ship at a time slid into the dock and unloaded. We were the first nurses to land in Sicily. The ship was carrying ammo and mules. Later we learned from the Harbor Master that he was expecting the 10th Field Artillery in this convoy...not ninety-eight nurses.

Our landing, as part of Joss force, was totally different from what I had imagined. I had been expecting the worst but, thank God, the beaches had been secured. My friends from the AAA were guarding the unloading convoy and, as I stepped on the dock, they shouted, "Welcome to Sicily, June". It was an incredible sensation. As I was restrapping my luggage, some one shouted, "Air Raid". Dropping everything, we ran for cover. They were our own planes, coming back from a mission. The jubilation didn't last long as German fighters engaged our fighters overhead in a dog fight. One of the American planes was shot down and my AAA friend took me in his jeep across the fields to the downed plane. The pilot was okay. He gave me his parachute seat as a souvenir, and I used it constantly. We had never been issued pillows.

Just as we got back to the beach, another dog fight erupted and again we ran away from the beach to the safety of a high stone wall and pressed our bodies against it. At that moment, I wished that my helmet was full length--head to toe. When the firing and fighting stopped, an old man ran out of the stone house in the orchard and welcomed us in tearful English, "I'm from Toledo, Ohio many years ago." A sudden burst of anti-aircraft fire and the drone of two Jerries right overhead sent us all sprawling flat on the ground. We all watched spellbound as one German fighter was shot down. The pilot bailed out at the last minute. We piled into a big truck and were whisked through the streets of Licata to the sound of much cheering and surprised shouts of "Signorina". They dumped us out in an almond orchard, where we sat, waited for further orders, and wondered where our men were. We weren't far from enemy territory--and just a short sprint from the sea. Soon a Colonel arrived and took us back through Licata to our hospital, three miles southwest of the city. Were our men glad to see us. They had landed D day on Orange Beach. During an air raid, an LST loaded with 2nd Armored men and equipment was hit, broke in two, and sank. The Navy asked them to go back into the bay and help pull men out of the water.

Within two hours of our landing, we went on duty. We lived between a makeshift airfield and an ammunition dump, just a bomb's drop from the harbor. There we pitched our pup tents in a rutty, stubble-riddled field in front of the hospital tents. Fleas, flies, lizards, mosquitoes and ants were everywhere, creating misery for us. Water was rationed, just a canteen full a day for drinking, none for bathing or laundry. To enforce the water ban, an armed guard was put on the water trailer. I went down to a nearby sulfur creek to do a bit of open-air bathing. Sulfur water doesn't suds and my skin felt awful. All of the hospital's bloody linen was washed by hand in a scant amount of water. Then it was hung to dry on the shrubs or scattered about on the ground to dry in the sun. We had only three small, inadequate 1.5 KW generators for the whole hospital and had to fight for ages before we got four 5 KW generators.

I shared a pup tent briefly and meagerly with another nurse

and Vino her unhousebroken dog. Vino had been smuggled over from Africa in the motor-pool equipment. Using a pick axe and shovel under a hot Sicilian sun, we dug our own fox-hole in a shadeless area in front of our pup tent. To ensure a softer landing, we lined it with straw from a nearby hay stack. To our regret, the straw was infested with lice and fleas. Vino's fleas weren't trained either and spent more time on me than on him. He barked only between 2 AM and 4 AM and toileted himself ONLY on my one woolen blanket and parachute-seat pillow, while I was working in the operating tent on an hour's-unlimited basis.

I told Vino's Mom how to train him, but she thought it sounded cruel. So I suggested that she diaper him with those Birdseye diapers we brought overseas. She actually did just that and as he ran through camp with his wee diaper on, the men were hysterical with laughter. When it fell off, she ran after him with bigger safety pins. I told her that the next time he soiled my blanket or woke me up I would kill him. As hospitals have no weapons, she asked how I would do it. My detailed description was horrifying even to me. Assorted complaints to the Chief Nurse, who slept like a log, only brought the snide remark that obviously I was not a dog lover. I wasn't anymore; Vino had changed that. Eventually Chiefy decided to swap pup-tentmates with me. Forty eight hours after the swap, nurse and dog were transferred to an Evacuation hospital. I hope the dog enjoyed that hospital as it was certainly named for him.

We worked hard all day and much of the night and were tired enough to sleep any place. Air raids became routine. At first I'd peek out of my pup tent to see who was getting the worst of it. After awhile, I'd just cradle my helmet in my arms and try to go to sleep again. We needed all the rest we could get. With a pup tent you don't have any privacy, you don't even have room to change your mind.

7-17-43 German bombers attack the airfield in the next field.

7-18-43 The ammunition dump on the other side of us blew up this AM. It sounded like a battle. Between the quinine I take and all that noise--I think my hearing lost points. For this part of the war, we are under the command of General Patton.

7-19-43 In support of the 3rd Division, we moved to four miles north of Agrigento. We followed the front lines, picked up the non-transportables in shock, operated on them, and kept them until they could be moved to the rear or flown to a General Hospital in Africa.

The nurses wanted to see Agrigento so we commandeered an ambulance for a watermelon-hunting expedition. We found a Sicilian who spoke French and, after much quibbling, we got several large melons. Agrigento was a fascinating but filthy old city, whose grey hovels gave it such a somber appearance. The shops had more merchandise than any we had seen in North Africa. One of the nurses wanted a bathing suit. The shopkeeper proudly brought out his best, and only, wool suit on which the moths had nibbled. It was for long-distance swimming, knee length, with wide bands of brilliant colors. Expensive too, only twenty dollars. The suit looked like it came from a Smithsonian exhibit.

The men are complaining about moving so often, packing and unpacking a hospital unit, and pitching all of those tents. But how about the infantry? They Truscott-trotted and fought their way across Sicily until the GIs' feet were worn to nubbins. At one point, they marched about a hundred miles in four days. Our platoon inherited a nineteen year old, married, Truscott-trot victim whose feet were really shot, but his eyes and tongue worked overtime. One day he told me he'd hate to be my husband as he couldn't afford to buy my clothes. I laughed and asked how he thought that I would be a clotheshorse. He said, "You always look so neat and pressed." Actually I washed my fatigues, hung them up to drip dry, pressed them with my hand, laid them under my bedroll, and slept on them. There were no Quartermaster laundries in Sicily until the campaign was over, instead, we used boards and tubs. Once we had 15 POWs to do our hospital laundry.

7-22-43 After the Third Infantry Division captured Palermo, we had a breathing space. When we got march orders we had to borrow twelve 2 1/2-ton trucks from them to make our next move. Moving frequently was a way of life for us.

Being in a convoy on the northern coast was a nightmare. There were no shoulders, no guard rails. From the road it was a sheer drop to the sea below. The roads were built for mules and sure-footed donkeys. All bridges were blown out. The British "Diversion" sign marking the detour, for us meant "Aversion". The rough terrain tortured your spine and battered your buttocks. Sitting on a wooden seat in the back of a truck, is a jolting experience. The ever-present thick dust suffocated my soul. In that scalding heat, with barely any water to drink, I wondered why the ancient Romans had ever spent any time there.

Sometimes, two nurses were assigned to the operating tent: one for days and one for nights, but you frequently ran many hours over your scheduled time. We utilized old plasma tubing and glucose bottles and made our own Wangensteen sets. Everyone had to use mosquito netting. One very hot day in Sicily, while attempting to bathe out of our helmets in the shelter of our wall tent, one of our enlisted men, completely inebriated, opened our tent flap and staggered in. We screamed for him to get out. Not even glancing at our naked bodies he replied thickly, as he reached for our canteens hanging on the foot end of our cots, "Zat's okay, jus' bringin' fresh drinkin' water." With that he filled our canteens, returned them to their places and left.

Nights, when we sleep out under the stars, the latrine screen is our dressing room and our helmet is our wash basin.

7-19-43 Scorching Sicily
Dear Family,

We just finished moving again to a new area. Before the sun sinks any further behind the mountain I want to tell you as much about this spot as I can. We won't be using tents tonight, just cots under the sky. We're high up on a hill with mountains on all sides except one, and that has the sea. Ancient cities with old and modern ruins are perched on two of the mountains. I cooked my supper over canned heat. I'd saved the food from packages you sent sometime ago for just such an emergency. I had a half canteen cup of bouillon, a half canteen cup of cocoa made with part of a "D" ration bar, water and some condensed milk, a tiny can of cold corned beef and some very stale, old brown, tasteless crackers. The cocoa boiled over and the bouillon water spilled because the ground was so lumpy. Bad news, because water is rationed here. Usually they have an armed guard on the water trailer. This was originally a grain field and the stubble is quite high. My stockingless legs are scratched to shreds. About two hundred yards from my vantage point on the hillside, the hospital tents are going up in a race against darkness. I think we should all join a circus when we get back to the states. At the head of my cot, I have my one piece of hand luggage, on top of that are my two field packs. For a pillow, I have a parachute seat.

To screen myself--somewhat--from the prying eyes of the enlisted men, I put up two poles at the foot of my cot and hung half of my pup tent over it. It's so dark now that I can only see the reflection of the paper. The moon should be up soon, it has been so gorgeous the past few nights, but it gives the enemy too much help. I prefer the real dark, dark nights. Fondly, June

Five more days and we moved to a field outside of Corleone. The thistles were knee high and covered with millions of snails. The ground was the usual dry, rutty variety.

7-24-43 Sicily
Dear Family,
Gypsies again, on the move, sleeping outside. The snakes and snails are thick. My sweet, new tent-mate is old enough to be my mother. She's gung-ho for any of my daring suggestions. Her home is only 21 miles from you. I burned the thistle, snail- infested area on which we were going to sleep. It roasted the snails, but we just couldn't eat them because they reminded us of raw oysters. Ugh. Our former Goum neighbors loved the snails and ate them raw. The Goums are native African troops, but they have French officers.
We have a few trees here within walking distance. The mountains are more beautiful than the last place. I'm still on night duty in the OR. The ground is so rough, latticed with mammoth cracks. You can sprain your ankle if you step into one. At night, it is dangerous to walk around because we maintain a strict blackout; no flashlights permitted. Guess you know, my green cat's eyes come in handy. We have a GI who also has cat's eyes, but his pupils are elongated, just like a cats. On my fatigue trouser leg there is a small narrow pocket--in which I carry a miniature deck of KEM cards and hook my flashlight on the outside. Goodnight and sleep well, June

Al Jolson had a troop show. After the show, Jolson spied two of us nurses and promptly cuddled us to him, one on each side, one of the Auxiliary doctors took our picture. While Jolson was biting my left ear, I was kicking him. I liked him better when he was singing, but the GIs seemed to enjoy both acts.

7-23-to-28-43 At Corleone. Here we have a two-holer wooden latrine. Quite a luxury. You feel like a Queen on a throne. The lumber is rough and splintery and the latrine screen doesn't quite go down far enough to the ground. You can tell who is sitting in residence by the size of their feet. On top of some high rock formations outside of the city, the natives told us they keep their prostitutes there. We didn't try to verify their story. It looks like they'd need a very, very long ladder to get up there. Many times we have set up our hospital in a dried up river bed. All of the huge, high bridges that went over the riverbeds have been bombed. One night in my topsy-turvy Sicilian world, we got a rush march order in the middle of the night. Our ambulance was creeping along in the blackout hanging on the side of a mountain. I was sitting with the driver to help him see the road. Squinting in the dark I thought I saw a soldier with a gun beside the road and I told the driver to stop. I stuck my head out the window and said, "We're looking for a place to set up our hospital." The guard exploded, "My God women, the bridge is out ahead, we're waiting for artillery." We had a terrible time turning around.

7-25-43 The news commentator said Mussolini left Italy. The same day a barefooted, ragged Sicilian woman with two little boys barged into my tent. She didn't know that their leader had left them. She had thirteen children, four sons in the Italian army. She hadn't seen them for years. One son was in Naples but when I told her that Naples was in Italy, she didn't believe me and wasn't quite sure where Italy was or how far away. Her youngest daughter saw a Negro soldier drive by one day and was so frightened they hadn't been able to get her out of the house since. Everyone in this country is white. Airplanes were also too much for her to comprehend. After the initial invasion, a stray bomb killed some Sicilian men and two cows in a field. She told me her family salvaged the meat, but she seemed unconcerned about the dead men. We were so starved, we collected two dollars from everyone in the unit and sent our cook out to buy a cow for supper. He bought a cow for $200. an incredible price. It was so tough, stringy, and old we couldn't eat it. So much for letting a cook, who was a mortician, do the shopping.

7-28-43 Now near Trabia. This time we are in an olive grove, the red clay soils our clothes and gets up our nose. The sea is almost within diving distance of our tents. My tentmate and I took off in the direction of Palermo. Rides were a dime a dozen; we got there in record breaking time and just browsed around. An Irish friend of mine stopped over later to take me to see the cathedral at Monreale. A priest met us at the door, took one look at me, and said, "You can't come in". I asked why and he answered, "Because you don't have any stockings on." My friend nearly blew his stack. He said to the priest, "What the hell are you doing looking at her legs for anyway? Pax vobiscum." With that, he took my arm and we brushed past the priest and toured by ourselves. Imagine anyone living like we do having a pair of hose of any kind. The Sicilian women I had met had very hairy legs but no stockings.

7-30-43 Somewhere in Sicily
Dear Family,

We move so frequently, I forget to write because my stationery is packed in my luggage and I haven't had time to open it. We live in an olive grove and the red clay dust permeates everything. Our chief nurse has never given us permission to go anywhere when we were off duty. My tentmate and I decided to go over-the-hill, like our GIs do. They had the same problem with the Colonel. We had a great time. The natives flocked about us, and even tore at our clothes to get us to pay attention to what they are trying to say. Here I have language problems. If they would write their questions, perhaps my Latin would be a big help. Sign language isn't bad, and a smile in any language is great. We bought melons, grapes, almonds, peaches, and cactus pears. Our soldier's whistle at anything that looks like a female, it's so harmless. I whistle back at them, if the chief nurse isn't around.

I was invited by the 3rd Division to a dinner dance in Palermo at the beautiful Whittaker Mansion. From a tent to a mansion that's hard to take.....coming back to the tent is so dismal.

Did I tell you before about one of our drivers who accidentally killed a cow? He felt so sorry for our poor patients, who had nothing to eat but C rations, that he stole some vegetables so the cook could make stew for them.

It's incredibly hot. The last time we bivouacked four nurses played bridge. Visualize our tent with the top full of flak holes, slime trails on the canvas left by the big snails at night. We sat on our army cots, used the ground for a playing surface. Each of us in our underwear. With the temperature a usual 130 plus, we had our laundry pails filled with sea water in which we soaked our feet. Around our head and neck we had a small wet hand towel. Our canteen with our precious daily quota of drinking water was covered with one of our wet wool socks to cool the water by evaporation. I always felt like we sweat "C" ration gravy.

In one of our moves I had a wall tent by myself. It was dangerous. I came back to my tent from the OR in the middle of the night and there was our new Chaplain, a priest, quite drunk, on my cot. Until we got rid of him, my surgical helpers would have to flush him out. The war brought out the best in most people, there are always exceptions.

We had our own POW camp next to us at one of our many setups.

I'm too tired to remember just which one at the moment. They were Slavs and seemed to be very happy to be with us. They did our hospital laundry by hand and also helped carry patient's litters. Just a small wire fence surrounded their area and no one ever tried to escape. I'll send you a picture of them. We develop our film in x-ray solution. I'm so tired of war, June

Sicily, undated letter.
Dear Ruthie,

Field hospitals have about 200 men and 18 nurses. Once we were near another Field hospital whose CO was regular army and a regular guy. Their nurses and our nurses decided to have a dance for our enlisted men, our CO gave his permission. We had heard some Red Cross workers had just arrived in Sicily and had opened a club for the GIs.

Our CO gave one of our nurses his recon and driver and permission to contact the Red Cross workers to invite them to our dance. The Red Cross workers were so excited about joining us for the festivities, they all promised to come, and said they would bake a huge box of cookies for the party.

The appointed day arrived. When our nurse went to pick up the women for the dance, they had lost interest and had fragile excuses why they couldn't come. But we knew. Why dance with a private when you can cuddle a colonel?

The Chief Red Hen, fawned over our nurse and smilingly plunked a large box of cookies into her arms, saying they were for the men. God bless our buxom emissary, she turned on this creature and said, "Did you ever see a man dance with a box of cookies in his arms?" With that she threw them into the dirt at the feet of the Red Hen, got into the recon, and came steaming back to the field. When the CO heard the limp excuses offered, he started to chew on his mustache. By his authority, none of us were to censor this story in the men's letters home.

One day shortly after we arrived in Sicily, when walking down the street by myself, I saw this older General approaching me. I saluted him, he returned the salute, then he grabbed my left hand, patted it, and said, "Thank you so much, honey, for coming here." I was very touched. Really. Love, June

X-ray crew

FIVE

Sad, Sad Sicily

3-1-43 Today we set up our hospital in Pollina, a little town near Cefalu. More misery and sorrow. Worked 'til we were ready to drop. When the push was over and the shock ward was empty of patients, I took off down the road for a walk, wearing my helmet. It was early in the evening. A vehicle came up behind me and the men called out "Wanna lift, soldier?" I turned toward them and said, "Yes." Were they surprised and pleased to see an American woman.

They were very drunk and offered me a drink of their wine. On the back of their weapons carrier they had several corpses of their buddies they had dug up and were taking them to be 'replanted' (that was their word). They wanted me to go with them and I did. It was so sad as they told me about their buddies being killed. I cared about all of our soldiers who served, who died. When the soldiers fell in battle, before the troops moved on, they buried them and marked their graves so they could be picked up at a later more convenient time. They told me it was about two weeks since their buddies had been buried.

Aqua Dolci, Sicily
Someplace, sometime today I met a LOOK photographer.

8-7-43 Today we were assigned to II Corps.

8-10-43 Sad Sicily
Dearest Family,
Please send me as much 620 film as you can get every week, several cans of creamed mushroom soup and plain mushrooms and a box of Heath candy bars.

Curious Sicilian women come begging and peeping around our tents all day. They're not much older than I am but they have had so many children they're worn out. They're very poor, very sweet and so eager to communicate with women from another country. Working hard. Behaving properly. Love, June

8-14-43 Poor Sicily
Dearest Family,
Working like slaves. Too tired to write and it's always too dark to see when I get off duty. We were so close to the lines we could see our artillery fire and also that of the Germans. The Jerries have poor aim today. Shells landed in front of us and behind us. I'm well and as happy as one could be in this set up. Glad I have lots of energy. Don't know how the older nurses stand the pace. I finally got the slack suit and it fits perfectly. I love it. Our ingenious men made a shower out of a 250 gallon drum, a piece of hose and a shower head, and plopped some wooden duckboards on the ground and wrapped a latrine screen around it. Heaven smiled on me briefly.

Overtired, overworked and totally exasperated I blundered by asking the chief nurse today how she ever got her job. For years she taught school, tired of that, took up nursing and graduated just a year before I did. Her dad had a friend in Washington, a Pentagonite with pull. She stood outside the surgery tent, her nervous tic was to pick at her left elbow when she spoke. "My, you certainly are capable." She has never, ever helped care for a patient, no matter how rushed we are. Maybe it's not part of her job description. She's a paper shuffler.

In our pell-mell existence, we received our first naval casualties. A ship right off shore from us was bombed and strafed. Even our dentists were doing minor surgery we were so swamped. We have surgical priorities that must be operated on first: belly or chest wounds take precedence over orthopedic surgery or some simple debridement. Even if the patients are the enemy, if they fit the category, they come before our soldiers. We have surgical auxiliary teams that come to our unit to do the surgery. They work non-stop 'til the shock wards are emptied of patients. The doctors were specialists in chest, belly, or orthopedic surgery.

At first, we used to line the inside of the surgery tent tops with clean sheets; it was supposed to keep the dirt from falling into the wounds. It was cumbersome work for the enlisted men and so time-consuming. We needed a sewing machine to sew the sheets together, but when the machine arrived, there weren't any needles for it. Our infection rate was almost nil, despite the wounded coming to us from straight off the battlefield. Many times there were maggots in their wounds and when you carried them on the litter, the maggots would roll out of the wounds onto the canvas.

Working in the shock wards, giving transfusions, was a rewarding, but sad, experience. Many wounded soldier's faces still haunt my memory. I recall one eighteen year old who had just been brought in from the ambulance to the shock ward. I went to him immediately, he looked up at me trustingly, sighed and asked, "How am I doing nurse?" I was standing at the head of his litter. I put my hands around his face, kissed his forehead and said, "You are doing just fine, soldier." He smiled sweetly and said, "I was just checking up." Then he died. Many of us shed tears in private. Otherwise, we try to be cheerful and reassuring.

I've seen surgeons work for hours to save a young soldier's life, but despite it they die on the operating table. Some doctors even collapsed across the patient, broke down, and cried. There are many dedicated people here giving their all. Very tired, June

Hot Sicily
Dear Betty,

Had a little time for myself late today and went swimming. Afterwards, took a long walk along the beach far away from the hospital to daydream and pretend I was at Camp Waushara. In the distance, I heard some fellow calling, "Signorina, Signorina." Looking back, I saw a beached landing craft with machine guns on deck, and a sailor running towards me. I didn't answer but started to run as fast as I could. The beach was rocky and hard on bare feet. The instant he caught up to me he prattled in his limited Italian and I prattled in my limited Italian. Finally, to clear the decks I said, "Okay, sailor, what's your real problem?" You should have seen the look on his face -- no signorina, one Americano. It was delightfully funny. The sailor turned out to be a Lieutenant JG and contritely took me back to his craft and introduced *me to his shipmate -- the quiet son of the Kingfish from Louisiana.*

Knowing how the Navy lived, I asked my new acquaintance if he had any food to spare, more specifically any ice cream. He had some, and promised that every time he saw our Red Cross on the beach he would come ashore with my favorite food. Love, June

Hot & Dry Sicily
Dear Family,

Next stop Brolo. We lived in a river bed. In rummaging through a little war-ravaged village, GI-Pepper-Belly and I discovered a Nazi medical depot. We figured it might be booby-trapped, and took turns throwing stones into it. When nothing exploded, we went in to investigate what they had left behind. It looked like they had left running. One of the favorite Nazi tricks was to booby-trap a fountain pen.

We took all of the dressings and some alcohol burners and a most interesting set of surgical instruments in a beautiful chromed box. Unfortunately one of our doctors wanted to see the instruments when we got back and then refused to give them back to us. That's what Captain's bars and no conscience do for some people.

We also discovered a large shed with huge bags of filberts leaning against the wall. We were so hungry we ate some and liberated a bag to share back at camp. It was very heavy. We alternated carrying it on our backs. We were bent in half. Everyone made filbert brittle in their mess kits by melting sugar and pouring it over the solid layer of nuts. Delicious. Love, June

8-16-43 Sicily
Dear Betty,

Today, I had a ride in a car, which had springs. Our backs and ovaries take a terrible beating riding in the back of a truck over pock-marked roads. We moved to Falconie. Saw General Patton and General Wilson.

Yesterday General Patton was visiting wounded patients at the 15th Evacuation hospital. He spied a patient who wasn't wounded and asked what his problem was. He didn't like the answer and using his gloves slapped the sad soldier across his face. Lucky it wasn't one of my patients I'm sure I would have hit him back. When I was in eighth grade, my short-tempered teacher hit Bill, our slow-paced neighbor boy over the head with a fat Geography book. I grabbed the book out of her hands and bawled her out for hitting him. She flunked me in deportment. A bomber crashed very close to us, but the crew bailed out safely. Went swimming. Love, June

56

8-17-43 Messina fell. We could see Mt. Etna smoking. I helped the 15th Infantry celebrate Messina's fall over fried chicken and fried potatoes. The British were going to occupy that area so we rejoined our main unit at Aqua Dolci to help care for the remaining patients.

8-23-43 This night, orders came that we were to leave at 5 AM for Corleone.

8-25-43 Somewhere in Sicily
Dear Ruthie,
Everything that's miserable happens to us. The other evening one of the fellows and I were swimming way out in the Mediterranean. Suddenly it looked like there were volcanoes erupting or a fleet of ships steaming rapidly toward us. Then they became black swirling spouts rushing our way. The breakers were huge and the sky darkened rapidly. With arms propelled by pure adrenalin, we swam frantically as though we were Olympic champs. The shoreline is cluttered with mammoth rocks and we were washed up on shore like broken driftwood. We clawed our way up the bank. It was about 8:30 PM. and the men had just finished striking our tents as there was a march order for 5AM.
The salty water came in huge swirls from the sea. Our cots and all of our belongings were out in the open, unprotected. I froze wearing only a wet bathing suit and swimming cap. The wind was terrifying. I covered my cot with a pup tent half and shoved my luggage under the cot. Then I crawled under a truck to wait out the storm. It lasted about an hour, at least it seemed that long. After it quit, I drained the water off from the cot and crawled in under the shelter half. Then it started to pour again. Have you ever been so discouraged and cold that you couldn't cry? Well, I was. I thought morning would never come.
Before it got light we started back to Corleone to take care of Darby's Third Ranger Battalion. Love, June

Sicily, undated letter
Dear Ruthie,
We're on the range with the Rangers, sounds like a song title, doesn't it? They are so special...the roughest, toughest nicest characters we've ever encountered. Some of their officers held their night maneuvers not far from our hospital so that their men wouldn't forget the sound of battle and get too comfy. It's hard to get comfy on an army cot in 110 degree plus weather. One night, the able-bodied men stretched a tent out on the cracked, rough earth

and pegged it in place. They got a generator going to give a bit of light and decided that they wanted to dance with the nurses. Our windup, olive drab Victrola was on its last legs. You'd just get in a soldier's arms when some joker would turn out the faint lights and you'd get kissed. Lots of raucous laughter and clapping would come from the stag-line. They were mostly in their teens, scared but brave.

Many of them have malaria and most of the nurses have malaria, but we had to work with temperatures of 103 or more. The GIs frequently offered me their cot saying I looked worse than they felt. The Army Surgeon had recommended a 14-day period of treatment in a hospital for malaria. Because the troops and the hospitals moved so fast they couldn't abide by this suggestion. The male patients, however, were then evacuated to Africa. The nurses stayed on duty in Sicily. Since I had jaundice I can't take atabrine to prevent malaria. Now that I have malaria I take quinine and my ears ring constantly like a high-pitched siren. One of our platoons is taking care of the Artillery units that are shelling the coast of Italy. Chilling again, June

Somewhere in Sicily, undated letter.
Dear Betty,

At the airfields, the anti-aircraft gun emplacements are dug down into the earth. Many nights the local female population, mothers and daughters, came calling on the fellows offering affection. Their officers would bust the non-com in charge. It didn't help much, as it was like a merry-go-round. Every few days the same guys are getting demoted or promoted.

One of our GIs spoke assorted languages fluently. Whenever he went scrounging for food, he'd take me, his favorite chow-hound, along. He had met Baron and Baroness Cammarta and they invited him to bring a couple of friends for lunch. They lived in their summer villa in the field adjoining our hospital. Their winter home in Palermo had been bombed. The whole family from grandparents to grandchild and innumerable servants lived in this spacious mansion. It was so cool inside... such a contrast to our hot tents. The farmers around there harvested and threshed grain the way they did centuries ago.

When I was off duty, I climbed mountains for diversion or went hunting fresh eggs. Ten lira each (10 cents) was the price they asked us. AMGOT (American Military Government Occupation Troops) would only let us pay five lira. The problem was to find the Sicilian who would sell them for that price. Sicilian hens are temperamental and lay at only a certain time. After struggling through the usual "Uova? Quanto costo?" the Sicilian would, by a series of motions and pointing at his watch, tell you that at such and

such a time his hens would have laid so many eggs and that you should re-
turn. One or two cold, boiled eggs taste like steak when eaten slowly--about
thirty minutes per egg. Fletcherizing this way filled up my empty shrunken
stomach. Thought you might enjoy these items. They say it all.

Gi Chow Inspires...

Since his entry into the Army, the average soldier has eaten and drunk many concoctions which have not only given him indigestion, bad dreams, but in many cases, the urge to write poetry. In his thoughts about love, battle or the routine job, the GI manages somehow or the other to make some references to food or drink. Today's poems are a digest of some of these gastronomic experiences where the Muse forsakes her laurel for the cookbook.

Ode to an Egg

You, subject of the world's old riddle
You, who look so well on pan or griddle,
To you we sing paeans of praise
Oh, happy mem'ry of happier days.

Sunny smile couched in snowy lace,
Ruffled, you retain that pleasant grace.
Even clothed, as when poached
Your culinary magnet isn't approached.

Here not coddled or watched with care,
Spurned on any sergeant's bill of fare,
To rekindle our love oft have we tried,
We'll have you in any shape, except "dried."

Life for us just won't start
Until you resume your integral part.
The riddle's answer isn't easy pickin'
Who came first--you or canned chicken
   T-4 Cecil A. C (last name is missing) Stars & Stripes

Our most beautiful nurse lost one of her upper front teeth. Our
dentist was on loan to the infantry and the CO wouldn't send her to the
rear to a hospital that had one. For days she stretched her upper lip over the
offending space when she spoke. She was so embarrassed to look like a Jack-

O-Lantern.

Orders came to move up, again in convoy. We ride in the back of a 2 1/2-ton truck. The occupants of any vehicle that come up behind us, start to chat with us, and hand us bottles of wine and food. 'Toothless' started to drink the wine and got so sloshed that she started smiling at every vehicle and would point to her mouth and say "See I lost my tooth and my CO won't let me get it fixed." She'd shout out his full name and rank. It was delightfully funny. Word travels fast in a convoy and the very next day the CO lent her his recon to go to a dentist. Please keep writing. Love, June

Somewhere in Sicily
Dear Mom and Dad,

One of the GIs in an AAA outfit was a native-born Sicilian. He was detailed to go up into the villages and buy chickens and eggs. He took me with him in a weapons carrier. We drove on things that couldn't be considered roads. In one of the villages we came to, way up in the hills, he parked on the street and told me to wait there for him. As soon as he disappeared from sight the people came out of the houses and touched my clothes and my hair.

One of the younger ladies invited me into her home. It was on a corner, threadbare, with only two rooms. The main room had two doors exiting on both streets. The lady who invited me, put two wooden chairs in the middle of the room. As soon as I sat down, villagers crowded in around me until the room was packed.

They really grilled me. First question they asked was "How many children do you have?" Next, "How old are you?" and finally "Are you married?" When they found I was twenty-two they thought it was a crime I wasn't married. They thought I was an antique. They had never met anyone from America before, and the last thing they had expected was to have a nurse visit their village. I was wearing fatigues and they traced my insignia with their fingers. So many people wanted to touch my hair they kept changing places with each other in order to do that. I was wearing bright red Revlon nail polish. That was new to them and they had to touch that too.

Then my hostess brought me an eight-ounce glass full of wine. It was so thick and dark it looked like purple soup. While I was trying to explain to her that I didn't drink wine, she wiggled into the kitchen and reappeared with a raw egg and was going to break it into the wine. Smiling, I finally managed to explain to her that I would love the egg and would take it back to camp with me and have it for breakfast. She just smiled and hugged me. Then she reached up on the bare walls for a small pin cushion, hanging on a nail. It was made of rags and held together by a tiny bit of embroidery. She

60

pressed it into my hands. Tears came into my eyes. I didn't want to hurt her feelings by refusing it but I had nothing to give her--only the fatigues on my back. Just then, my driver arrived with a supply of chickens and eggs. I told him about the wine and he explained to them why I couldn't drink it.

We went to other villages. Many had water running down the gutters, which were filled with all sorts of trash and human discharge. You'd see a little bare-bottomed tyke toileting himself in the gutter at the top of the hill. Not too much further down, a woman would be washing out a dish in the same gutter water. Much love, June

9-3-43 Somewhere in Sicily.
Good morning family,
        8th Army invaded Italy.
        We're having the second rain of the summer. It only lasted about three hours. The sky was gorgeous where the rain clouds were trying to break up over the mountains and along the distant seashore.
        Did you ever send the mushroom soup, candy and cookies? Today we got our first chocolate bar since we were in Ferryville, North Africa about four months ago. I'll ration it to myself so it will last longer. I'm sending your Christmas gifts soon and hope you will like them. Am well at the moment and behaving, Love, June

9-8-43 Dearest Family,
        Italy surrendered to the Allies, but in our isolated field we didn't know about it. Unsuspecting such a great event, several nurses and our friends from the 48th Medical Bn. drove into Corleone just as it was getting dusk. The town was "Off Limits" to all troops, so we were the only Americans in the city--we thought. Everyone of the 25,000 inhabitants were out in the streets celebrating. They mobbed us. The jeep would barely move. The Baron and Baroness and AMGOT officials took us to a balcony on the second floor of their headquarters overlooking this vast mass of people. They cheered and we smiled, waved, and nodded. Then we'd shout "Viva la America", "Viva la Britain", "Viva la Italia", and they'd answer the same in unison. Sometimes they'd shout "Bueno Americano".
        We started all the church bells ringing. It was soul inspiring. Lights came on in house windows that had been blacked out for ages because of the continued air raids. The crowd moved up to the church and, choosing two of their oversized saints, mounted them on a candle-rimmed platform and started a procession down the street from one end of the city to the other. The priest in his flowing robes, with little altar boys trudging behind him, led

the parade to the accompaniment of a tiny band. Various people would give gifts of money. Then the procession would stop while someone in the crowd would climb up and pin the money on the saint's robe.

All of a sudden the tempo of the music changed. We rushed to the head of the procession to see two AWOL GIs swinging out on a trumpet and drum they had 'borrowed' from the band. The priest just speeded up the tempo of his chanting. It was a night to remember forever. Love, June

9-10-43 Somewhere in Sicily
Dear Mother,
Send me the following items. My collapsible electric iron, brown and dark green anklets size 9 1/2--3 pair, film 620-828 as many as you can buy, 2 packages of good bobby pins, 1 package medium lead for an Eversharp pencil, small hand-mirror, candy bars, pecan rolls, 2 pr. panties small size, 2 bras size 34. We moved again. The flies are terrible here, but it is much warmer than when we were in the mountains. Love, June

9-10-43 Orders came to move to Termini to stage for the invasion of Italy. We staged and staged. Orders were given and then cancelled and then given again and cancelled. Happily we missed the initial landings at Salerno.

9-14-43 Commendation:
1. You, your officers, nurses and enlisted men are commended for your excellent performance of duty throughout the Sicilian Campaign.
2. You have helped care for over 12,000 patients, 3909 of whom were American Battle casualties. Through your untiring efforts, skill, and devotion to duty, you have rendered the highest type of surgical care.
3. I congratulate you and your unit for your exemplary performance of an arduous task. Signed John P. Lucas Major General, USA, Commanding

9-17-43 Somewhere in Sicily
Dear Ruth and family,
Have mom send me that blue ribbed sweater I knit myself, also the parts of that dark navy blue one I started, and the rest of the yarn plus a pair of knitting needles, size five. I had the front, back and one sleeve done. The other sleeve wasn't quite finished. I'll need them this winter. Also some 828 film.
Last night a five-inch-long centipede type creature got into my cot.

I felt it crawl across my foot and killed it before it could bite me. Anything that has over two legs, bugs me. Love, June

9-25-43 Sicily
Dear family,

The Admiral of the Fleet threw a big party at the Prince's Palace in Palermo. A friend of mine, a skipper on an LCI invited me to attend. The problem was how was I to get the forty miles by land to the dance. He just didn't have a jeep. He called me from Palermo and made me promise to meet him at the harbor in Termini. I walked miles to get there. Fortunately there were other nurses on the dock from an Evacuation hospital. They had been driven there. Ship Ahoy! A minesweeper arrived to pick us up for the trip. The SS Philadelphia and Boise were in port. Douglas Fairbanks was a naval officer on one of them. We had such an incredible evening. What heavenly food, gallons of ice cream and cases of Coca Cola, I thought I had died and gone to heaven. There was a storm at sea on our way back to Termini, no casualties however.

It was lucky I went and that the trip back took much longer. It was just beginning to get light when I stopped at the latrine on the top of our hillside on the way to my tent. I saw a huge soldier bending over one of our nurses, his hands were under her mosquito netting, reaching for her throat. I kicked a rock and screamed. He ran to the road. My friend was so terrified that she couldn't scream. My screams alerted our men but they couldn't catch the fellow. They threw a 24 hour armed guard around our tents for a few days. We really couldn't spare the men for such a detail. We lived in terror for a long time after that.

At that same location on one of the very hot days, an ammunition train sitting on the tracks at the foot of our area started exploding from the heat. Shells in all directions.

Sightseeing in Palermo, examining the skeletons in the Catacombs, swimming and sailing at lovely Mondelo Beach, and trying to beat the Navy out of their huge Coca Cola supply helped pass the time, while we waited to invade Italy. One day I managed to get a whole case of Coca Cola and started to hitchhike back to camp with it. A soldier in a jeep gave me a ride. I promised him one bottle for the trip. Everyone who passed us and saw the Coca Cola begged to buy it for $5.00 a bottle. No sale. I shared it with our nurses. Love, June

9-26-43 I went to a 60th Infantry party.

9-27-43 I went to a II Corps dance. All combat units were trying to enjoy themselves before sailing for Italy and more war.

9-28-43 Our hospital received a commendation from the Commanding General II Corps.

During this campaign our Supply Officer had to travel long distances and contact several medical supply depots to get what we needed. Intravenous fluids were our greatest need and they were in short supply. Fresh vegetables or fruits were not issued to us but could be secured from the natives. We treated 2800 cases both medical and surgical. Many times we had a complete turnover of patients in a 24-hour period. We were understaffed for nurses.

I received the following letter from a former patient at Fort Custer who was temporarily in an infantry replacement depot in North Africa.

10-10-43 Somewhere in Africa
Dear June,

It isn't often that I get this way, and when I do I don't put it down, but I've got so much time--to think and to write. So I wrote this job in blank verse (I couldn't say it in rhyme--it would sound like the lyrics to a jive song by Sammy Kaye). It's thoroughly unoriginal. It's what a lot of others think. But I had the time so I wrote it down. I call it "I'm Selfish". It isn't a very good title. As a matter of fact it isn't a very good poem, but I feel that way, and after the war I want to live that way in Wisconsin, or Brooklyn, or Rochester. Here it is.

If I were to tell you what I want
When I return from the war you'd laugh.
I'd be a big disappointment to all the speakers
The orators and statesmen and reporters;
Because I don't really much want
What they say I want,
And I don't need what they think I need.
I'm selfish.
You don't talk about what I want,
You don't bull with the boys about it,
You just want it;
At times you ache for it.

I sometimes read in the papers or magazines

And someone says that the boys at the front
Want to "Win the Peace".
I don't want to "Win the Peace",

I don't really think I know what it means,
I don't care who Wins the Peace
As long as I get what I want,
And so does everyone else.

I'm not interested in post-war economics
Except that I have a job and enough money
To raise a family decently.

I don't care who gets what corridor
Except that the people in it like the idea
And my son doesn't have to fight a war about it.
I don't care a damn thing
About reparations, war debts, lend-lease,
As long as no one gets hurt in the counting.
I'm selfish.

Do you know what I want?
What I'm fighting for?
I'll tell you-----

No big ideas, no four syllable words
No platforms for greedy politicians
That's not it.

I'm fighting for my own place to live
Anywhere in the country, anywhere I want to.
Good food, and clothes, and shelter
For my wife and my kids and me,
For a little place that's all ours.
And a good open school for the kids
Open to all ideas, I mean.

I want to vote about how many
Should be on the Supreme Court,
Or whether we should raise or lower the tariff,

Or what kind of taxes we should pay,
Or should we spend or balance;
I don't want a plebiscite where all vote "yes".

I want to pack up the wife and kids
And go away for a weekend;
Where I want to go
When I want to go
For how long I want to go.
And I want everyone all over to do the same.

I don't want to hear speeches,
Except at election time,
Or dedicating a bridge, or a dam, or a library.

I don't want to be yelled at over the radio,
I'd rather hear Bob Hope
Or a Dodger broadcast.

All I want the Army to do
Is beat Notre Dame and Navy
So I can win in the pool.

I want to kiss my wife any time
And not by decree.
I want to take my son fishing
And discuss life,
And not be whipped for "sabotaging the effort".
And everyone else to do the same.

I want to go to any church I please;
I want to hear both sides of the question.
And when I want to say something
I don't want to have to look over my shoulder
For secret police.
And everyone else to do the same.

That's why I want to win the war,
Let the talkers talk about what I mean,
They make it sound big and profound,

They make me sound big and profound,
But I'm not big and profound
I'm selfish. Alex

10-13-43 Italy declared war on Germany. I'm a patient in an Evacuation hospital.

10-20-43 I was invited to Palermo by the daughter of a brewery owner. She gave me a case of small bottles of champagne to take to Italy, and took me shopping so I could buy a whole stalk of bananas. They were seven cents apiece and they never ripened to taste like anything resembling a Chiquita banana. They were woody and dry.

Today we received seventeen 2 1/2 ton amphibious DUKWs for our move to Italy.

10-21-43 We got orders to go to Italy in a 300 vehicle DUKW convoy. The British put us up for the night at Messina in their hospital. That was the first time I had slept on a bed since I left New York.

SIX

Up the Toe of Italy

The Straits of Messina were never defended so the Germans and Italians evacuated thousands of their soldiers to fight another day.

9-9-43 At 0330 hours, our troops from the 5th Army, VI Corps landed on Red Beach 2 near Paestum -- they were the first American Army to invade Italy in World War II. Our Ranger friends from Sicily, those wonderful dead-end kids, went to Maiori. LCIs of the British and American navies shuttled our troops from their transports to the beaches through German mine fields. It was a bloody fight; the Texas 36th Division lost about 7,000 men in their part of the landing.

On the advance to Naples, the 5th Army included the 45th, 3rd, 34th, 36th Infantry Divisions, 82nd Airborne Division, and the British 7th Armoured Division.

10-22-43 At 1030 hrs, LCTs ferried our hospital's heavy trucks over to Italy across the Straits of Messina. We traveled in DUKWs and came ashore at Reggio Calabria in southern Italy. DUKWs are seven-ton amphibious trucks that could carry 25 men on land, or 50 men while afloat, or 5000 pounds of general cargo. Comfy they're not. That night we bivouacked at Giosa Taura, the next night at Nicastro. Trip-weary, we spent many days in convoy, over rugged mountain roads with hairpin curves. To make each curve, the DUKWs had to back up and that slowed us to a snail's pace. All along the way we bartered for fresh eggs, chickens, potatoes, and fruit to supplement the awful C rations the Army furnished. Other bivouac spots included Belvedere, Salerno and Avellino.

At night, we'd find a small level area to camp, put two DUKWs fairly close together, throw a tarpaulin over the dividing space to keep off the rain, and proceed to fry the chicken and potatoes. Once, we discovered a German ration dump that contained fresh-frozen apricots. It was our dessert for the day, a most unusual occurrence.

Potpourri

Like a lot of raging fires,
My heart is filled with wild desires
Of ice-cream sodas, chocolate malted,
Former knick-knacks now exalted.
I miss the lowly hot-dog stands
That are never found in foreign lands;
Miss the Cokes and candy bars
And meals sandwiched with mild cigars;
Miss the crowded five-and-ten
And nickle music mixed with gin,
The corny jokes of soda jerkers,
Lunchtime rush of office workers--
I miss these things that I recall,
But miss my sweetheart most of all.
            Pfc. J. B. Wallis: Stars and Stripes

October 1943 Somewhere in Italy, only GOD knows where.
Dear Family,
         The past week, we suffered through a rugged session: freezing by night, choking on dust all day. Maybe we'll be lucky and get to live in a building. The Bilron was for me, the Army doesn't stock any here. The doctor wants me to take it because I had jaundice.
         In the August 9th issue of Life Magazine, pages 69-73, is an article about Dr. Randolph Lovelace. I was his part-time scrub nurse in Rochester when he was on a fellowship at Mayos. He'd wait until all the nurses were finished scrubbing in Kahler surgery and then come around looking pathetic and hopeful and ask for volunteers to work with him, as Dr. Charley Mayo

had given him a couple of thyroidectomies to do. A classmate of mine and I volunteered. We were captives until Ginny fainted while holding the retractors one day. I was at the sink working on the soiled instruments when Lovelace shouted for help. I turned. There was Ginny on the floor, her very long arm still holding the retractor in place. Then I became the lone captive. Lovelace would jump out of airplanes at incredible heights to test his theories and those of his two cohorts. The L on the BLB oxygen mask stands for Lovelace.

Too bad the frame for the painting of the harbor at Palermo was broken. It was painted by one of the locals; I hope it wasn't torn. It was a long time in getting to you. Please keep sending me food. Love, June

Dear Family:

Men from a battalion of the 45th told me that when they arrived in Italy they shuttled back and forth from the beach in different directions during daylight and under cover of darkness a few times to make the Krauts think there were a lot more troops arriving. If that explanation is garbled--and you are confused too, the ruse worked. Love, June

10-28-43 We arrived in Caserta and are attached to the 5th Army, under Lt. General Mark Clark. Here, we set up our 400-bed hospital in an Italian-German barracks. It was heavily camouflaged with scenes of tall trees painted on the building. For the first time, we had civilian help to do the laundry and clean the building.

Too bad we weren't attached to Allied Force Headquarters. They lived in the 1,200 room Caserta palace: in it was a 40-room royal apartment. The palace was surrounded by acres of formal gardens, statues, pools, and fountains. Being envious of such living quarters is useless.

Field Hospital checklist of clothing and equipment for Nurses, APO 758 US Army.

This was my list of what was authorized for me. What was authorized and what I got were two different things. If two were authorized sometimes I'd get only one. Small size was the loose use of the word "small". Frequently I was given a man's small. Wearing men's stuff I was well camouflaged. You, couldn't tell if I was human, much less a female. Nothing fit properly.

1 Bag, utility; 3 Cap, Seersucker sm.; 1 Cap, Service, OD 21 1/2; 1 Cape, OD sm.; 1 pr. Gloves, leather 6 1/2; 1 pr. Gloves, wool 6 1/2; 1 Insignia, Officers; 2 Jacket, Seersucker sm.; 2 Jacket, wool, OD 10 R;

2 Necktie, khaki; 1 Overcoat, Field 12 sm; 1 pr. Overshoes, women's sz 6; 1 Raincoat, sm.; 1 Scarf, beige; 2 pr. Shoes, low, service 5 1/2 A; 2 Skirt, wool, OD 12; 1 Sweater, beige, 36; 9 Uniform, cotton, 12; 5 Waists, cotton, 32; 6 pr. Anklets, wool, 9 1/2; 1 Cap, wool, knit med; 1 pr. Gloves, mosquito 6 1/2; 1 Jacket, field, winter, sm; 2 pr. Leggings, canvas 2R; 1 pr. Overshoes, Arctic, women's 6; 4 Panties, winter, sm; (On July 4, 1945 I was issued 4 pair of summer panties) I still celebrate the day for that reason; 4 Shirt, HBT (Herring Bone Twill), Spec. sm; 2 pr. Shoes, field 5 1/2 B; 4 pr. Stockings, wool sz. 9 1/2; 4 Trousers, HBT, Spec. sm.; 2 Trousers, Outer cover sz 12; 1 Trousers, wool liner sz 12; 4 Vests, winter, sm.; (July 4, 1945 I was issued 4 pair of summer vests); 4 Waists, wool sz 34; 2 Jacket, tropical 10 R ; 2 Skirt, tropical sz 12; 1 Cap, service, summer 21 1/2; 4 Shirt, Seersucker sz 12; 4 Slacks, Seersucker sz 12; 1 Trouser, wool, OD 29x29; 0 Shirt, wool, OD; 1 Undershirt, wool 34; 1 Underdrawers, wool sz 30; 1 pr Shoes, men's G.I. 5 1/2; 1 Overshoes, Arctic, men's sz 6; 1 Bag, Sleeping (didn't arrive until 1944); 1 Jacket, pile liner sz 12 (didn't arrive until Feb. 23, 1945).

Dear Family,

Twenty letters today. I'm on night duty, twelve hours and it's really rugged. We're having an air raid again. I have six wards of patients. Some of them are frantic. I've given the worst ones all their ordered sedation. Our buildings are completely blacked out, but the soldiers wouldn't even let us use a flashlight so we could continue our work. I'm in a closet charting. I can hear the Germans go overhead time after time and then you hear the bomb as it bursts. You just keep on doing whatever has to be done. There is no place to hide. No bomb shelters. I'm so very tired. Three and a half hours of sleep wasn't quite enough for me. Suppose I'll ever be able to sleep again? The moon is too lovely tonight. That always helps the enemy along. They don't have to drop so many flares to see where to drop their bombs effectively.

Love, June

Dear Parents,

My lifeboat-mate from the trip to North Africa is now sharing my tent. When things get too serious around here, she takes off her restraining undergarments, puts on a baggy set of men's long johns, and starts toe-dancing around the tent, while reciting assorted verses of The Shooting of Dan McGrew. Every now and then she varies her routines by grabbing the baggy knee of her long johns and pulling them up slowly to barely show her ankle, while she rolls her eyes to heaven. Then it's belly laugh season until we hurt and have to stop.

Mom, the light socks and ankle socks arrived. Thanks very much, but, please, remember I wear size nine, the ones you send are too large. Just like the panties. I still wear small, you always send medium or large and they just fall off me. Lucky I wear fatigues to catch them. You wouldn't want me to drop my drawers in public. We have no place to shop. I don't mean to be cross. You and dad are my life-line and I couldn't do without you.

Love, June

Dear Parents,

The rainy season chalked up a new record this month. Despite the weather conditions, we averaged an air raid every other night. The patients needed more sedation than usual because of it.

The quality of food improved a smidgen in Italy. Many times we were too busy to eat anyway. One of our GIs, a great scrounger from the hill-country back home, would come into the ward almost every day with fresh vegetables for me. He carried the tomatoes, potatoes and peppers inside his shirt, which he fluffed out to look blousey, so no one knew what he had. Then he'd wait until other officers from our unit had left the room. While he was dilly-dallying, he'd visit with the patients. He usually had a good snoot full of wine, plus some Blue Heaven jags. One didn't dare to ask where or how he got the loot. He was very tall and slender, but he looked so lumpy on vegetable days. He had a little sister my age and I guess he thought I looked a little peaked. I was touched and grateful.

My only distasteful assignment so far during the war was to interview all of the patients who came in with a venereal disease. I sat on their cot with my clip board and filled out army forms. What was her name? Where did she live? How many times did you have contact with her? Etc., ad nauseam. I was regaled with the most lurid details. One wag told me he had gonorrhea so often he swore it came with his C rations. He also told me that he didn't care what the female looked like--he'd just put a flag over her face and do anything for Uncle Sam.

There had been a regulation in effect that if a soldier got VD his pay was docked while he was being treated. The men quit reporting it, went untreated, got seriously ill, and were no longer fit for combat duty. They stopped docking their pay. Enjoyable Ella Fitzgerald came to entertain the patients.

We have this resident psychiatrist who follows me around asking for permission to psychoanalyze me. He said something must be wrong with *me as I was always so cheerful and no one should be cheerful in a war zone. I told him to see a shrink himself -- he is so depressing. He must have chronic ulcerative colitis; his bowels are always in an uproar about something. Love, June*

10-31-43 Today I sent a Christmas-New Years V-mail to my parents. Designer, unknown. Here's a description. In large double lined letters--MERRY CHRISTMAS--across the top of the page. Below it seven large twinkling stars under which were three mountains with ten pine trees in front. On the left hand side, an American flag on a stand. On the right, a tent hospital. A road leading to the mountains separates the flag from the hospital. Beneath it, this poem.

Out of the dark and lonely war
Out of the dreadful cannon's roar
A bright sweet light of joy and cheer
A merry, victorious CHRISTMAS and a HAPPY PEACEFUL NEW YEAR. At the bottom of the page doubled lined letters--HAPPY NEW YEAR.

11-14-43 Somewhere in Italy
Dearest Family:
I hope the packages you mentioned arrive soon; I'm very hungry for homemade cookies. My pajamas are all worn out too and my anklets are fini. It's raining bucketfuls. So thankful, we are in a building. We'll probably be back in the field soon, it's our destiny. Love, June

11-15-43
With the 5th Army at the front. If you ever want to know the true nature of a campaign, find out how the infantrymen are going into battle. If they're riding, with their barracks bags stowed neatly in the two-and-a-half, then it's going well. If they're walking, then it can still be going well, although slower. In this campaign, the boys are climbing. They are also crawling and wading and sliding and marching but primarily they're climbing: up mountains and down mountains, carrying their single blanket and the extra package of K-rations, toting their rifles and machine guns and mortars and an extra ten pounds of mud on each foot, fighting the weather and terrain as much as the well-entrenched Jerries. *Sgt. Walter Bernstein, Stars & Stripes*

11-26-43 Somewhere in Italy
Dear Family:

The Bilron, film, cookies, candy and moldy cake arrived today. Was the cake still warm when you wrapped it? The sleeping bag is a godsend, at least I'll be half warm this winter. We had a turkey dinner yesterday, someone must have made a mistake; we aren't used to elegant food. The first sunshine in weeks. Maybe the rainy season is over and the soldiers can get down to some serious fighting. What mud does to those poor soldier's feet. Glad Bud is in the Air Force.

Please read the book "The Last Days of Pompeii". As usual, I was the last person in the unit to get a pass to go to Pompeii. I ended up taking the tour with twenty-three men, some male officers, and the rest enlisted men. The Italian guide went into detailed explanation of everything, until he got to the street that had the deepest ruts worn into the solid rock by chariot wheels. I wondered how many centuries it had taken to form the ruts. This was Prostitute Parkway. A phallus was chiseled into the rock by each doorway.

Guideo stopped at this house which had a rather large locked, box riveted to it. With a great flourish he unlocked the pièce de resistance or the penis de resistance (take your choice). There was a Roman soldier standing in full uniform with a monstrous erected penis lying on a scale. The other part of the scale was piled high with gold. You're right--they balanced. Sorry, Chiefs, but I laughed. The machos didn't appreciate that. To confound them more, I took a picture for posterity.

Guideo then moved on to a house that he said I couldn't go into. Only the men were permitted to see this. So I waited outside, curious about what I was missing. When the men started coming out much later, I told Guideo that I thought it was unfair to restrict my seeing the whole tour. One of the officers turned to the guide and said "Let her go in". I went. There for posturarity were the Roman's favorite sexual positions. My one thought was that in those days they didn't live to be very old -- so they were limber enough to try anything.

The patients are in a good mood today. They're playing some ancient records on an antiquated Victrola with a near defunct needle. It's not soul-inspiring music.

Ruth, I got some pretty handmade silver butterfly pins for you and Betty. An Italian civilian barber and his little boy are assigned to my wards each day. The soldiers that can walk to the back room barber shop do so; the others he shaves while they are lying in bed. Every morning, he breezes in and says "Goodda-morning--Shava--da haircut." Everyone laughs and we all imitate him. His little boy buzzes along behind him carrying the water for the shave.

74

Italian women sweep and scrub the floor. They sweep all the dirt and cigarette butts into a corner. Then they pick the butts out of the dirt and take them home to their husbands. I've told them some of the fellows have contagious diseases, but they still do it anyway. Maybe they have the same diseases at home. Love, June

11-29-43 Italy
Dearest family,
    We're back in tents. Chilly isn't it? I was invited to a dinner party last night at 5th Army headquarters. Good food, good companionship.
    My Christmas gifts arrived. Thank you. The sweaters feel wonderful. What I wear can't be called regulation, the colors and designs don't jibe with the Army. Can't wait to try the popcorn as soon as I can find some dry wood. I got a crummy little potbellied stove, but nothing to burn in it. The wood I've found so far is wet and green. Using my little hatchet I tried to chop it. It was like rubber. My fingers were frozen and blistered. Not wanting to take up swearing, I hired an Italian man to cut some wood. It's not safe to walk in areas that the engineers haven't swept for land mines. I can just see the headlines in a paper back home "Freezing Troops Given Stoves" and everyone who read it felt good about their sons and daughters. Stoves do not a fire make. It's like a gun without ammunition.
    Mother, sorry you think my letters lack a lot of detail sometimes. That's censorship. Are they lacking in humor too? I can't tell you just where we are now. But I can tell you that we drove over here in a DUKW convoy. Took us about eight days from our starting point in Sicily. By now, that's long enough ago to be in the history books. The latrine screen, or lack thereof, en route was brutal, though now all of that seems sort of funny. We had a nurse who couldn't go with a coeducational crowd around; by the end of the week, she was really ill. The last night, when we did have a latrine screen around our slit trench, it was placed just a whisper away from the kitchen tent. She warned all of us to stay away. We did, but one of the youngest enlisted men walked in on her by mistake -- one latrine screen in the dark looks like another. The fellows in the kitchen heard all of the fireworks. Plus that, they got a first person, exaggerated, revolting account from the soldier. Such fun, we have no secrets, June

11-30-43 Today, back in America, the bituminous coal-miners got a wage increase and turned out the highest weekly production in 16 years. Harold Ickes said the new contract and wage increase will be like adding another hour of production to each working day. I wonder

75

how much of the war effort depends on coal for the factories turning out war materiel. Until the miners got a lucrative contract, they were dragging their butts while our soldiers were hoisting their rifle butts, one wool blanket, some ammo, a packet of rations, and a canteen up to the fighting front. They didn't get a pay increase. But they fight each day and night an unlimited number of hours. I've often wondered if these miners had sons in the combat zones.

...With Ga'lantry
The mocking voice of Death
Beckons seductively;
Across the littered heath--
Speaking not angrily,
But choking off breath
Of mere humanity--
Aye, and so firmly.

A voice half unreal,
Belching and thundering,
Summons with steel
Men to the numbering;
Charging all kneel,
The right and the blundering,
And with humility.

Certain that voice I hear
Amid the shelling,
All shades of sound so clear,
Loud and compelling;
Somehow habitual fear,
Calmly dispelling,
Gives way to gallantry.
Pvt. Roy Daniel--Stars and Stripes

This poem, written by a combat veteran, is accompanied by a sketch of two young helmeted soldiers with their rifles, staring at the grim reaper whose feet are snarled in barbed wire.

12-4-43 Somewhere in Italy
Dear Betty,

After the terrific rains last night, the ground in our tent is a veritable stream. You should see us wallow in the mud, like piggies.

Yes, I liked that leather jacket, too. I reckon you can have it, if you want it that much. Perhaps I'll be too skinny to wear it if and when I get home again.

I've received the loveliest gifts so far. A friend at Fort Custer had his chief nurse do the shopping for him. He told her to buy whatever she would want if she were in my place. She wrapped everything in individual packages...nylon bra, panties, slip, hose, housecoat, satin bedroom slippers, Revlon nail polish, polish remover, cuticle oil, emery boards, combs, nail files, Lentheric perfume "Miracle", candy, powder, rouge, lipsticks, powder puffs, a silk slip, toothbrush and tooth powder, and a miniature deck of KEM cards. When I wear the lingerie it'll make me feel like a female again, at least underneath the olive drab-drab-drab. Our neighbor Karl sent me a huge box of Johnston's mixed salted nuts. Lt. Fitzgerald sent soap, cigarettes for trading, canned chicken à la king, Kleenex and gum. My roommate from Rochester, is stationed with the Navy in Hawaii, sent Roger & Gallet toilet soap, satin pajamas, bras, panties and food of all kinds. I know I shouldn't have opened my packages before Christmas, but I was so excited I nearly burst. Bless everyone who thought of me. My new tentmate had made me promise that I wouldn't open any of my packages early. Before she got off duty and caught me, I had to hurry and rewrap everything.

The legs of our cots were sitting on rocks to keep them out of the thick mud. She thought if we put the pieces of cardboard from our packages under our cots that we'd be warmer. But all that happened was it attracted all the field mice for miles around. She was scared of mice. Naturally they got into our food packages. As we don't have any bathrobes, we have begun to use the inside wool lining to our coats. It has large cutouts under the axillae. They are ugly but warm. *Love, June*

Lines found near A Submerged Field Hospital:
Now is the season of rain and thunder,
When you go to bed above and wake up under.
And though you're rugged as a Turk or Saracen,
You wish to God you were back in garrison.
Churchill once mentioned tears, sweat, and blood,
But forgot the worst of the lot--mud.
Mud on Privates (first class and bucks)

Mud on Sergeants, Jeeps, and Trucks,
Mud on you and mud on me,
And on 2nd Lieutenants, M.A.C.
Insidious mud that sticks like glue,
Reminiscent of C ration stew,
Mud that's impossible to get off ye,
Mud that looks like GI coffee.
Generals all whoever you may be,
Bend an ear to this GI plea.
Listen and heed this hopeful refrain,
War postponed on account of rain.
                    J. R. Bastian: Stars & Stripes

12-7-43 Italy
Dearest Family,
        My new tentmate and I had our first 24-hour pass and we went to Naples to a dance. She's Catholic and took me to mass. People put five lira (five cents) in the collection plate and took out 4 lira change. The poor souls were dirty and ragged, and there were chickens running in and out of the church. Recently, she got married and hasn't told anyone as the Army frowns on that. Other nurses who married overseas were sent to another theater. This war tries more than men's souls. Love, June

        Because of the almost constant rain we now have a mess tent. Our sanitary facilities are of the semi-permanent type, even grease traps and soakage pits. One night in an air raid, I dived into one and one of the soldiers landed on my legs, we were a mess. Garbage is given to the Italians who haul it away for their animals. Mosquitoes are everywhere. We have repellent, bed nets, and headnets. Venereal disease is rampant. To try and control it, officers give frequent sex-morality lectures and hand out condoms. I often thought of the engineering officer in North Africa who smuggled his French mistress to Sicily. Our TO didn't call for mistresses for men. I wondered if the engineer hid Frenchy in the motor pool equipment like my pup tentmate did her dog, Vino.

        At the moment, we have two major campaigns behind us and are now in the middle of the Naples-Foggia campaign.

12-8-43 Italy
        Our hospital is on Highway 6. To avoid moving the wounded

from 30 to 50 miles further back to the nearest Station or General Hospital, we admitted 113 battle casualties in a two-hour period. Our admitting clerks were really rushed. The Army Surgeon's office sent us several surgical auxiliary teams to do the operations. These doctors are so talented and devoted and work incredibly long hours. In a 48 hour period, 84 casualties were operated on. We only lost one of these patients.

12-12-43 Commendation from II Corps for our hospital.

"As a result of my personal visits, combined with reports of visits of officers of my staff I wish to commend you, your officers, nurses, and enlisted men for the efficient manner in which you are caring for the sick and wounded soldiers, not only of the II Corps Command but of the entire Fifth Army Command. The wounded to whom I spoke were outspoken with praise for the attention they are receiving.

In particular, do I wish to extend my commendation to the NURSES for their cheerfulness and attention to duty as they go about caring for the wounded under the most adverse conditions of weather.

I am confident that your hospital is doing everything possible to provide care for the sick and wounded in such manner that reflects credit to the highest standards of the Medical Corps of the United States Army. Equally confident am I that this high standard will be upheld by each member of your organization in the battles to come!" Major General, Geoffrey Keyes U. S. A. Commanding

We just heard that last month Senator Styles Bridges was investigating Lend Lease shipments of 450,000 yards of diaper cloth to North Africa. So that's where the cloth went.

SEVEN

Christmas in Italy

12-23-43 Italy 1 AM
Dearest Family,
    Last Thursday's Stars and Stripes had this great Bill Mauldin cartoon called UP FRONT. Five unshaven infantrymen in full Army gear, steel helmets, rifles, ammunition belts and canteens are hanging by their fingernails on a precarious mountainside. All the soldiers are looking up... stupefied at their sergeant who has just ordered, "Hit Th' Dirt Boys".
Mauldin has captured the war with his sketches and comments. My favorite coined word of his was "garritroopers"; they were affected non-combatants, too far forward to wear ties and too far back to get shot. Both Art and Bob from home have been good about stopping to see me. Because they are enlisted men, Army regulations forbid them having chow with me in our mess. We have to stand out in front of the Colonel's tent to talk to each other. The old goat thinks he might miss something otherwise. I should have scalded his ears with fictitious, titillating tidbits. Guess my strategy is slipping.
    It's getting quite cold here in the daytime. I have to wear my wool-lined field jacket. As soon as the sun sets, the cold is vicious. Will I ever be warm again?
    It doesn't seem like Christmas-time without snow. We wallow through mud instead, and it's not very pleasant. It's the poor soldiers I worry about

who have to bail water out of their foxholes, and don't get to take their shoes off for days at a time. Trench foot is horrible. The suffering of our young men is awful. No one at home will ever believe or understand us. Love, June

Christmas
"They'll have pumpkin pie as usual,"
I heard one doughboy say.
"Not at our house," said another
"We have mince-meat pie that day."
And so the boys got started
And talked of things back home;
Their thoughts were pointed westward
Their guns were laid toward Rome.
Soon came a rude awakening
As a shell whizzed overhead
Then one who had been silent
Looked up again and said:
"We'll do what the Captain told us
The night before he fell:
Have a Merry Christmas fellows
And give the Jerries hell."
            Cpl. Robert E. Burns: Stars & Stripes

12-25-43 Italy 4 AM
Merry Christmas family,
        I went on duty at 7:30 PM, gave my evening medications and treatments, and dashed over at 8:30 to the recreational tent to sing "Cantique de Noël "for the fellows. Then back to duty and passed out the Christmas packages the American Red Cross had donated for the sick and wounded. Oranges, apples and English walnuts tied in a big white hanky with a red ribbon around it; also, a box containing a deck of cards, three packs of cigarettes two bags of candy, and several writing cards. Earlier in the afternoon, the Italian Red Cross passed around Italian nut bars.
        My two wardmen, who have magnificent voices, and I sang some carols for the patients. Then we tucked them in their hard, cold cots. The men never complain. You can't help loving all of them. Love, June

Dear Folks,

Christmas night wasn't something that we expected. During a furious storm, tents blew down, all the others leaked through the flak holes and tent flaps, some ripped down the center. We managed to keep the tents erect over the patients by having everyone in the unit cling to the poles. Pyramidal tents were the only ones to weather the storm. The stove pipes became disjointed and posed a terrible fire hazard. Mud was everywhere. Many of the patients are only 18 and 19 years old. They had to grow up too fast and fight for America. Many are homesick and scared about their wounds.

Love, June

On three occasions in December 1943, when all surgical hospitals around us were filled to capacity, our unit received the overflow of battle casualties. We admitted all through the night. Surgical auxiliary teams were called. Three arrived that night and two the next morning. A second ward tent for the operating room was pitched and five tables were in operation until all cases were finished. Each surgical team brought a nurse who scrubbed. Some teams had a nurse anesthetist. I circulated and supplied the needs of all the teams plus working in the shock ward. Previously, the teams arrived without any nurses.

The majority of our wardmen had never worked in a hospital before. With our training, most of them became skilled and dependable. Above all, they were caring persons--gentle persons. It was a joy to see them working with the wounded.

Serving the patients meals without the benefit of trays was a hassle. Food was just slopped together Camp Kilmer style. Shortages were a way of life. Tinware, canteen cups, towels, and wash cloths were liberated by the patients when they returned to combat.

12-27-43 Italy
Dear Parents,

Max and I visited the Isle of Capri, after I came off night duty the last time. Capri was founded by the Greeks, but there are Roman cisterns there to catch the rainwater. The island is only about four miles long. We took the ferry from the mainland. It took us over two hours to get there. The sun was just setting. The island is beautiful from the ferry. Sheer rocks go straight up from the sea. At the harbor are several quaint little shops and all sorts of fishing boats along the waterfront.

We took an open-air taxi up a long, steep, winding, narrow road to the beautiful Hotel Quisisana, which is an Air Force rest camp. The gardens surrounding it are magnificent. There is even a theater within this mammoth hotel.

Here, you forget there is a war on. Everyone looked at us as if we had just crawled out from under a rock. I don't know how they let us shabbily dressed infantry folks in there. Probably Max traded them a tank for a night at the hotel.

We went shopping upon arrival because we had to return to Italy early in the morning. The shops are open at night. Where we live, people don't shop, there aren't any shops. Here, they have very little to sell...polished wooden boxes and oil paintings. I bought an olive-wood match holder 1 3/4 " wide by 2 3/8 " long with an elaborate inlaid floral and bird design on the front. Most of the shopkeepers speak English because of the big tourist trade they had before the war. It's nice not to have to think in Italian. When we were near Naples I sent you several long necklaces of branch coral. They were a dollar each. Did you ever get them? There the craftsmen would even make you a large brooch from coral depicting your hospital for about two dollars. As we have to carry everything on our own backs, I try to travel light.

For supper we had pork chops, braised carrots, mashed potatoes, bread and peanut butter, coffee, and pudding. We don't get fresh things like pork chops. Our meat is dead but not edible.

There was a GI stage show that evening in the theater. My room had a single bed with an INNER SPRING MATTRESS. All I've slept on since I came to Africa was a cot with a lumpy bedroll under me or sometimes just the ground. I also had a desk, straight chair, overstuffed chair, wardrobe, and wash sink. Where I live, Mother, we don't have furniture. I have an army cot, trenching shovel, some rope, and a galvanized pail -- that's all. Although I was dead tired, I slept fitfully as I started having malarial chills again. At 6:30 the maid called me for breakfast. At 7:30, we took the funicular five hundred feet straight down. We boarded the ferry and returned to the mainland and the rugged routine of war again. 'Twas lots of fun being peaceful and cared for, if only for fifteen hours.

Mom, I gave Max that sleeping bag you sent me some time ago as the Army finally issued me one. He said the first night he slept on the ground in it he kept feeling something sharp jabbing him every time he turned over. Couldn't tell if it was a strange bug or what, so he crawled out and got his flashlight. It was a bobby pin. He said he couldn't go to sleep after that...all he could do was daydream. Refreshed, June

Listen, Mister

Were you ever hungry, Mister?
Not the kind that food soon gluts,
But a gnawing cutting hunger
That bites into your guts.
It's a homesick-hunger, Mister
And it digs around inside,
And you find you can't escape it,
For there ain't no place to hide,
Were you ever dirty, Mister?
Not the wilting collar kind,
But a stinking, slimy, messy dirt,
Or the gritty kinds that grind,
Did you ever mind the heat, Sir?
Not just the kind that makes sweat run,
But the kind that drives you crazy
Until you even curse the sun.
Were you ever weary, Mister?
I mean dog-tired, you know
When your legs don't want to go,
But we keep on going, Mister
You can bet your life we do,
And let me tell you, Mister,
We expect the same of you.

Pvt. David C. Furgason: Stars & Stripes

This poem sums up how we lived and worked and felt. Meanwhile, people back home were going on strike in factories and griping because sugar and gas were rationed. By this time, many of us were having lots of dental cavities, thanks to the lack of a decent diet. Our dentists didn't do root canals, they just yanked 'em out. I had to have a bridge made. Then the fun began because our dental drills were run by leg-power, making the process painfully slow and erratic.

1944 Somewhere in bitter cold Italy
Dear Family,
    Don't die of shock. The Chief nurse invited me to go to the 3rd Division New Year's Party because she said I could and would talk to anyone. Dad, do you think that was a compliment? The party was in a 500-year-old church on a mountain top. At midnight both sides fired a barrage -- up in

84

the air, not at each other.

My date was much older and obviously not in a party mood. He was barely civil. Maybe his friends were killed in "Purple Heart Valley". Maybe he'd gotten a Dear John letter that week. I knew the pain of all that and could have commiserated with him. Perhaps he was expecting Betty Boop. With me, he got the Betty but no BOOP. He offered me some liquor. I told him I didn't drink; didn't need the crutch and I was perfectly happy on canteen water. After that exchange--civil dropped one step lower. I contemplated asking to have him fired off in the next barrage. Years ago, I scrubbed with a doctor who had the same manner. His excuse was he had pruritus ani. That's legitimate.

During 1943 we admitted 6343 patients. Love, June

EIGHT

The Struggle North

January 1944 Somewhere in Italy

We were finally authorized washing machines; none arrived. The hospital was divided into three sections containing 120, 120 and 160 beds. We felt like rubber bands, 18 of us to be stretched three ways. Knock off one for the Chief Nurse, who was a paper-shuffler. Sometimes, one nurse could be responsible for 60 patients.

When the terrain permitted, hospital tents were pitched in the form of an olive-drab cross with a pyramidal tent as the center hub. This arrangement shortened the distance you had to walk, and made it easier to care for the soldiers, especially in bad weather, which was the only weather we had.

1-1-44 Somewhere in Italy
Dear Family,

Terrible rain and windstorm. 3rd Division pulled out. Alex was wounded last night and sent to an Evacuation hospital. The ambulance driver said he kept asking to be let off at our hospital. They told him his wound wasn't severe enough to stop at our place. The drivers just love to tell that to wounded officers.

During the night someone stole my gold-rimmed Shaeffer pen and pencil set. A patient I had at Fort Custer gave it to me as a going overseas gift so that I would write to him. I had been charting in a little wall tent and left it on my packing-crate desk. Tired and lonesome, June

1-10-44 General Sir Henry Maitland briefly inspected our hospital.

1-15-44 Somewhere in Italy
Dear Mother and Dad,
Today, after I got off duty, I hitchhiked over to see Joe E. Brown (his mouth is really big) in a GI show. He seems to truly love performing for the troops. The show was so funny, I laughed until I hurt. We have so little to laugh about. Love, June

1-18-44 Somewhere in Italy
Dearest Family:
We now have a mix of wounded, medical patients, and battle-fatigued soldiers. Each category tugs at your heart. The wounded were happy to be missing only one arm or leg. Col. Robert T. Frederick commander of the First Special Service Force (Devil's Brigade) comes to visit his men. They seem to be like a family. He's a very caring person, usually only Lieutenants or Captains from other outfits come to visit their men.
One patient with malaria and trench foot had just received a letter from home. He gave it to me to read as we had known each other at Fort Custer. Apparently, he had gone through a court martial. His famous father wrote that the only way he could redeem himself in his eyes was to die on the field of battle. I thought of Jesus asking the accusers to cast the first stone if they were without sin. Each day my life is filled with more sadness about man's inhumanity to man. I have a terrible earache but as usual I have to work. The patients need me.
One newly admitted Army officer announced to the ward at large that he came from a long line of Navy brass and that he preferred being cared for by British Sisters. Because they were older and more mature, he felt they gave him his due respect. I reminded him that it was hard to tell when he was in pajamas or naked just how important he was and suggested that he return to a British hospital. He was full of condescending conversation. Then, His Nibs really started spiking with malarial fever. I gave him my Kahler-Mayo Clinic best care. My platoon CO had the cot across the aisle from his Royal Highness and watched and listened with great amusement, along with the other 28 officers in the one tent and 30 GIs in the connecting tent. With lots of TLC, he recovered and left.

Many days later, he appeared at the tent flap with a gift for me and a public apology. The words must have seared his larynx. The gift was a pair of nylon hose. At first, I thought it was some left over "trading material" he used on the native girls. But from the apologetic look on his face, I believed him when he said that he'd sent home for them just for me. With combat boots, nylon hose aren't a priority, but it was the giving and fibbing I appreciated.

A few days ago, I was working on the battle-fatigue ward. It was time to give medications and rub backs before lights out. As I finished with this one very young soldier and was tucking his blankets around him, he said, "My mother always kissed me goodnight when she tucked me in bed." So I kissed him on the forehead. He blushed, covered his head with his blanket, and everyone else called "Mommy, Mommy." Love, June

Reverie At Night
Often I dwell in thoughts so deep,
So somnolent, they make me sleep;
Solemn meditations of yesteryears' mirth,
Retrospective mood quietly giving birth
To dreams of childhood's days gone by,
And valiant memories averse to die.
I see my home set against a pleasant hue,
And the glory of the sunset, bright and new.
And the lights at parties softly effused
Where young, pretty girls were easily amused.
I see the flowery meadows where I was wont to play.
Yet above all things in memory's long array
"Tis you, dear mother, standing in the sun
Venus blessed, smiling; my dream is done.
Pfc. J. J. Orlando: Stars & Stripes

1-19-44 Humphrey Bogart and wife were poured out of the recon car to visit our patients. Tubs and wash boards are still being used for hospital laundry.

1-21-44 Units from the 5th Army headed for Anzio.

1-22-44 Flew to Foggia today with friends. Would hate to bail out en route. D-day: Anzio troops established a beachhead.
Today's Stars and Stripes cartoon UP FRONT by Mauldin is

so sad, so true. Three exhausted, dejected infantrymen are sitting on the ground in front of a shell-riddled building, their rifles resting on the wall behind them. A tired officer is standing on the left, hands in pockets. The caption "We'll be here quite a while, men. You can take your shoes off tonight." Perhaps the cartoon was about the soldiers from K company on Jan. 4-5, who were trying to join up with I company and take San Vittore. It was a 40-hour, house-to-house battle where men fought from roof-to-roof, from-room-to-room.

1-24-44 My tentmate was married again, this time by an Army Chaplain. The Army didn't approve her Italian marriage. She has many relatives in Italy and they dug up their buried treasure (hidden from the Germans) to find gifts for her. Her Italian speech is so upper class that whenever we go anyplace together, the natives treat her with great deference. We moved again, to Presenzano.

1944 January...Somewhere in Italy
Dear Family:
Max and I just got back from the opera "La Boheme"; it was wonderful. The ride back in the jeep was bitterly cold. His camp is near our hospital, only way back up in the mountains. We drove up here to the little hut that he lives in. Now he and his sergeant are frying hamburgers over an olive-wood fire that we built in the old corner fireplace. The hut is made of stone, only two rooms. One is ten by ten and the other is ten by five. We have blacked out the one window with a GI blanket.
Max is the supply officer for an Armored unit and he and his first sergeant are alone here--the rest of his outfit is on the Anzio beachhead. Two Army cots, two five-gallon water cans and this typewriter and a telephone constitute the furniture. The terrific windstorm we had New Years' blew down the olive trees that we are burning tonight. They make a beautiful iridescent fire.
This typewriter will not get a battle star for good performance. It doesn't space and the keys stick. We're listening to a German broadcast. The music is good. Today, I had a half day off from duty and nearly fainted from the shock. It has been lots of fun. Happily, June

2-1-44 We were all given early Mother's Day V-mails to send home. The directions for using the V-Mail....Print the complete address in plain block letters in the panel below, and your return address in the space provided. Use typewriter, dark ink, or pencil. Write plainly.

Very small writing is not suitable.

The sketch is a soldier in the turret of a tank holding a radio handset in his hand. In a balloon above his head is a picture of a mother wearing glasses. The puffs of smoke coming out of the muzzle of the tank's gun spell MOTHER'S DAY.

I started malarial chills again. Very sick.

2-9-44 Somewhere in Italy
Dear Family,

It has been a hellish bit of night duty. Admitting critically wounded patients on the double, getting them cleaned up, starting I.V.s, changing dressings, getting them something to eat (if they could), and giving medications. You have to keep involved records of everything for the Army; that's as it should be.

To compound the misery, it started to pour and the tents leak. They are filled to over capacity and there is no place to put the poor soldiers to keep them dry. We're high up in the mountains and it gets bitter cold, noisy too. The big guns boom all night long and shake the ground. My fingers are so cold I have to warm them over my candle so that I can hold the pen to write.

The Germans bombed and strafed a hospital on the beachhead a few days ago. Latest reports listed 23 dead and 68 wounded. The dead included two nurses, six patients, 14 of the hospital personnel, and a Red Cross worker. The dead patients were in the receiving ward with wounds suffered at the front and were waiting to be operated on. The hospital was more than half a mile from the nearest military target. Fragmentation bombs were dropped on the operating and administrative areas and the ward tents. Two litter bearers were hit while carrying a "chest case" to the operating ward. The men tried to hold up the litter but they had to let it drop. The report said the patient has a chance of pulling through.

Incidentally, we, too, were scheduled to go in on the beachhead but our orders were cancelled at the very last minute. Mother, I feel your prayers for me are getting top priority. We were also scheduled for the Salerno landings, and they also were cancelled at the last minute.

I wish you could see me tonight. For a change, I swore that I was going to be WARM. Over the first layer, (my long woolen underwear, a wool sweater, a wool olive drab shirt), I wear a pair of men's fatigues. My GI shoes, which are two sizes too big for me, are also men's. They are covered with mud to the tops. Wearily, June

2-14-44 Italy
Dear Betty,
        I was told to report to the CO's office. Lordy, lordy, I thought as I headed to the inquisition tent, what hot water am I in this time? Instead of being greeted with the usual scowls and frowns, the monster and monstress beamed at me. General Saville had called them and asked permission for me to be the hostess for the 64th Fighter wing dance in Naples. Chiefy had her overnight bag already for me to use, a musette bag was more my style. I didn't know who this General was, but they committed me to go and gave me time off duty. We rode in style in a car, with a driver, for the long trip. The young pilots kept me dancing to gorgeous "String of Pearls" kind of music. The Air Force has a different lifestyle. Suppose the monster would let me put in for a transfer, again?? Does water run up hill? Love, June

Krauts bombed not too far from 5th Army headquarters we're just across the way from them at the moment.

2-16-44 Another hilarious UP FRONT Mauldin cartoon in the *Stars & Stripes*. A huge barrel of Vermouth sits in a cellar. Three bullet holes have pierced the front of the barrel--each is spouting vermouth directly into the three canteens, sitting on the ground. Three combat soldiers lounge on either side of the barrel. The caption "Go tell th' boys to line up, Joe--we got fruit juice fer breakfast".

1944 Somewhere in Italy
Dear Family,
        February 15th an Air Corps friend took me up front to watch them dive-bomb the Benedictine monastery, we call it Monte Cassino. It was a beautiful, but sobering, sight. I still see the faces of all those healthy, vital young men who were maimed and killed trying to take the area. For my money, I think Roosevelt put the bombing off this long so he wouldn't lose the Catholic vote.
        About 3 AM last night, in the middle of a storm, one of our nurses went to the latrine tent. As she walked through the opening flap, she heard someone move. She turned on her flashlight. In the corner was a soldier. She didn't recognize his uniform. In that brief flash of light, he hit her over the head with a sharp rock and gashed her scalp wide open. She screamed and fell backward unconscious, out into the rain. None of us on the wards heard her scream because of the storm. Eventually, the rain revived her. Covered with mud and clotted blood she staggered back to the ward. Of course, the

soldier ran away. Maybe he was a German. Tonight, they are posting a guard around the nurses' tents again. But it won't last. We can't spare the soldiers to do it. I have my ears so tuned they can detect the brush of a hand on the tent canvas. Will I ever learn to sleep again? Soundly? I think not.

Packages from home do nearly as much good as letters. There is nothing to buy in the way of food, no stores just devastated countryside. We sit and read the labels over and over and picture the stores back home. Clean and neat with food stacked on the shelves. No, I'm not hallucinating. Love, June

Grocery Destroyer

Three times a day you see him run,
His mess gear in his hand,
You'd think that Jerry was around,
He runs to beat the band.
He gripes about the food each day,
But always asks for more,
He eats enough to fill six men,
And is hungry as before.
He says someday he's going home,
That shouldn't hurt the Army,
A man who eats the way he does,
Should buy his own salami.
        J. Curtis: Stars & Stripes

Somewhere in cold Italy
Dear Betty,

One of our very sweet, older, pediatrics-trained nurses nearly brought the ward tent down with laughter today. For months she has looked for stoppers or caps to be used on a test tube containing a lab specimen. Medical supply never answered her requests. Because our headquarters company just joined us at this location, she went to their office tent to complain. There was no one in there, but on the makeshift table, she spied an open box of rubbers (condoms), just the type of thing she had been looking for. She thought her requisition had been filled. Grabbing the box she hurried back to the ward, started putting them on her specimens, and then proudly showed the patients her lucky find, saying, "Aren't they cute?" Despite their severe belly wounds, their boyish laughter ricocheted off the mountains. Cold and tired, June

Mind's Embrace
Steel-helmeted and grim,
I lie along a mountain rim,
The quiet tread of dusk brings thoughts of you
The dark green earth which seeks my thigh,
Is not the same that you and I
Once lay upon, with faces turned to autumn's blue!
I dream the times your hands were velvet on my brow,
And I had but to reach and touch them.
Now Multi-colored worlds make for the space
That lies between us. I must content
Myself with wishes, lover-sent.
A vision spun--a mind's embrace!
   Cpl. William R. Fitts: Stars & Stripes

Dear Ruth,
  Today one of our Piper Cub Field Artillery observers was potting along when out of the blue a Luftwaffe pilot started chasing him. The Piper flew straight at the mountain and at the last moment made an almost right-angle turn to avoid disaster-- but the fighter just went SPLAT. We all cheered.
Love, June

2-29-44 Away from my tent--in Italy
Dear Ruth,
  Four days I've been a patient in this General Hospital, waiting for reports on assorted x-rays of my very painful left leg. I keep banging my shin on those sharp corners of the army cots, which are crammed so close together in the ward tents. It's difficult to avoid them in the daylight but in the blackouts, when you're in a rush, it's murder.
  It's quiet and warm here, no booming guns, and the ground doesn't shake. The buildings are lovely with all that gorgeous plumbing. It's a three-hour ride to my unit, so none of the nurses can come to see me and bring my mail. Love, June

During March 1944, Operation Strangle was started by the Air Force, saturation bombing of areas on the march to Rome.

3-3-44 Moved to Corona to care for the 88th Division

3-15-44 Somewhere in Italy (this letter was badly censored)

Dear Family,

Just got back from a few perfect days at the rest camp. As usual, I was the last on the list to get leave! Saw many old friends from Africa and the Tunisian campaign. CENSORED It was so nice and warm at the rest camp I can't get used to the quiet. Ed is still in Sicily and Alex is still in a convalescent hospital.

Here is my activity while at the rest camp. (Because of the drastic censoring the sequence of events may be altered time- wise)

Went shopping, played ping pong, sang songs CENSORED. Climbed Mt. Vesuvius with two doctors who said they had enough lunch packed for three. When I told them I couldn't go because I had known since I was a young child that if I climbed Vesuvius it would erupt, they laughed so hard I was embarrassed into going with them. Besides, the clever approach about having lunch for three intrigued me. At least it was original. A cloud descended on our tour group and we got separated from the rest at the edge of the crater. We promptly sat down and waited for the cloud to rise. As we couldn't see each other, we did hold hands. If you're going to die, holding hands is more comforting. We could hear the sounds of bubbling, boiling lava. It was so frightening. As I was the only female in the party, the guide missed me as soon as the cloud cleared and he started to search frantically calling "Signorina". The wind was so strong up there that we didn't hear him call me. It all turned out okay as we kept our heads and our seats and waited for him to find us. I knew you and Alvin and Myrtle would know that I'd climbed Vesuvius when you heard the news of its eruption March 19th. None of you laughed at me about my prediction. When we got back to camp, I went bicycling with some of the officers back from the front for a rest. CENSORED I got a look at myself in a mirror on this trip and saw how awful my uniform looked and I could see all of the places it didn't fit. Everyone told me that with all those C rations I ate I'd fill out the pleats, but I don't want to look like a bean bag. Went to Capri in a rowboat with four characters I knew from the 34th Division....168th. They rowed and I chatted. Finally, one of them asked, "Could you actually stop talking?" I said, "Yes" and never uttered another word for the rest of the trip to Capri. They tried kneeling in the boat and begging me to talk. It was useless. We visited the Blue Grotto and Villa Fourtino, shopped, ate dinner, and took the ferry back to the mainland, where I took their laughing pictures for posterity.

An A-20 pilot had promised me a ride in his plane in North Africa. I hadn't seen him since. When we met again at the rest hotel, we went flying----me in a piggy back position by the back of his head. Diving over the bay was a real experience, then we flew over Vesuvius just as it was beginning to really rumble and spill -- the first time since 1872. We ate dinner at Vesuvio airport and he brought me back up front. He couldn't quite get used to seeing the flashes of artillery across the sky and the burning mountain sides. The Air Force is lucky that way. They drop their bombs and go back to civilization. We have to stay here and take it 24 hours a day, seven days a week, year in and year out CENSORED.

Today, there was an accidental explosion at an ammunition dump and we got in the casualties from that. One soldier driving by in a truck had a piece of shrapnel go right through his heart. The other was an Italian civilian whose scalp was peeled completely back to the base of his skull. He had 2nd degree burns of both arms, face, chest and legs, a compound fracture of his left leg and a badly fractured hip. He's still alive this evening, which is a miracle. A painful miracle. He begs us to let him alone and let him die.
Love, June

The *Stars and Stripes* enlightened all who read their eagerly awaited edition that we have firemen in the Army and all their trucks are painted olive drab. Off duty the boys play checkers, sleep, read, or sit on benches in front of the firehouses, like the Smokey Stovers at home. Quarters for the 10 local platoons range from ancient buildings and modern warehouses to station houses they had to build themselves. One outfit has a high ceiling that's frescoed with 16th century art.

Like firemen all over, they like to recall the fires that burn in their memories. The favorite recollection of S-Sgt. Luther E. Brown, Antigo, Wis., goes back to Mers El Kebir, near Oran, where they spent all night chasing a fire around in circles. "We first got the report of a fire about 10 miles away." Brown related. "When we got there, it was gone. Then we got another alarm on the same fire in the other direction. When we got there, no fire. Finally we caught up with it behind us. It was an airplane, limping home, on fire." Major Engels says his boys have only one worry -- that they'll be called upon to put out the one really big Naples fire--at Vesuvius. P.G.

3-26-44 Still in Italy
Dearest Family,
On my few hours off this afternoon, I grabbed my camera and sauntered down one of the nearby back roads to an ancient (600 years old) little village which had been bombed and rebombed. I spied and picked some dainty wild flowers. Just as I was turning up a forbidding, but interesting, looking lane, a British sergeant shouted "Lieutenant, that road is mined." I backtracked

gingerly. He offered to show me what was left of interest and where it was safe to walk. We borrowed the key for the old cathedral, which was badly tattered from the previous bombings. Perched high in the back was a 300-year-old pipe organ, the kind worked with hand bellows. The sergeant called a dirty urchin of fifteen to play for me. You'll never guess the concert he played. "You are My Sunshine", "Beer Barrel Polka" and "You are Always in My Heart". I sang with joy.

The music brought a bedraggled Italian man into the cathedral. He said that the mayor and his family wanted to meet me. We all went to what was left of the mayor's home and the usual glass of wine was forthcoming. It was so strong I thought I felt my hair curling. I managed two small sips and then suggested we go outside and take some pictures. They were delighted and gracious. As a farewell gift, they gave me a beautiful bouquet of camellias.

When it was time for more exploring, we were joined by a couple of handsome Scottish Guards. They suggested we go to their billets and meet their landlady. After going through a maze of filthy alleys and stairways, we finally arrived. A crotchety misshapen, bearded, old Italian gentleman met us with shouts of "Signorina, bella, bella!" Hanging on his arm was an 18-month-old youngster with the curliest hair, rosiest cheeks and dirtiest face you ever did see. In a shrill old voice, Gramps proceeded to sing..."Santa Lucia". Of course, he was from Brooklyn, Philadelphia and Rhode Island.

To those I met on the way back to the hospital, it was "Buon giorno" (bwohn JOR-no) to the Italians, "Cheers" to the British, a salute and hello to our men. How I needed that delightful break. Love, June

A Buck Sergeant from the 45th Division told me that his outfit had taken this particular mountain and were knocked out three or four times and finally they were relieved by the French 2nd Army. Roy was left with the French and the soldiers built fires at night to cook their food. The fire was a great target for the German artillery and they plastered them. Roy spoke to a French officer about the fires and he said, "A Frenchman has gotta have a hot meal in his belly, and then he'll fight well in the morning."

3-27-44 Received the following Dear John letter by V-Mail and mailed it and my thoughts about it to my parents.

June Darling,
Had intended writing to you on Saturday evening and at the same time take care of a lot of old correspondence which I've accumulated over

a period of months. Was OD that night and, after making early rounds, I stopped at the Club for supposedly a few minutes but got stuck in a bridge game, which lasted out the evening. Had a few good cards and also a lot of bad. Haven't played much bridge since............left.

Yesterday was another beautiful day, just about as nice as any spring day could be. Went for a long walk in the afternoon and then last night went to the show in Bay Shore with.........the WAC officer. The picture we saw was "Up in Arms", very good but somewhat misleading as to the grand and glorious life of the Army Nurse Corps.

Received two letters from you this morning, darling, both quite old, and another on Friday written March 14th. Am very happy to hear that you have had the opportunity to go to the Rest Camp for a little vacation. It was long past due, and I know has been pleasant. I still so much wish, however, that you might have been returned to the States instead and still hope that that day will not have to be too far in the future.

Darling, there is something I have wanted to write about for the past several weeks and is something I feel should be discussed. Regardless of the final outcome, I feel that it is no more than fair to all concerned that I tell you now, otherwise I'm afraid that some day I might feel the perfect heel and be ashamed even to face myself. If you've not already guessed, I am referring to the love tangle I've become involved in.

On one or two previous occasions, I've mentioned .... in my letters. Whether you had ever thought or wondered if I was becoming too interested in someone else, I don't know, but it almost seems that at times you must have.

Our friendship started very casually with an occasional date, never dreaming of or having any desire to go steady with anyone. In a short while, however, it became quite apparent that ours was to be more than just a casual acquaintance, at which time I laid the cards on the table and told..... all about you because I did not want to find a one-sided love affair developing, and then some day for her to be badly hurt. After that I felt much better, had a clear conscience and things went along fine. Months went by and friendship turned to love, I know we both realized it but were afraid to face it. Was even afraid to admit it to myself, not knowing just how to cope with the situation. She felt much the same, not wanting to hurt you nor wanting to be hurt herself. I never once thought it would be possible to fall in love with someone else nor that I could be so much in love with two different persons. I found that I was wrong.

.........was transferred and has been gone five weeks, which has given me the opportunity to think this through more clearly and on an unbiased *basis but still has not enabled me to arrive at any satisfactory decision. Darling I've had many sleepless and worried nights but can't see through the fog I'm engulfed in. This, June, is just one more and important reason why I want you to return to the States now, because I don't want this to drag out indefinitely. It has been more than difficult to write this letter, darling, but at least I now feel as though a heavy weight has been lifted from my heart and mind. My love,.......*

Mother, Daddy and Ruthie, it is cruel "To lift the weight from a man's heart and mind," who is living stateside in great comfort and luxury in his custom-tailored uniforms and dump it on another's heart and mind, who is living in a tent in the mud, being rocked by artillery fire in the mountains, and harassed by low-flying German fighters. I can understand civilians not knowing how war is fought, but I cannot understand how officers can be so naive. He says. "Return to the States now." Am I supposed to go to General Mark Clark, letter in hand, and get permission to leave the battle zone? Lying creatively, in a short letter, I gently let him off the hook. In spirit, I joined the legion of soldiers in ETO who received a Dear John letter. "Love postponed on account of war" became my battle cry. Just, June

4-1-44 Today, we moved again to another cold miserable field. My tentmate was sent to the States to give her unborn child a chance at life. Her husband will be rotated to the States soon.

4-12-44 Was interviewed by Korman of the Chicago Daily Tribune. I told him that the same American officers follow us about year after year, but they all get promoted and we don't. Maybe it's because we lived in garlic plots, sheep fields, potato patches and anyone stupid enough to live in those places couldn't be all that bright. We're good soldiers, just following orders. Actually women have gotten the short end of the military stick from day one.

4-15-44 This year, for Mother's Day we were all given Bill Mauldin's V-mail cartoons to send to our Mothers. It's a picture of a shattered building, a shutter hanging by one hinge next to an open window. Willie in steel helmet is dangling his mess kit out of the window. His buddy Joe is outside kneeling on the ground his rifle pointed at a mother hen, her chicks at her feet. Empty ration cans litter the ground. A sign over the shattered building reads "Hold yer fire, Joe--it's Mother's Day."

4-19-44
Dear Ruth,

Last night, they showed a movie in the next field called "Phantom Lady", a mystery thriller, which wasn't too bad. It helped break the monotony.

Today, we had a USO show at camp. This is the first one I have ever seen and found it was crude and corny. Maybe they think our tastes have deteriorated since we came overseas. The patients told the girls the show smelled and hurt the poor things feelings. Although I agreed with the soldiers, perhaps they shouldn't have been so frank, after all the girls came a long way to entertain us. We all thought they could better use that USO space on the ships or planes for ice cream made in the States. We don't like the awful stuff made here with condensed milk. However, no one asks what we want or like before they send over that type of USO show. We get pot-luck everyday, in every way, in everything.

The diarrheas going around are debilitating and humiliating. Some male officers I know are so weak they could barely walk. They couldn't make the latrine in time, so they just dug holes in the dirt in their tents and used them. When they ran out of places to dig, they moved the tent to fresh ground and started to dig all over again.

We got a couple of young nurses on detached service from a hospital in the rear. I don't think they volunteered to come to our primitive facilities. One of them was recently married, but they soon separated her from her spouse. She refused to go on duty and care for the soldiers. Instead, she retired to her cot and decided not to eat. Her attitude didn't make sense to me, but I felt her pain. I brought her one meal on a tray; she took it and threw it on the ground at my feet. That was the last time I tried to help her. Petulance didn't pay when we were pups.... remember? Love, June

Undated, Italy,
Dear Ruthie,

We recently got a grumpy, bony, regular army nurse assigned to our unit. Her speech, gait, and appearance showed more male hormones than female. She accused one of my wardmen of trying to kiss her. If he did, his buddies must have bet him a year's pay. Kissless reported him to the Colonel, demanding that he be court-martialed. Every war needs its moments of humor. Our officers promptly assembled and held court. They busted the GI from corporal to private. Within a respectable number of hours, they promoted him to corporal. I think they are still laughing. Love, June

4-25-44 Italy
   5th Army also gave us a V-Mail Mother's Day card to send home. It depicts a GI with a 5th Army patch on his sleeve, sitting on a wooden ration box, writing a letter home. His desk is an old packing crate, his shelter half is supported by a piece of wood, his steel helmet and combat boots lie on the ground. The caption over his head.... "Dear Mom" on MOTHER'S DAY

4-26-44 Italy
Dear Ruth,

   Irving Berlin was here today at the hospital to entertain the soldiers. We had a PA system set up to service the wards, as most of the patients couldn't walk to the show.

   My night shift had been exhausting, I'd barely gotten to sleep. One of my tentmates woke me and told me my hero had arrived. Pulling my fatigues over my pink satin pajamas, I ran. I didn't have any insignia on and my pants weren't tucked into my unlaced boots. Sitting in the third row on a plank seat I was having a ball singing all of my old Berlin favorites when he stopped the singing and asked me to come up and sing for the fellows. Not quite dressed for the occasion I was so embarrassed.

   The soldiers sitting around me picked me up and passed me hand-over-hand and dumped me on the platform at Berlin's feet-- just like a sack of potatoes. By that time, my pajamas were showing at the neck line and I was scared and breathless. Berlin asked me what I was going to sing, and for the first time in my life, I couldn't think of a thing. He had a voice like a peach seed caught in a sausage grinder and had already sung all of the songs that he had written that I knew by heart...including my favorite "White Christmas", which the men always sang as "I'm dreaming of a white mistress." My mind was in a whirl 'til I recalled a new, stupid song one of our nurses kept singing all the time, usually off key, but with great gusto. So I said, "How about Paper Doll?" I have often wished that Mr. Berlin would have laughed. Instead, he said, "I never heard of it and don't even know who wrote it." I didn't know either who had written it. Well, that changed things, and I wasn't scared any longer. I tapped Mr. Berlin gently on the shoulder and turned to his enlisted man pianist who smiled at me, I guess to give me courage. "I'll bet you know it," I said to the pianist. He said he did, as his fingers rippled over the keyboard. He asked what key I sang in. "Soprano", I replied. He started to play. My larynx felt frozen stiff as I sang the first few bars. Too high a range for me under that stress. I stopped and said "I'm not Lily Pons, how about pitching it a bit lower?" He laughed, the troops laughed, and I finished the song with the appropriate words.

Some of our Jewish doctors, sitting in the back of the tent, were hysterical with laughter. Berlin had planned to have a meal with us, and our CO even had his bed sheet washed and ironed to use as a table cloth for the big event. But after my faux pas, Berlin did not stay to dine. People called me Paper Dolly for days after that. The CO is furious with me. The feeling is mutual. How come he rates a bed sheet? Guess 'cause his skin is so old.

It rained all night and part of the day, but when it rains at least we don't have an air raid. That is one thing to be happy about today. Love, June

Moments of pure bliss are rare but appreciated. One of our other platoons was set up in a beautiful valley, complete with a tiny stream, flowers blooming, and birds singing. In the midst of paradise, a sick nurse was confined to her tent for a week. As usual, she woke early and was enjoying the sights and sounds when the bugler broke into her reverie. Instead of reveille to welcome a new day, he played "Easter Parade" to welcome Easter and hopes of a better, peaceful world.

Dear Ruthie,
There are more dumb songs being sung here. This is the latest from my Field Artillery friends. Don't show it to Mother.

> *I just called up to tell you that I'm ragged but right*
> *A thief and a gamblin' woman drunk every night*
> *I got a porterhouse steak three times a day for my boys*
> *Is more than any Sadsack 'round this town can afford.*
>
> *I got a great big electric fan to keep me cool while I sleep*
> *A great big handsome man to play around with my feet.*
> *I'm a rambler and a gambler and Lord am I tight*
> *I just called up to tell you that I'm ragged but right*
> *Roll over baby--a chicken ain't nothin' but a bird.*
>
> *We may be dark skinned lasses, but Lord what do we care.*
> *We've got those streamlined chassis and a do or die air*
> *We'd like to spend an intermission in your V-8*
> *We'd like to see you later, but we never late date.*

We got the hips that sank the ships from England, France and Peru.
Now if you like Napoleon--it's your Waterloo.
Our reputation is gone with the wind--so let's breeze it tonight.
I just called up to tell you that I'm ragged but right.

Roll over baby--a chicken ain't nuthin' but a bird
In Macy's basement the customer is always right.
If you can figure out the weird lyrics, put another star in the
living room window. Busy, busy, June

Somewhere in Italy
Dear Parents,

An old friend turned up from Sicily, dirty, bearded and exhausted from the long drive and furious that his outfit didn't have any of those neat little American jeep trailers he'd seen en route. He thought it would be nice if I went along to help him hunt for one as I had such good vision. I discovered one but it was on a British jeep--Lend Lease don'tcha know. That didn't bother him a bit. He liberated it, and we drove merrily away.

Miles later, we came to a small simple bridge over a gully, he stopped his jeep, cleverly named DAMIFINO, and said "You always wanted to know what it was like to throw a hand grenade. Here's the place to try it." After the explosion, I thought we should return the trailer as some poor underpaid British GI would be docked a year's wages. We returned it unnoticed.

One of my former patients from Ft. Custer finally arrived overseas as a 45th Infantry replacement, tracked down my whereabouts and brought me a gift....a palm-sized Beretta registered in my name in New York city. I hid it and the bullets in the bottom of my bedroll until I saw him again and gave it back. The Colonel would have skinned me alive if he had known about it. We aren't permitted to carry guns of any sort. Squirrel and rabbit hunting is all you ever taught us, Dad. Love, June

5-9-44 Somewhere in Italy
Dear Ruth,

The cereal, olives, and mints arrived in good shape. Do you suppose you could send some potato chips and homemade dill pickles? Today, we put up mosquito nets on all the beds in the hospital. We also got some pillows for the first time.

It was very hot today and soon we'll be able to go swimming, if the Colonel gives permission and lends us some trucks. We have suits that we made out of our worn-out seersucker dresses. A transcription from BBC of

Fred Waring's program is coming over the loud speaker now. It sounds like home.

Tonight, we're having an Eddie Cantor movie. Before the movie started, I went for a walk down by the river. That's where I go to recharge my batteries in that peaceful setting. The moon is in a beautiful phase. The water trickled so musically over the rocks. Oh, to stay there forever.

Someplace in this rat race of my life, our CO picked up with a Belgian striptease dancer called Beatrica. She has black-at-the-roots blonde hair, with purple tints on the end. He'd bring her to mess and ask us to eat with her. We lost our appetite. She told us that her show was kicked out of NY prewar. Our CO's dalliance was costly.

On another date with Beatrica, he did not take his new camera and it was stolen from his tent. About that time, we had a striker, an Italian soldier who had defected from his unit. Everyone assumed he had liberated the camera because he disappeared into the countryside that same day.

Here at this location we had wooden two-holers. A great treat for the seat. Love, June

5-10-44 The eve of the major assault on the Gothic Line defenses. We got letters from Generals Wilson and Clark promising new drives to destroy the Hun and drive him out of Italy.

5-12-44 5th & 8th Armies launched big drives on the front. Very heavy casualties.

Somewhere in Italy 11 PM
Dear Ruthie,

I'm too busy and too tired to write, but we must keep in contact; it's all that keeps me sane. We're working now from 12-15 hours a day, never sit down, except to eat, all day long. My legs ache, my back aches (those army cots are so low), and my head aches. For days we have had nothing but non-transportable surgicals.

I'm with another platoon because of the big push; they were swamped and I was sent to help out. That's right, we see war at its worst.. Such young soldiers, too. Nineteen-year-olds and they can't even vote against our horrid, war-loving president. They're so patient and never complain. In one whole ward, sometimes there aren't enough arms and legs to go around. I won't be able to write much or often so don't be angry with me. Following are some reasons why.

Bed 6 penetrating wound of the left flank, penetrating wound face, fractured mandible, penetrating wound forearm. Penicillin 25,000 Units 3-6-9-12-3-6-9-12, morphine 1/4 gr. prn., 1000 cc 5% glucose in saline AM & PM. On third day evacuated to a rear hospital.

Bed 5 amputation right leg, penetrating wound left leg, lacerating wound of chest, lacerating wound right hand. Penicillin 25,000 units 3-6-9-12-3-6-9-12, morphine 1/4 gr. prn. 500 cc blood AM & PM, 1000 cc 5% glucose in saline AM & PM. On third day evacuated to a rear hospital.

Bed 4 massive penetrating wounds of abdomen. Expired.

Bed 2 POW (prisoner of war) lacerated liver, sucking chest wound, penetrating wound of diaphragm, possible gas bacillus in chest wound. 10:20 PM. T 103.2, P 138, R 30, BP 98/50. Shock position, two units of plasma, morphine 1/4 gr. prn, 25,000 U penicillin q 3 h, 3000 cc 5% glucose in saline, output--from chest drain 1000 cc., catheter 700 cc., nasal oxygen, Wangensteen suction. TPR. 11 PM 105 (rectal), 142, 46; TPR 12 PM 106 (rectal),80, 22. TPR is abbreviation for temperature, pulse and respiration.

One time I had a patient who had apparently had a hand grenade in his hip pocket. When he tried to pull it out it went off. Amazing it didn't kill him. Tired and sad, June

To Patriots

I would not like to think that some young boy
With rosy cheeks, blue eyes and downy lips
Must die, while I, secure in my employ,
Parade his fellows to their warbound ships.

The older ones can die--I do not care:
They've seen their bubble build, now watch it burst.
But it is sad to see those dying there
Who have not laughed nor wept nor kissed nor cursed.

You would not hold yourself in such esteem
Nor speak of sacrifices as you do
If you could hear six-barrelled mortars scream
And know that they were killing kids for you.

Lt. C. Kilmer...in Stars & Stripes

Somewhere in Italy
Dearest family,

Just had a nice lukewarm bath in our homemade shower tent. Water was heated on an old round stove and piped to a series of tin cans with holes punched in their bottoms from which water drizzled slowly out. Tenting just covered the sides. It's breezy, but we think it's nice. There are some mighty big flak holes in spots but that just ventilates the place well. I don't think there are too many GI eyeballs peeking in. Such a view might blister their peepers and scar or scare them for life.

Pitched horseshoes with the enlisted men this morning; I held my own. I haven't played since I was at Uncle Albert's. It rained last night, and the nights are so cold. Love, June

Max

NINE

Anzio to Rome

Went through Texas staging area in Naples. There was a filthy, semi-toothless old crone who sat out in front of our building and cracked nuts in her teeth. Then she picked them out of her mouth and laid them on a paper plate so the sun would dry her saliva so she could sell them.

Boarded LST 352 at Naples 2000 hours. Left for Anzio- Nettuno area. Arrived early next AM, air activity and artillery fire. We took over 47 patients from another Field Hospital two miles east of Nettuno. The first two days we lived in a "dug-in" ward tent. Then we moved into 'dug-in' pyramidal tents. In the next two days we admitted 128 more patients and had to open additional wards. We were assigned to II Corps. That means we'll be split again into three small surgical units and assigned to the infantry divisions that are spearheading the next push for Rome.

1959 letter of recollections from a nurse who served on Anzio prior to our arrival there.
Dear June,
I was with the 56th Evacuation hospital on Anzio from January until Easter Sunday 1944, one of the reasons I give special thanks at Easter. To

our left was the 93rd, abutting us on the right, I think was the 94th. Directly behind us was a tent of Red Cross girls. Bombs killed the chief nurse and assistant chief nurse of the 93rd, also one of the Red Cross girls. We took care of several injured at the 56th. I remember a young MAC officer lost an arm. I gave his anesthetic. Another time, antipersonnel bombs hit a ward of the 94th, exploding an oxygen tank serving a patient and killing him, and spraying our ward with missiles, causing injuries to some of our patients. Later, bombs killed one of our nurses and injured another, both chest wounds. The one killed was Ellen Ainsworth. Her family left her body there. I visited the Anzio Cemetery in 1958 and found her grave. The Cemetery is very beautiful and well kept.

Another time, at night, antipersonnel bombs were dropped. I was on duty and had a patient, under anesthesia, being operated on. Flak began raining through our operating tent. I reached down beside me and put on my steel bonnet. The doctor, scrub nurse, and circulator all got as far under the operating table as possible. I started to, but thought I can't do that, I've got to protect my patient. Then I said to the others, "Don't you think you ought to be ashamed?" I leaned over my patient to protect him as much as possible. Imagine my surprise when Gen. Clark and some other VIPs came to our unit and pinned a bronze star on me for bravery. Our OR nurse got a Silver Star and there were some others I don't remember. My chief nurse anesthetist later told me that one of the doctors had put my name in for the medal. Love, Lonnie

Dear Betty,

Sorry for the long delay in writing, but we moved again and have been very busy. We are restricted to the immediate hospital area as it isn't safe to leave. There is nothing to write about but the wounded. We live down under the ground in sand-bagged damp, smelly foxholes, like moles in a blackout. Each hole is big enough to accommodate one army cot. It is timbered and sandbagged on three sides and the top. It's cozy, confining and for this area I'm happy to be underground. A pyramidal tent tops it. The hospital generator is sandbagged, even the mail tent. Patients, in the past, have been killed in their cots from strafing etc.. The ward tents are also dug down into the ground, but there are no sandbags overhead. It's just not possible. The huge Red Crosses are supposed to be protection, but the enemy didn't always observe that convention. The tent-mate I had in Sicily, remember the one who had a dog she diapered, was wounded in the leg here at Anzio.

On arrival, I was told that more medical alcohol was drunk here on the beachhead than was used to sterilize surgical instruments. In other locations I used to put grape Kool-aid crystals in the alcohol bottles and label them POISON.

Soldiers from a combat engineering battalion were the first to break through to the beachhead forces. Happy Day. A chaplain, who had been a patient of mine at Capua, stopped in the operating tent to bring me some fresh doughnuts. All doughnations are gratefully accepted by this hungry helmet-rack. Love, June

With Immortal Honor
The warmth,
That once you called your own
Which gushed forth so eager
On the ground, is now
A beacon-star off in the mist.

So, if-- At some far-flung parade or fete.
A patriot stands forth to read
The list of braves who died
Upon the plains.

Your name--
Though long-forgot,
As if it were naught,
But earthly clod Will be whispered then
By the lips of God.
Cpl. Peter J. Carter: Stars & Stripes

Memorial Day, 1944 We started our move to Rome. Over strange terrain, driving blackout at night, passing tanks and other armor on narrow roads, and then establishing our hospital in pitch-dark was a operation we had done numerous times before. Our units leap-frogged each other en route. We were attached to Clearing Stations taking only non-transportable patients. In the push from Cori to Rome, I stepped out of the OR for a few moments one night just to change the scene. Heard Jerry coming and got behind the biggest tree I could find. He strafed the full length of the road in front of our hospital tents. We're with the 3rd Division.

Assi-Ameur, North Africa 1943

Fort Custer 1942

Removing clothing
from bed roll

Sicily 1943

Christmas nightmare 1943

109

My Sicilian movable home

Field Hospital loading for Sicily Invasion

On the move again

*Our camouflaged
Caserta, Italy hospital*

Endless stream of wounded

110

As I sit on my ass...

Hospital laundry

Corona, Italy 1944

My little French friend

Nurses leaving Naples staging area for invasion of southern France

Signorina

35¢ each
egg

Canteen cup cooked eggs

Greetings to the first troops in Rome

Shower unit - Cassino

Tired, dirty in convoy

We are dumped on the beaches -
Invasion of southern France

*Retreated from Saralbe factory Christmas Eve
in the Battle of the Bulge*

Hungry French children

*"Do come and bathe at my house" -
BOOM! Herbitzheim, Germany*

*Near neighbor's artillery -
France*

My tent without the top - Anzio 1944

10th Field Hospital, Italy, 1944 - brushing my teeth

Combat nurses -
fighting snow

Beautiful Bedelia, Battle of the Bulge, 1944

Mud and snow - everywhere

My home sweet home, on Anzio

Anzio beachhead wards

Serving patients mess - Italy 1944

*Crashed behind our tent -
France 1944*

GI's Anzio homes - 1944

Packed, ready to convoy

Too pooped to move

Sign of the times

Booby trap

It's not the Mayo Clinic

One of our many locations - we had a floor

Bathing in the rivers - no privacy

the water was an ice cold mountain river!

Better than a slit trench

10th Field Hospital Nurses - I'm the short shrimp reading the letter from home

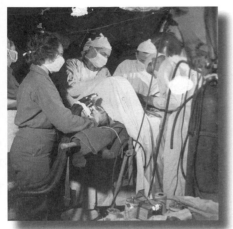

Surgery - France, February 1945

Charting - Allach, June 1945

Chow time

KOTEX - supply Sergeant Danby

Dachau Headquarters, July 1945

Typhus wards - Allach

Dachau bodies in boxcar, April 1945

Dachau horrors

*Hitler's Doll House -
Salzburg, Austria*

*Dauchau, Gemany -
trainload of corpses*

Nurses' quarters at Dachau -
formerly SS officers apartments

Entrance to Allach, displaced persons' camp

1945 German jet

Reaching Italy's toe

Irish ice cream courier

Driving Goering's car

Invasion of France aboard USS MARIGOLD

VE Day Paris

Just pretending

Damrite and me

Homebound aboard USS Westpoint

Cigarette butt snipers

Description of Hell

Air conditioned home

Tanking to church

*Allach
Concentration Camp*

OFFICER'S PAY DATA CARD

JUNE M. WANDREY, ..., 1st Lt., ANC
(Name)   (Serial number)   (Grade and arm or service)

Over...O...years' service ...2nd...pay period ....years completed

----------, 19......

Monthly base pay and longevity .... $ 166.67

Additional pay for....F/S................. 16.66

Rental allowances.................. ....

Subsistence........30 day month... 21.00

Date ...1 Jan 1945...... Total, $ 204.33

Dependents (state names and addresses):

Evidence of dependency (mother) filed with voucher No. ....

----------------------------------, 19........

Accounts of ....

Allotments, class E, $ 100.00 $.......... $..........

Insurance, class D, $...3.30......   Class N, $...3.30

Pay reservations, class A, $.........................

Other deductions, $.........................

Subsequent changes in above data with dates thereof:

WD. AGO. 65-1 # 496318

WD. AGO. 65-10# 143221

Changes affecting pay will be entered here and maintained up to date.

W. D., A. G. O. Form No. 77
March 26, 1942   16—27679-

125

1944 Italy undated letter
Dear Family,

An ambulance load of six work-and trip-weary nurses had quite a scary, terrifying experience. About 9 PM we were told to move up toward the front. By following such-and-such a highway, we would find one of our enlisted men posted on the road to flag us down. We knew the front had advanced rapidly, so if we were only expected to go a limited number of miles we wouldn't get too near the front. We drove on and on, and it became very dark. Occasional antiaircraft tracers lit up the sky. One could hear the German planes overhead. We donned our steel helmets in case of a strafing. Our ambulance Red Cross isn't visible at night. There was hardly any traffic. It kept getting darker. We had to drive blackout, and the road was littered with wrecked German vehicles and craters. Progress was slow. We asked the few GIs we met along the way if they had seen a hospital convoy. No luck. We'd been creeping for ages, and decided to check the speedometer and drive only two miles further. After two treacherous miles...suddenly an oncoming jeep crept into view and we hailed it. We could hear small arms fire. The lone occupant had a fit when he found we were nurses. "For God's sake--take 'em back" he yelled at our confused driver. We turned around, and after an eternity of creeping and searching, we found an Infantry Clearing Station that had a field phone. We contacted our headquarters and told them where we were. They directed us to go to another Clearing Station where they would meet us. By this time there was such heavy fog one couldn't see to drive safely. Permanent squint marks have formed between my eyes. Somehow we made it. They gave each of us a blanket and a litter to sleep on and pointed out a cave in the distance. We crawled in the cave, collapsed on the litters, and pulled a blanket over our shoes, helmet and all. Other soldiers were also sleeping in the cave. Soon I'll be an authority on different kinds of snoring. Half-an-hour later just as we'd begun to doze, one of our officers, who had hustled up from our headquarters, arrived, loaded us back into the ambulance, and guided us to our correct area. By then it was just getting light. We helped finish setting up our hospital, which the enlisted men had begun hours before, and got the surgical tent in order. Numb from the cold and fatigue, we curled up on the ground and went to sleep. This field nurse business, isn't for the faint of heart. Love, June

6-4-44 ADVANCED ALLIED HEADQUARTERS ....excerpts from the *Stars and Stripes.*

A special bulletin tonight revealed that units of the 5th Army had crossed the city limits after a day's fighting in the suburbs of the

Italian capital. Resistance to the Allied forces apparently was bitter in the outskirts but declined as the penetration deepened.

Radio messages addressed to the people of Rome by Marshal Pietro Badoglio, Italian prime minister, and General Sir Harold Alexander, Commander of all Allied armies in Italy, called Romans to prevent destruction of the city as the German forces withdrew. People of Rome were asked to neutralize demolition charges, protect public utilities, railways and communications, remove barricades, keep off the streets and note the location of booby traps and mines so that Allied engineers could deal with them when they take over the city. The Romans were also asked to remain calm, hide their food, and go about their regular business.

"Citizens of Rome," the radio called throughout the day, "This is not a time for demonstrations."

The Arch of Titus, erected in 70 A.D. to commemorate the Romans' triumph at Jerusalem, yesterday witnessed the entrance of Allied troops into Rome -- the first time in all history that the "Eternal City" had been conquered from the south.

6-5-44 Italy

We were the first American hospital to enter the city. Soon there was a large sign stretched across the street saying WELCOME TO THE LIBERATORS. As the Germans fled the city, we took over a building that they used as a hospital. Their dead patients were still lying around; they hadn't had time to bury them before our troops arrived.

One of our Catholic nurses dated a war photographer who took her to the Vatican to meet the Pope. Pius was upset that she had come into his presence wearing pants. How sad that in his elegant surroundings he knew nothing of the life of a combat nurse. Maybe he thought she wore white silk hose and white starched uniforms in the muddy fields where she lived.

One of our platoons, led by a Catholic doctor, stopped the convoy on entering Rome. He and the other officers went into the Vatican and met the Pope. The doctor was later reprimanded for stopping and was confined to quarters while that platoon was in rest camp.

6-6-44 The Allies invaded France. The moon last night had a strange ring around it.

6-7-44
Dear Family,

Rome is beautiful, the cleanest place we have been in 16 months. Even the people look civilized and wear clean clothes. Ever since we've been overseas, the natives have stood outside of our mess tent and watched us eat, waiting for the scraps we might leave. It spoils my appetite seeing the hungry look on their poor faces.

If the Germans keep running as fast as they are now, could be we'll be home before the New Year. At least I'd like to think that way. It gives me hope. A good set or two of tennis would really put me in good spirits. Love, June

6-8-44 Established hospital in Bracciano

6-9-44 We were given V-mail Father's Day cards, designed by Cpl. Bill Gordon to send home. Superimposed over a large 5th Army shoulder patch is a typical scene: pup tents, campfires, with the mountains behind. A soldier stands saluting an image of his pipe-smoking father emerging from the smoke of one campfire. The message is "A Salute, Dad, on YOUR DAY, June 18th. The bottom of the card is rimmed with stylized stars and stripes.

Our drinking water comes from Engineer-operated water points. If it comes from other sources, it is heavily chlorinated and almost makes you ill when you drink it.

6-11-44 This month we cared for the 3rd and 88th Divisions.

6-12-44
Dear Parents,

Back to Rome, in tents on the banks of the dirty Tiber admitting anyone who needs care. It rained all night and today. I wore combat boots and turned my trousers way up so they wouldn't get wet from the long grass. Love, June

6-15-44 Italy
Dear Betty,

Today was my turn to go to the Vatican; I wore my dress uniform with a skirt. I went with our Catholic chaplain. Two Catholic nurses from another hospital joined us as we were crossing the Piazza S. Pietro. The Swiss Guards wear the most colorful garb, big black tam-o-shanters, blue and black leg-o- mutton blouses, and knee breeches. They carry staffs. The men who guard the Pope have helmets with plumes, spears, and multi- colored garments on the same order as the Swiss guards. They are the Papal colors of the early Roman Empire. There were thousands of GIs at the audience with the Pope.

We stood in the front row. The Pope stopped right in front of me. He's as small as I am. I gave him a big smile and he extended his ring to me to kiss. Methodists just don't go around kissing old men's rings as you well know, so I didn't. If one thinks of the sanitary aspects of that antiquated custom, it's repulsive. Instead I extended my hand to him, gave him a happy, hearty handshake. We chatted briefly. I told him I came from Wisconsin. Also about the great fishing there and put in a good word for Father Nurnberg. Are he and Mom still discussing religions? The Pope blessed a rosary and gave it to me. I'm going to give it to Mrs. B. when I get back. It isn't safe to send things home.

Perhaps I rattled his Papal cage, but I meant no disrespect. His position I salute. The Catholic nurses on either side of me wanted to hit me over the head after it was over. They were burned up because he didn't speak to them and wasted his attention on me. They broke out a package of cigarettes and started to smoke in the Vatican. To me that was a sacrilege. The Vatican is a wonderful, incredibly beautiful building made so by the paintings and sculptures. The Judgement Day is magnificent. There must be a thousand rooms in the compound. I think even an atheist would be moved by the Holy nature of this place.

I have an infected finger from a jab with a dirty needle in the OR. The sulfadiazine I'm taking has made me absolutely sluggish and it doesn't become me. Love, June

6-16-44

Dear Ones,

Rome is so lovely. The ancient buildings are awesome. Mussolini has built some magnificent state buildings. Yesterday, I went swimming in the first fresh water lake I've seen in years. I swam until I was thoroughly exhausted. It was so like Camp Waushara. There was a big hydroplane pier where the upper crust and politicians used to anchor on their way from Rome to India.

A friend from the Field Artillery took me flying in a Piper Cub over Rome, the Pontine marshes, Civitavecchia, the zoo, and St. Peters. He brought me this song that everyone is singing.

"You gotta accentuate the positive, eliminate the negative, latch on *to the affirmative, don't mess with mister in between.*

You gotta spread joy up to the maximum, bring gloom down to the minimum, have faith or pandemonium's liable to walk upon the scene. To illustrate my last remark, Jonah in the whale, Noah in the ark. What did they do just when everything looked so dark?

Man, they said you gotta accentuate the positive, eliminate the negative, latch on to the affirmative, don't mess with mister in between." Love, June

6-26-44 Mac took me flying over Bracciano and I saw all the sunken German planes in the water. We went swimming and used a DUKW for a float and diving platform.

6-26-44 Italy
Dearest family,

At the moment, the war is on hold and everyone is having parties and I am invited. One was in a lovely villa occupied by an Ordnance group. While dancing with this officer, I kept getting great whiffs of gardenia fragrance. He didn't look like the type to be wearing gardenia. I mentioned that gardenia was my favorite flower and that I had always wanted to just cover myself with them. With that, he whisked me out into the garden. There was a high gardenia hedge surrounding the villa, just loaded with blooms. People pinned them all over my uniform jacket and every time one got the slightest brown tinge to it, a whole new batch was picked just for me.

I celebrated my 2nd birthday overseas by flying over Rome, the Pontine marshes and up along the coast observing the German wreckage in a Piper Cub. Diving around in one of those things is a real stomach flopper. Afterwards, we made some ice cream by hand. I threw a few spoonsful of powdered eggs, canned milk, water, lemon powder, corn starch and sugar together and poured it into a gallon pail. We put the pail inside of a large can, packed ice around it, and turned the little pail by hand until the ice cream froze. After adding some fruit cocktail to it, we stuffed ourselves.

On my birthday last year, I also had ice cream. After spending weeks on a cot with yellow jaundice, my birthday was a day to get up. Ed drove to Tunis with some ice cream mix and had some French acquaintance who had an ice box freeze it for him. Our food lately has been terrible, nothing but C rations. I'm losing weight because I can't eat the stuff--hash and greasy beans and then beans and greasy hash. What I wouldn't do for some fresh strawberries. Love, June

7-2-44 I was hostess for a Field Artillery unit's enlisted men's party, held north of Rome at Lake Bracciano. The GIs were swimming and holding hands with the young Italian girls, having a wonderful time. The officers were playing bridge. They had mail call and shortly after that one of the hill-billy soldiers came strutting into the tent to tell his CO that he had just become a father again. The CO said that was impossible because they had been overseas over two years. The soldier replied "Well what's wrong with that, there's two years difference between my brother and me." After the soldier left they told me some weeks before the same soldier came dashing into the CO's tent shouting "Colonel, they's scraping the road." "That's fine," replied the Colonel "it will be easier for you to drive." "Ya, Colonel, but they's scraping it with airplanes."

The washing machines we were authorized last January finally arrived.

7-6-44 Italy
Dear Betty,
We nurses were moved into the rest-area Hotel Excelsior in Rome. It was gorgeous, the food was gorgeous, and the plumbing was gorgeous. Months ago, I had Mother send me that black taffeta formal with a pink satin bra top covered with gold sequins, just in case I ever got some place I could dance. This is the place; I decided to wear it to a dance the first night. You could easily tell me from the Italian girls and those in uniform. I was having a wonderful time dancing with my friend Ed. Another officer repeatedly kept trying to cut in. Ed kept telling him to get lost. Finally, he asked, "Is she your own personal girl friend?" Ed said, "Yes." The guy didn't believe him and said so, with that they promptly squared off. Ed, a Golden Gloves boxer from Texas, hit the officer, who fell backwards and shot way across the dance floor, missing all the dancing legs. I stood there in amazement for a moment or two, then walked up to my room.

My door had barely closed when that gruesome twosome, my CO and Chief Nurse, pounded on the door. They thought it was disgraceful that I had been out of uniform and that two men had fought over me. Oh, yes, I MUST mail the formal home in the morning. Damiflwill. My tenure at the rest camp may be iffy. It was okay that father's (pimps) appear nightly at the hotel entrance with their scrubbed daughters to sleep with the officers. The girls said they were working their way through the local university and earning tuition money. No one in authority complained about that behavior. Nearly tearful, June

7-9-44 There was a small notice on the bulletin board at the hotel saying that Jascha Heifetz was giving a concert for the troops at the Teatro del Opera. No one I asked wanted to go, so I went by myself and originally sat way up in the top balcony. When Heifetz came out and saw the small audience, he had a temperamental fit and was so nasty he wasn't even going to play. We all shouted, convinced him to play, and clapped enough for a thousand men. It was a quality audience and a superb performance.

7-10-44 Today we moved back to Capua by truck convoy. Now we're assigned to AFHQ (Allied Forces Headquarters) attached to SOS (Services of Supply) and 7th Army.

7-11-44 Italy
Dear Family,
Yesterday we moved again, crossing the Pontine marshes. The ground floors of all the houses are flooded thanks to the German Army. You probably remember when they flooded them to retard the progress of the Allies. You can't retard these Allies because we aren't retardable types. General Clark told us months ago "We are here to stay". The poor farmers are the ones who suffer too; most of their crops are drowned. It was one of the most beautiful rides that I've taken in convoy in a long time. Everything was so fresh and green. We all got our faces badly sun-and-wind-burned. Our skin has gotten tough after living outside all of these months in every kind of weather. Maybe I can do an ad for Noxzema some year. We don't complain anyway. It has been weeks since I heard from Bud. Is he still in India flying the "hump"?.
We have a nice area here, but the flies and mosquitoes are so terrible that we have to wear long sleeves and trousers tucked into our boots. In the hot Italian sun, that is punishment.
Last night they showed the movie "Thousands Cheer" for the troops. It was a musical with scores of big names represented. The sound track was worn-out, like all movies we have overseas.
Just hated to leave that lovely hotel in Rome and all the comforts of civilization. The Italian civilian, who we had here for a striker, brought me some cherries on a branch. I didn't ask where he had liberated them. He disappeared when our men moved back here by boat. Giuseppe has a girl friend in Florence and no doubt headed that way. I still don't know why he isn't in the Italian army. So many young Italian men roam the streets in the big cities, all dressed in civilian clothes. They're so happy to have the Americans fight and die for them.

Yesterday we passed a convoy of French ambulances. Their drivers are all pretty French women doing their bit for the war effort. These little ladies go right up to the front all the time, the same as our ambulance drivers do. We are living next to a corn field, I only hope that it gets ripe before we have to leave here as my mouth is watering already.

We have the cutest little white puppy, belongs to the enlisted men who work in the kitchen. They got him in Rome. He has so much pep and the boys toss him lightly from one to another just like he was a ball, and he loves it. Love, June

7-13-44 Somewhere in Italy
Dear Betty,

Yesterday it was hotter than hot. We decided to go swimming in the ocean, for Midwesterners that's really different. The breakers were huge and they knocked us down as fast as we could get up. We hadn't been in the water over an hour when the angriest, blackest clouds appeared over the mountains. We dashed for the villa, changed our clothes, hopped into the ambulance, and started for camp. Then it really began to pour.

My tent sides were up and my cot was soaked. It was mighty cold too. My pleasurable swim turned into a downpour of misery. I had to take a complete bath in ice cold water to get all of the salt water washed off. Every time I licked my lips I got parched from the salt.

Recently, our CO has been in such a good humor, I don't quite know how to take him. His Belgian bombshell took him swimming for the day. His delicate skin hadn't seen sun in decades and his whole back came off in one sheet. He ordered me to special him in his misery. The whole unit is biv-ouacking together. He dug out a musette bag of photos that he stored under his cot. It was full of snaps he had taken of his affair, and he insisted that I look at all of them with him. Apparently, he wanted to show someone how macho he was. At this point in the war, I have no starry-eyed illusions about the human species. When I asked him why he kept the trashy pictures, his answer was typical, "I'm going to throw them overboard one by one when we go in the invasion of southern France."

Mother said Mike is near Foggia in the Air Force. As soon as I can hitchhike to an airport and find a plane going that way, I'll go and visit him. After my last ugly special assignment, I need some fresh air away from this place. Sickened, June

7-15-44 Flew to Foggia in a B-25 to see Mike at Cerignola. Spent the night with my toothbrush at the 34th Field Hospital and saw three nurse friends from Custer.

7-17-44 Italy
Dear Betty,

Mike went on a bombing mission at 3 AM over the Ploesti oil fields in Romania. I wanted to go along, but they were afraid to take me because no one knew I was here. If we got shot down and survived, what would happen to me. When the mission returned, one plane was on fire and most of the men bailed out just short of the field. One airman's parachute didn't open. Everyone was screaming, "Pull the cord, pull the cord." The pilot landed the plane safely. Mike was ashen as he got out of his plane. A dud had gone between his legs and lodged in the canopy above his head.

Much later that day, Mike and Jim flew me in a B-24 Liberator to Pomigliano as I had no other way to get back to where we were bivouacking. As they had no reason to be in that area they told me they would just do a rolling touch-down and I should jump out of the plane, duck, and run as fast as I could to the edge of the airport and disappear in the brush. I did as instructed, barely touching ground in my race. Working my way back to the road, I got a ride with a Negro from ordnance. He thought my jump and run exercise sounded exciting. I asked to be let off about half-a-mile from camp and nonchalantly walked the rest of the way just in time for the confusion of chow-time. Love, June

General Nathan Twining was the Commanding General of the 15th Air Force. Five hundred planes went on the raid, ten men in each plane. Mike's group of between 36-40 planes, under command of Colonel Steed, were known as the Flying Horses. Their target was the Amerino Romano oil refineries. The flak was heavy, intense, accurate. On the return trip, they were attacked by 12 ME 109s.

7-19-44 Moved to a staging area with the 45th Division northwest of Pozzuoli. Guess we are going to invade southern France with them. The rest of our unit is going with the 3rd Division. Our unit is taking ten days of medical supplies, figuring 50 patients a day. The list included gauze, plaster-of- Paris bandages, intravenous solutions, dressings, sutures, penicillin, and other drugs. Each officer was allowed a bedroll and Val-pack. I'm almost used to inconveniences of all kinds.

7-26-44 Italy
Dear Family,

We had chicken tonight for supper, the first time since last Christmas. Was it good. Germany has to collapse some time soon. When people are as hungry and homeless as those we see, they'll do most anything to have peace. These fair-weather Italians side with whomever is winning. They're living centuries behind the rest of the world. It's hard to believe that sophisticated Roman life ever existed here. Over the last centuries, they seem to have gone backwards. From what we see, most of their farming is done by hand, not with machinery.

We've hit a uniform snag. They took away all but three fatigues outfits. Then they moved us back to the city from the dusty potato patch in Pozzuoli. Naturally, all of the nurses based here in Naples still wear their dress uniforms. The officials won't allow us out on the streets in fatigues, so we sit in our hot rooms 24-hours-a-day.

My staunch shadow and I had had it, we walked boldly out the front door of this prison-like building. We planned to hitchhike to the Red Cross to take a bath. We just got to the bottom of the steps when a ferocious-tongued, rear-echelon Chief Nurse spied us and fried us. We told her it was tough--we didn't have anything else to wear and if she didn't like it that was tough too. Our GIs say TS when they are burned up, I didn't have a TS card to hand her. That isn't lady-like anyway. Off we went--to the baths. Maybe God is writing my monstrous infractions down on latrine-o-gram paper, using a big black dirty pencil. Love, June

7-27-44 Italy
Dear Betty,

At the crack of dawn, Beebe and I slipped out of the staging area, while all others were asleep, and hitched a ride to the Naples airport. We decided to fly to Cecina to say goodbye to old friends at the front. They don't mind our fatigues; they've never seen us in a dress. Cautious-but-kind covered for us, by signing us in and out of the building each day, messing up our cots, then remaking our cots when no one was around. We arrived in Cecina dusty, tired, and excited. Unfortunately, friend Max had already left in his jeep for Naples to say good-bye to me.

Word spread fast that we had arrived, and many of our other old friends showed up to welcome us. They brought roast beef sandwiches and canned pineapple. Then off to the nearest hospital to borrow a swimming suit. The water was sloppy warm. Later we played soft ball. That night they had a dance in a villa on the sea shore, even the chaplain came. The moon was

135

beautiful. We slept at a large tent hospital, and the next day we planned to fly back to Naples. Some day I'll fill you in on the exciting details of getting back. Love, June

7-28-44 Unfortunately King George of England arrived at the Cecina airport as we were trying to find a plane going south. All the medical brass was there to greet him, and we didn't want that Chief Nurse to see us. In our fatigues we would be very noticeable to greet a King, besides being a long way from MBS.

All planes were grounded for the invasion of southern France. We were scared stiff as we were part of the invasion force. George, my engineer friend, drove us to the airport at Follonica, and we cruised the planes until I saw a familiar number on a plane I had flown in before. We stopped to check it out. The pilot was just getting ready to fly to Naples to pick up a load of ice and beer for a pre-invasion Air Force party. He told us this was the only plane authorized to go any place until the invasion was in full bloom. My memory for long numbers paid off. I thought it would be a good idea to take the jeep along in the plane to Naples. We would have transportation back to the bivouac area, and the pilot could use it to get the beer and ice. We convinced our now-apprehensive-driver that it was a good idea. Using strips of adhesive from the plane's first-aid kit, we covered the units identification. It looked nice--we smeared it with dirt to match the body, pushed the jeep up the ramp into the plane. George and I sat in the jeep. Beebe became the co-pilot. We sang en route and had a wonderful time.

Just minutes before we got back to the Naples bivouac area, the nurse in charge of our platoon had her suspicions aroused when Max arrived, half-dead from the long jeep drive from Cecina, and asked for me. She couldn't find me and told him to wait in the threadbare, slum-like reception room. When I appeared, she gave me a cheerless, cautioning lecture and five minutes to speak to Max...no more. It was the last time I saw Max in good health.

When my quiet, normally law-abiding, reserved friend and his jeep got back to Cecina it was chow-time. His CO asked him where he had been all day and what he had done for amusement. He told him that he had flown to Naples for the day in his jeep. Everyone knew that was humanly impossible and they guffawed loudly. George had the last laugh.

8-2-44 Italy
Dear Family,
Last night, Bill and I drove out to our headquarters to get some laundry soap so we could keep clean in this filthy slum. It's worse than Chicago's worst, where I used to work. People sleep on the filthy sidewalks at night. Last night, two little boys and a man were curled up next to the stone fence near our door, not even a rock for a pillow. All along the streets are sale tables covered with grimy, grey pig's intestines, feet, heads, with slivers of lemon arranged between them. The flies are black on top of the flesh. The dust and dirt from the smelly streets blow in layers over the meat. Behind these tables, a sloppy Italian hawks his wares. Incredible that people could eat that stuff. The stench of it in the sun is overpowering. One has to rush by it. A good pig sty would be more acceptable. These starving people have no choice. Help, help, June

8-9-44 Our men and all hospital equipment were loaded on 17 half-ton cargo trucks and an equal number of half-ton amphibious trucks and put aboard seven different Liberty ships. Seventeen surgical teams and the 6703rd Blood Unit were attached for the landing. In the initial wave, surgical technicians from the 27th, 51st, and 59th were sent in lieu of nurses. Once on board, the men sat and waited until 8-13-44 when they set sail for southern France. Usually the Navy fed them well but this time Army hospital personnel had to do their own cooking. B rations were in short supply and the deck became their mattress. These men were scheduled to go ashore at H plus 4 to H plus 6 hours.

8-12-44 Eve Curie came to visit the nurses in the Naples staging area out of pity or curiosity I couldn't tell.

8-15-44 At 0800 Operation Anvil-Dragoon D-Day landings took place on the French Riviera. They were planned to seize the French ports and to divert the northern German troops. The men of my platoon were scheduled to debark at 1130 hours D day at beaches 262A and 263 with the 45th Division near St. Maxime, France. For the invasion our platoon had four general surgical teams, one orthopedic team, one maxillo-facial team and one shock team.

8-16-44 For the invasion of southern France, nurses from two Field hospitals and two Evacuation hospitals loaded on the USS Marigold, a recently converted hospital ship. We were part of operation Anvil-

Dragoon, attached to the U.S. Seventh Army under General Alexander Patch. It seemed all the local Italians knew exactly where we were going.

8-18-44 At sea
Dear Betty,

It seems to me that I owe everybody, but have neither the paper nor the inspiration to write. Yesterday afternoon, we played shuffleboard and I didn't do too badly, considering my last game was three years ago. Met two flight nurses from my nursing school this week. They really lead a life of luxury, living in a gorgeous apartment in Naples, making frequent trips to USA. I've gained five pounds in the last two days, as soon as we get to work again that blubber will just be a memory. We can have all of the Cokes that we can drink and all of the candy that we can eat. Ice cream is served two meals a day. We also had whole wheat bread, first time in 18 months. WOW. Tonight they are having the movie "Life of Louis Pasteur", which was the rage when I was a junior in high school.

One of the merchant marines entertained us tonight with the cleverest skit about Hitler; he tickled our funny-bones. He speaks seven different languages fluently. The fellows have a wonderful little orchestra. Every evening they churn out dance music on the deck. It's incongruous: invasion ship painted white, all lights on continuously, band blaring forth. We want the Krauts to know that a hospital ship is coming.

Someone wants to play cribbage. I must go. Pray we will all survive the invasion tomorrow. We have no word of what befell our men who landed on the 15th. Fondly, June

At Anchor in the Pacific
Dear June,

My God, you have seen a lot and make me feel kinda insignificant; me only serving on a nice peaceful destroyer. We'll have to sink the entire Jap fleet to give me something to talk about when we get home. Too bad about some of our hometown boys, it won't seem the same. Father Nurenberg has bladder cancer. Hope to hell you read this after the Germans have surrendered and can come and help us mop up Japs in the Philippines, China and homeland. I'm taking my pharmacist mates to the base hospital tomorrow to help out with the many casualties. Last time out we cleaned the ship, I gave first aid lectures and calisthenics classes and did some hard reading. You are leading the interesting life, so do keep up the writing, my interesting friend. As Always, John

TEN

Of Bees and Rain

8-19-44 By 9:00 AM, the USS Marigold stood off St. Maxime, France. LCI 220, hung with drying laundry, shuttled the few injured from shore out to the hospital ship, then shuttled us ashore, where we linked up with our men and equipment. Drove inland to Rians. Set up hospital.

8-21-44 France
Dear Ruth,
France is beautiful. Lots of pretty mountains, but they need rain badly. There are many forest fires from incendiary bombs that have been dropped, and the ground is burned to a crisp.
The burning pine smells so good and tangy. It's too bad all of that timber was wasted. They could have used it to rebuild. The homes here are the same as in Italy. Yesterday, some French people brought us fresh eggs and melons for the patients who could eat and they wouldn't accept anything in return. For us that is a new experience. In Italy, they were always begging and trying to beat us out of our money.
Sitting here listening to some German propaganda I got inspired to write this letter before the Major comes around and catches me using the typewriter. Temporarily, my work in the operating tent is caught up for a

bit. There is only one patient in the shock ward right now, and his wounds aren't serious. This is the place we should have invaded last year, just by-passed Italy. It has been so long since we have been able to walk down a street and not have people clawing at you, begging for food and clawing at your clothes. In Italy, you had to keep remembering that the Italians were part of the Axis, allies of the Germans, until the very day our troops were heading for the beaches in southern Italy. They're turncoats from the German point of view. Reliable and turncoats are not synonymous terms. The Italians had difficulty deciding which side would put more butter on their bread.

A French woman captured seven German soldiers in the woods next to our hospital recently, using just a little Beretta. The fellows called her "pistol packing mamma". That is the type of cooperation that we have needed.

The fellows in one auxiliary surgical group got some German bicycles in the last village. The French didn't want them. They didn't want anything that the Boche had touched, so they gave them away. Any woman who had fraternized with the Germans when they were here has had her head shaved by the villagers. Wonder how long before we will get to Paris? When we arrived here the people shouted, clapped, threw kisses, and flowers. They came over and grabbed my hand and smothered it with kisses. It was a tearful, touching and humbling experience. Love, June

Serres, France. Operating with the 56th Medical Battalion we received 201 medical and 64 battle casualties and operated on 54.

8-23-44 France
Dear Betty,

First mail in three weeks just arrived. Last night, seven French people were handing some wine to an American officer. He had a live grenade in his hand, slipped and fell, while reaching for the vino. The explosion killed one man, critically injured two others and wounded three young girls. He wasn't even scratched. So Paris has fallen. I hope we get there soon. The bees are just thick in our area. We can't even eat in comfort the poor rations that we do have. Once you spread orange peel marmalade on a piece of bread, the bees pounce on it. A little French girl was eating some bread with jam and swallowed a bee. It stung her throat. She was allergic to the venom. Love, June

Near Grasse

I managed a trip to see how they made perfume. The tour guide showed us the shallow, square, wooden boxes that had a layer of fat in the bottom. Each day, fresh flower petals were packed on top of the fat, which absorbed the fragrance. When the concentration of fragrance was perfect, the fat was centrifuged. The solid, wax-like material was packed into three-quarter inch cubes, decorated handsomely with kings, queens, hearts, diamonds, spades and stamped MOLINARD-ILES D'OR-PARIS. The dies came in packages of assorted fragrances and sold for seven dollars. The guide said that the contents of one tiny cube was the equivalent of one ounce of perfume.

8-24-44 Moved to Batie. Beebe and I went scouting for fresh eggs; they charge us 35 cents apiece.

8-25-44 France. We're out of gas, so can't move any further-- front now over a 100 miles from us. Bet General Patton has gas for his Army. 157th Infantry moved into our area. We've been eating stewed tomatoes and lima beans three meals a day for days. The infantrymen throw hand grenades in the river to fish. Great results. Never had more fun fishing. Wonderful to have some fresh protein.

8-25-44 Somewhere in Southern France
Dear Betty,
Last night after moving to a new area, all of the nurses went swimming sans suits in the river that comes from the mountains in our front yard. It was so clear and cold, and we were so hot and dirty. Two of us walked to the nearest village and using my meagre French and a smile we bought 14 fresh eggs and a big bag of fresh pears from some people who lived on the outskirts. The lady was 22 years old her oldest child was three and she had two others. She thought we looked funny in fatigues and bandannas. This morning, I went to the river to shampoo my hair. The swimming cap you sent me completely disintegrated while we were living at the staging area in Naples. Love, June

8-27-44 France
Dear Family,
We're awaiting orders, just taking a break. It started to rain again, and the soil smells like fresh angleworms. My tent leaks, my sleeping bag is soaked, and all my luggage is in the same condition. I greased the seams of the tent with Vaseline as high as I could reach. Where I couldn't reach, it still drips on my head -- single-drop method of slow Chinese torture. I took off my shoes, waded through the mud to an ambulance, and played pinochle

141

with the enlisted men. One of them had bartered for some fresh eggs, tomatoes, potatoes and onions from a French family. I furnished the tank stove, and the fellows whipped up a tasty meal. Oh, yes, we salvaged a can of bacon from a ration dump -- that really put the finishing touches on our chow. The rest of the hospital ate lousy British rations of greasy hash. I'm down to the point where I take two vitamin pills and a cup of water for most meals. At least, I can keep that down. If we only could get all the mail that is tied up someplace for us, we might forget about our empty stomachs for awhile. I know they need the space on the ships for supplies so that the fighting can continue. Love, June

Undated note from France.
Dear Parents,

Our Marlene Dietrich look-alike is taking a helmet-bath and chatting like she had a merry maggot in her brain. We were discussing ailments, and she said she wouldn't be surprised at anything anymore...like getting a wart on the end of her nose or having a new tooth sprout out the side of her gums. She is hysterically funny, incredibly beautiful, with a sylph-like figure and is about 20 years older than I am. She should have been our Chief Nurse. Our life would have been more humane. The last time we were in an open-truck convoy and it started to pour, she told me it reminded her of her ex-husband. He had bought her a fur neck-piece for their anniversary. She promptly donned it, and on their way out to eat, it started to rain. A skunk stench emanated from the soaked seven-dollar fur. The young pilots want to date her; she laughs and tells them she is old enough to be their mother, and they don't believe her.

One of our courageous Auxiliary doctors and I hitchhiked to Veynes to look around. Only the CO has transportation. Sprouting webbed feet, June

8-30-44 France
Dear Betty,

The bees are so thick around here one can't sit still a minute. They get in your hair, crawl up your trouser legs or shirt sleeves, and then bite. The bees are making Cautious-and-Kind frantic. She's going into the latrine to dress; she maintains the stench is enough to drive even the bees away. I know it limits the number of times we use it.

Last evening, two French girls came over to our hospital on a tandem and they let my Sgt and I take it for a ride. Thought I might be stiff from the effort, but I wasn't. The seersucker suit arrived. Though it is too big in the *waist, that can easily be remedied if I can find some more thread. The Swiss Alps are gorgeous; we can get a good look at them. I can't bear to write much about our patients as they are the non-transportable variety and it's pretty heart-breaking. All I want to do is to forget about them. In Marion's last letter, she asked if war was really as bad as the papers say it is. Don't kid yourself, cherub, that I'm having a grand time. War isn't a joke, a fantasy. Civilians have no concept what the day to day drudgery, deprivation and fear is like. You know how the mind functions; one always remembers the more pleasant things in life not the unhappy moments, providing you are mentally healthy. I don't want your sympathy, just mail from home telling me about how I used to live.*

Brother writes that I should rough it like he has to do in the Air Force in India--living in a tent, using a slit trench, bathing out of a helmet, doing his laundry--CENSORED. I'm laughing. Flying the hump has affected his memory. He has a bearer to do his scut work and I have pictures to prove it. The Air Force patronizes the massage parlors, and his descriptions of what goes on isn't worth repeating. What does he think I've been doing in the past 19 months? Living in the open lots of times, pup tents, wall tents, finally a pyramidal; using slit trenches, once without even a screen around it; bathing in a helmet if we could even spare the water; and always doing my own laundry. Working many 16-20 hours a day, living on C rations, seeing mangled young men about you at every turn. Trying to smile when all you wanted to do was to wash your face and curl up on the ground to get a bit of sleep--while the ground shook and the men kept shouting "Air raid. Damn. Get those lights out." Meanwhile you hunched in a muddy, kitchen-slop ditch wishing your steel helmet covered you from head to foot. Or you didn't have a ditch, all the while, our guns were putting up a steady barrage of anti-aircraft fire. You just stayed there, hoping that their aim would be poor. I've lived with that so long it has become a part of me. When it is quiet, I worry, wondering what is going to happen next. Or some night to be getting a brief break from the operating tent you step outside into the blackness only to see Jerry go strafing down the road a hundred yards away. The bullets are beautiful streaks of red light as they come spitting death out of the plane earthward. You cringe next to a tree hoping that he'll leave soon or run out of ammunition. When it's over, you go back to the OR. Already casualties are coming in from the strafing. Two are dead, one a Chaplain. He was bending over and comforting a wounded soldier when Jerry went over the Red-Cross-marked clearing station near your tentage. CENSORED. Love, June

9-1-44 Southern France
Dear Family,

The winter here will be mighty cold. Guess we'll have to resort to longjohns to keep warm. These pre-fall nights are so cold my feet never get warm. We live in a clover field and the dew is very heavy on it in the late evening and early morning, so that one's feet and boots never dry out. Yesterday afternoon, one of the doctors and I went hiking to see the Alps. They are so beautiful. We came to a quaint little mountain village and stopped to chat with the people. We visited a pharmacy to try and buy some printing paper. They didn't have any, but the pharmacist invited us to the back part of his shop, which was his home. His wife fixed us a cool glass of grape juice. It was so wonderful. "Welch, Welch, Welch" kept running through my mind. They had both learned a bit of English when they were in school, 20 years ago. We bought some pears from a hawker in the next block and promptly ate all of them. Love, June

9-2-44 Went by open-truck convoy to Rives, 90 miles in the pouring rain. Beautiful mountains. Set up hospital and worked non-stop. Had 72 battle casualties and operated on 64. While we were eating outside, a young boy brought his sweet little sister with a big ribbon in her hair over to see us. We invited them to join us to eat out of our tin bowls.

Everyone has a story to relieve the pressure. A nurse from another platoon told of the night their tents blew down. Next day they ate outside, sitting in the open on a pile of cots. Eating was difficult because bees, which seemed to come out of the ground, got into every mouthful. One stung a gentle, thin, round-shouldered GI from Arkansas on the lip, which promptly swelled to twice its normal size. In anguish, he cried out the high-pitched hillbilly lament, "Some things are just more than a man can stand." It broke the dam and, despite his misery, everyone burst out laughing.

France--undated:
Dear Sawbones Saga Editor,

The next area we moved to was very lovely, surrounded by mountains on three sides. The prettiest little mountain stream, which had several deep swimming holes in it, ran right behind our tents. From 3PM to 5PM every afternoon the stream was OFF LIMITS to the soldiers, as that was the nurse's shower hour. The bathing suits that we had made were worn out. Some never had any. Besides our luggage was lost, so it was back to nature every afternoon. Cleanliness took precedence over modesty. Our laundry was done at the same time. Like the natives we'd beat the clothes on the rocks and then put a big stone on each piece and let the running water ripple through it for a rinse. Our last move took us by open truck convoy about ninety miles through the mountains. Fifteen minutes after we started, it began to pour and did not cease for the duration of the trip. By the time we got to the appointed area, it was beginning to get dusky and very cold. All of our luggage was soaked; we had nothing clean, dry, or warm to change into. Then came the usual orders to set up immediately, and we received casualties within an hour. Our shoes oozed water, we sort of sloshed when we walked, but work we did for twenty-four hours without ceasing. Then we took a four hour break and got a little sleep. The surgeons were bleary- eyed, the GIs dead tired, and the nurses bedraggled, and everyone was past the griping stage. The next morning the sun put in a belated appearance and dried some of our clothes and drove some of our worries away. It's funny how good a pair of dry fatigues can make one feel. The C rations followed us from Italy; we can't shake them. I only hope that soon a ship will arrive loaded with fresh meat for the combat troops here in France. Love, June

9-6-44 Somewhere in France
Dear Betty,

I've already worked 14 hours today in the operating tent. When I first got up, it looked like it was going to be a quiet day. Ten minutes later the ambulances started arriving in a steady stream. We worked and worked... three surgical teams operating without stop except for a snack at dinner and supper. Keeping them supplied with sterile dressings, instruments, and sutures kept me busy.

My best surgical technician on the day shift went AWOL, the only time he ever did that. He ordered a Pvt, who is on night duty, to take over for him. He reported to me that he was sick, so I told him to go to bed. With his kind manner and innocent face he fed me a whopper and I fell for it. Fourteen hours and he is not back yet and everyone is covering for him. We were swamped with work and could have used him. Next time I hear a 'sick story' I'll whip out a rectal thermometer and see how sick they are. After a recent 24-hour workday, I discovered that the Sgt. who was in charge of pitching our tents and putting up our cots hadn't provided one for me. I walked back to the big tent where some of our GIs were sleeping and crawled in the only unoccupied cot. I figured it was his. Feigning sleep, I heard him come back and stand next to the cot--breathing very deeply and fuming like a dragon. He stood there for a long time; I didn't budge. He hates women, think he started with his mother. No doubt she said to him, "My son the sergeant, is not Captain Savant."

Tomorrow is a gold star day, we are going to have fresh eggs for breakfast. Perhaps only one a piece. The cooks traded C rations for eggs. The other day a WAC Lt. came around with a wire recorder and asked us a few questions. When we were done, she said she was sending it to the radio station nearest our home for rebroadcast.

The French are so curious I have to keep shooing them out of the OR tent; they come to watch. After our arrival in Southern France, a British parachute Captain was admitted with two broken legs, suffered in the jump just days before our D day landings. The French cared for him and hid him from the Germans. We put walking casts on both legs. Today he turned up at our new area, miles and miles from where we had seen him before. He hobbled about with the help of two crutches. He is quite a character, speaks beautiful French. His call was purely social.

A friend went shopping for me today and returned with some fragrant French perfumes....Chanel, D'Orsay, Lanselle, Schaparelli. Love, June

9-9-44 Equipped with my 1937 French, I hitchhiked to Grenoble to shop for perfume. Lovely place. Eight people gave me their perfume brand and fragrance lists, as well as their cigarettes and toilet soap for bartering. Cattleya de Renoir, Mystere DORSEY, Crepe de Chine by F. Millot, Shocking de Schiaparelli in the torso bottle with the glass flowers on top, Caron's Bellodgia and Dana's 40 Carats. I went only to the posh perfume shops. The owners and clerks traded two and four ounce bottles of their best perfumes for a large bar of Wrisley's pine soap or a package of Camels. My musette bags were filled with ambrosial fragrances.

9-10-44 We moved from Rives to an area five miles NE of Salins and bivouacked for the night. Early in the morning, we moved to an area two miles north of Besancon and set up the hospital. Worked non-stop as the days ran into each other. Completely exhausted.

9-12-44 It was rumored that American troops who landed in Normandy are within the German borders.

9-14-44 *Somewhere in France*
Dear Betty,

For the past four days we have done continuous surgery, most French and German non-transportable cases, which take from three to five hours each. Surgical teams from our other two platoons have come in to relieve us for a short period so that we can get some sleep. One Auxiliary scrub nurse, who never cleans up the OR area when her team is done with surgery, is driving me to despair. Today, when I told her just what she could and would do from now on, she started bleating about being General Whose-its sister-in-law. I told her I didn't care if she was General Eisenhower's wife--she can clean up after herself like everyone else does. ah, whatthehell, archie there goes another promotion.

It has rained for the past 48 hours. If this pace continues, my big headache is how am I going to get the laundry dry to provide enough sterile linen to keep the OR running. The nearest QM laundry is 200 miles back and a good 24-hour run round-trip on these roads. We can't spare the man, time, gas, or transportation that long. We do the laundry in one small machine in cold water with no bleach. It is impossible to get the terribly bloody linen clean, although we soak it as soon as we finish a case. Water is 15 miles from here, but we always run out as we have only one small water trailer.

The undies arrived, but why the three sizes? I still wear small, the other ones fall right off. I wear men's small fatigues and had to cut 10-12 inches out of the waist and put in a drop-seat. So you see I don't need TWO drop-seats. Love, June.

9-16-44 Somewhere in France
Dearest Family,

Tonight, I took a ten minute break from the operating tent; it is getting like a cell for me. I walked down the road to our headquarters, that just moved in, and borrowed the Red Cross girl's typewriter. My fingers won't think without one. Today, we were supposed to get a break and have no more admissions for this stop, as one of our other platoons had moved up ahead of us. But the ambulance drivers missed their tiny sign and ended up again at our tents with a lot of non-transportables. We just rolled out the transfusions and started to work again. One of the patients was a little five-year-old, brown-eyed French girl with a shell fragment wound of her neck. Her long blonde pigtails framed her wee terrified face. I first saw her lying nearly naked on the litter and bundled her up in a scratchy wool blanket to keep her warm. She was chewing some Juicy Fruit the ambulance driver had given her, as though her life depended on it. She didn't cry nor have a word to say.

A young droopy-eyed Frenchman hung around the entrance to the shock ward day after day. I finally sent one of my men to ask him why he was there. He wanted to talk to me. Said he was Charles Boyer's youngest *brother and asked me to come to his house for dinner. My technicians had a conference and told me it wouldn't be safe to go, possibly all he wanted was to get some free penicillin...that he'd probably hold me for ransom until he got the medication. Their concern for me was worth a good laugh. I didn't go, only because I was too tired. It might have been very exciting. Love, June*

9-17-44 France
Dearest Dad,

Your 74th birthday is coming up soon, I thought it would be nice to come home for your party. Betty and I could sing "That Silver Haired Daddy of Mine," like old times. Will cousin Anna be baking her thirteen egg white angel food cake again for you?

We had fresh fish the other day for lunch. I couldn't help thinking of you and all of our fishing excursions. Our mess officer went fishing with four hand grenades. It really works quite satisfactorily. Just pull the pin, toss the grenade into the water, and duck. The concussion blows the fish up out of the water. Just between you and me, I'd rather be casting for bass or pickerel. Bud and I will help you make a new boat when we get home. Who would be so low as to steal your fishing boat? Had to be a stranger. Love, June

9-19-44 France
Dear Betty,

Spent the past 24 hours in bed vomiting, no reason for it but the terrible chow. Some General made the bright remark that the Field Hospitals had been such a howling success over here they'd sure be just the thing for the South Pacific, after this is over in ETO. I thought there were 55,000 nurses in the Army. They certainly aren't all over here. The only nurses I ever see are the few I work with. Perhaps they could get some stateside nurses to go to the Pacific. Love, June.

9-20-44 Hiked into Besancon. Got lost coming back and couldn't find our hospital again as they hadn't put out a sign on the road. Stopped for help at the Medics, 817 Engineers, AFHQ, 3rd Division--no one knew where we were located. I searched from 3 PM to 10:30 PM, was very frightened.

9-21-44 Lost in France
Dearest Family,

Yesterday I had the afternoon off, a rare treat, and went to a neighboring city with our GIs. By 3 PM I was finished shopping and sightseeing so decided to hitchhike home as it wasn't too far. But our CO never puts any signs out on the main road. I got lost, never could tell north from south. Even MP head- quarters didn't know where we were located. All the other MPs are French, who were no help at all, but are great on shrugging shoulders. At 10:30 PM, I finally found an ambulance driver who knew where we were located so I got home safely. Love, June

9-22-44 Somewhere in France
Dearest Family,
        Last night we tried to transfuse one of the patients, but the only available vein on his one arm had been used so often that it was badly thrombosed. The doctor decided to cut down on the vein. As he probed with a mosquito forceps, the GI holding the flashlight said, "Gee nurse, that vein sure is laxative." I said, "Bill, you mean elastic don't you?" He replied, "Ya, I guess maybe that is the right word, I don't use it very often." The whole camp is still laughing about the incident. Please send me some raspberry Jello, tapioca and popcorn. Love, June

Killer Joe

He's tough as they come--
A "Killer Joe" and then some.
I've seen him use the butt of a gun
With a bayonet raised in deadly run.
He'd march 'most anywhere and back
With horse-shoe roll and full field pack,
Wear his shoes right through the soles
And have his bunions fill the holes.
Whenever he ate, someone got hurt
With a bowl full of cuss words for dessert.
His face looks better with a gas-mask on
And he wears a helmet with the liner gone.
Yet--one day after a doubtful glance,
I saw him kiss a baby in war-torn France.
                    Pfc. Aurel C. Warren
                    Stars & Stripes

    Some of our hospital platoons moved 28 times in the first 32 days in France. Until the close of the invasion from the south, 63 separate moves were made. Our people are frazzled and our equipment is frayed. When I met a fresh-from-the-states officer recently, after

149

looking at the overseas bars on my sleeve he said, "June, you might have been born in the USA but you grew up here." Most people treat me like I was their little sister. It's very comforting and refreshing.

Undated letter from France
Dear Betty,

    This young soldier was admitted with extensive wounds of his right lower leg. Later in the day he was very perky because he knew he would be sent home with this wound. I asked if he would like to have me write a letter for him to his mother. He thought it would be wonderful and dictated a cheerful letter. The next night, when I came on duty, I saw flies sitting on his bandages and smelled the odor of gas (signs of gas gangrene). I sent a wardman to get the exhausted surgeon, who had gone to bed. The soldier had no reaction to the sensitivity test so the doctor started the anti-toxin. Despite every conceivable heroic measure, we lost him. The surgeon was distraught and broke down, and we both cried. The next day the doctor did a postmortem and discovered that the soldier had advanced galloping consumption too. When will all this sorrow end? June

ELEVEN

Mud and Misery

9-23-44 Was told to report to the Colonel at headquarters north of Vesoul. Why me? Together, we took off in the driving rain in an open jeep to look for a suitable site near Epinal for our next move. We needed a level field and a stream for our jerry-built shower unit. For over a month, we have had only helmet baths and a few soapings in an icy stream. Oh, would a hot shower feel good. The roadside was littered with demolished vehicles; one was still smoking, and the smell of burnt flesh filled the air. Today, Epinal fell to the Allies.

9-25-44 Moved to Plombeirre. Bivouacked for 24 hours. Rained non-stop.

9-26-44 Somewhere in miserable France
Dear Family:
> *If it wasn't against the family tradition to commit suicide, I'd do it, as wherever I'd go it would be warmer than it is here. We moved last night in the rain as usual. It hasn't stopped and there is no possibility of a change in the weather. We're freezing in this constant downpour. We have no stoves, and our tents leak all over, I got drenched even while sleeping. My head was almost as wet as if I'd had a shampoo. My sleeping bag was soaked, even*

though I had my trench coat thrown over it. Four days ago I washed out some longjohns; they're still as wet as when I washed them. I have nothing clean or dry to wear. I warm my hands over the candle so that my fingers will be nimble enough to hold my pen. I've lost sensation in my toes. Walking doesn't help as the ground is so wet and the mud so deep that it goes over the tops of my combat boots and up to my knees in some areas. Looking at the mud, you can't tell how deep it is until you step into it. The suction holds your leg down. You need to have someone pull you out. The only way to clean off the tenacious mud is to stick your leg, boots and all, into a pail of water and scrub. One nurse got stuck with both legs and it took two GIs to pull her out of the mud. The mud was so deep in one area we were in that when we got a march order we had to have tanks come and pull our equipment out of the field. I'm enclosing a photograph of it. And I have it nice. Just think of our soldiers fighting for our lives and their lives and contrast it with those fat Sons of CENSORED back home who got all of us kids into this. Those guys and the confounded strikers from the CENSORED union are making money hand-over-fist and griping about the tiny bit of rationing they have to cope with.

A very good friend of mine Max, a Lt. in the 6th Armored, was severely wounded recently in Italy. He thinks he isn't going to be crippled, so he's happy. His letter last night was rather cheery. What do you do, Mother and Daddy, when you run out of tears?

Last night, over the din of the pounding rain, came the old familiar boom of the artillery.

Some French women gave us three quarts of milk in exchange for a few cigarettes and dog biscuits. We boiled it. Some of the nurses tasted it, but it had been so long since we had had any fresh milk that it tasted like medicine, and we couldn't finish it. If you don't hear from me as often as before it's because I'm surrounded by so much misery, I'd rather not write, but I'll be thinking of you. Love, June

9-27-44 Moved to Remiremont; set up in a filthy French hospital the Germans had just evacuated. Our field artillery is firing over our head. This flank not too secure at the moment. Constant shelling. Swamped with wounded. Got to use the FFI (Free French of the Interior) shower. They gave us a specific time slot to do this. Most of us hurried right over and finished. One of our chubby nurses went late, took off her clothes, and hung them by the door on a nail. The shower was a fair distance from the entrance, had no curtains, only a four inch ledge of trim around the shower opening. Our GIs walked in at their scheduled time, she screamed and pressed her belly to the shower wall, and begged the first soldier to hand her her clothes. While the other men retreated rapidly outside the lone GI picked up her lingerie with his fingertips, and carried them shoulder high, at arm's length while he tried to walk with his eyes shut towards her--following only the hysterical sound of her voice.

9-30-44 Somewhere in France
Dear Betty:
Last night it froze and I nearly did too. I thought we'd get a break tonight. We've worked all day but the shock ward is still jammed full. Last night the Clearing Station in the next tent had the movie "The Hairy Ape". Have you ever seen it? It is sort of peculiar.
My technicians are unhappy tonight, and I can't blame them. Our CO won't order enough cots, so that the men have to sleep on the ground. Some of them had acquired cots by devious methods, but tonight the old creep took them away, still he has a cot! I sympathize with them but that's all I can do. For a Halloween prank one of our GI's is going into the Major's tent at 4 AM, hand him a urinal, and say "The latest thing in curb service, sir." They wanted my approval. Their suggestion tore me apart with laughter. Can't wait until prank night rolls around. Love, June

9-30-44 France
Dear family,
You can't beat this game, just about the time one gets the operating tent and shock ward cleaned out , the German snipers get busy and the shock ward fills up again. One of the GIs who just came in has a head wound, a lobe of his brain is protruding. He has never been conscious. We keep transfusing him with pint after pint of blood...hoping. We do everything we can to help him live, until his heart actually stops struggling. Between the big guns and the air activity and rush order surgery, we don't have time for relaxing. Betty writes of 90 degree weather. Last night it froze here. Love, June

9-31-44 France
Dearest Betty,
Yes, I got my ballot and voted. This was the first presidential election I have voted in, the first time I have been eligible. Voting is a sacred privilege. Thanks for the yummy Russian cookies you sent.
My leg has been so painful I can barely walk. Tomorrow I'm to have another set of x-rays. On the last set, there was a small area of marked density

in the region of the pain. The cots are jammed so tightly together that one can't help bumping ones shins.

About the broadcast, some WAC Lt. came to our area back near Grenoble and asked us all to make a short recording that would be rebroadcast in the States. Sort of a question-answer affair. Bet it surprised Mom. The enclosed snapshot was taken after the end of a very weary day. One of our GIs was experimenting taking portraits. Love, June

10-1-44 France
Dear Liz,

We have some French civilian litter bearers, as of today. Helps us out a lot. Besides, the French like our food and cigarettes. So you are lonesome since your husband went overseas, but you have plenty of diversion at your finger tips.

As for me, I want to be sent overseas, very badly. I'm tired of the noises of war, the trauma of war, the sleeplessness of war, the hunger of war, and the incessant griping. If I drank, I'd become a chronic alcoholic and forget it all. We had one GI who was SOMEBODY before he became a GI. Booze and barbiturates finally did him in. The last time I saw him he was zonked out in a snowbank. Guess he got to go home. Love, June

10-7-44 Somewhere in France.
Dear family:

My pyramidal tent has a stove. When I could find wood scraps for it, it was slightly warmer, but not warm enough to dry my woolen longjohns that needed laundering so desperately. Fortunately this was the land of Eau de Cologne and oh, did I cologne. Love, June

France 1944
Dear family,

How smug can Mrs. Grump Rump get? Just consider the source, Mother. I wish she was here with me right now. The shells are coming in and going out frequently. Maybe one would have her name on it. Some are landing so close the building jars, all four floors of this massive old hunk. We had a bit of air activity this morning, just enough to keep things from getting boring. When you hear the boom and then a sound like someone tearing a sheet--those are our own shells going out, but when the procedure is reversed--DUCK. The ration dump moved again so now we are back on C rations. I have a terrific cold. Every time we move into a building we all catch colds. These old buildings are so drafty--big shell holes all over. No, I won't be home for Christmas this year, maybe next year. Love, June

10-10-44 France
Dear Betty,

Was invited to Major General Truscott's dinner party held in a big ward tent. When my date and I arrived late...people were sitting in chairs all around the perimeter of the tent. It looked like a wake. The General gave me a corsage and expected a kiss for it. Not from me. Whether any of the earlier recipients kissed him, I didn't ask. My refusal spurred the General into humorous pantomime posturings, attempting to lure me in front of all those strangers into giving him a kiss. Not from me. I was grateful for the corsage, but I never grovel. He made me feel like a prize yearling in the auction ring. It was demeaning.

The most memorable thing about the evening was that they served roast duck. As we have the same mess allowance, I often wonder why we never had the good stuff to munch on. I figured the corsages came out of the taxpayer's pocket. I'm a taxpayer. My ride back to camp was almost threatening. IF my date is BUSTED in grade I can plan on wearing a neck brace. Phooey, June

10-18-44 Bruyeres, France
There Were No Flowers, No Champagne, For Doughboys Who Liberated Bruyeres

Figures of the townspeople slide warily through the dismal streets of Bruyeres this afternoon, their wide-eyed faces mingling with the stubbled, weather-darkened countenances of GIs. The civilians start to go about their business and the soldiers pursue their warring activities, the two groups paying little attention to each other.

Although advance American elements only yesterday afternoon made their first penetration of this small city at one of the most important crossroads of the Vosges, there is little of the flower tossing and wine pouring that marked the communion between American and Frenchmen along the long route of the 7th Army up from the Riviera.

Cold rain beats relentlessly through inadequate clothing and there is little to relieve the dismal atmosphere which preys upon men's spirits. Frenchmen contemplate their broken houses and GIs peer ahead into the grey to find the enemy, whose artillery fires a registering shell into the town now and then. Long winter, with its numbing discomforts, never seemed nearer.

The old mayor of Bruyeres stands in the main intersection of the town in the center of a little group of civilians and soldiers. Many of the buildings which look down on the strange, uncheering gathering in the street have been hit by shellfire and have poured rubble over the sidewalks like sick men vomiting. With intense bitterness, the old man addressed himself to an American. The Americans, he says, have shelled Bruyeres out of all proportion to military necessity.

"You have smashed our buildings and killed and injured our people," he says in a high voice, his flimsy cardboard collar quivering. "Twelve people have been killed and 25 badly wounded."

"There were Germans in the town," the American answers.

Yes, there were Germans. Ask lst Lt. Carl A. Patterson, Bryan, Texas, who led his C Company platoon in under the machine gun fire which came from the railroad station in deadly arcs.

T-Sgt. Fred Costilla, Beaumont, Texas, will pause in the opening of his K ration to tell you how impressed he was with the interlocking system of defenses among the buildings at the southern edge of town, where the Germans had made a stand against the American doughboys who advanced over open ground to close with them. Pvt. George Haymons, McRae, Ga., could recount how he and others in his infantry platoon had walked forward under a roaring barrage of German shells, possibly directed from OPs in Bruyeres, and had gladly availed themselves of the shelter of a railroad tunnel as they fought toward their objectives in the town.

There had been Germans in Bruyeres and some 200 of them were made prisoner last night and today.

The mayor may or may not have wanted to see the Germans driven from France. But if he did, he didn't want the doing of it to cost his town anything.

Bruyeres shows more of the marks of war than most of the towns which have stood along the trail of the 7th Army's advances, but there are a hundred towns in North Africa, Italy or, for that matter, England, which have suffered much more. The thing is that the Germans' insistence on fighting from every defensible wood, hill and building is going to bring a mounting toll of civilians and their property. Those who are closely affected are going to find their burden a difficult one, especially if they cannot see a France beyond their front doors, beyond a cobbled street in a small town of the Vosges.

This article in the Stars & Stripes by Pvt. George Dorsey makes me angry with the French people. It reminds me of the experiences my adopted brother had in France during WWI.

10-25-44 Moved to Grandvillers, we got lost again in blackout driving. More small arms fire. Exhausted working.

10-27-44 France
Dear Ruth,
Remember how finicky I used to be about the stationery I used? Things and times sure have changed. Please excuse the scraps that I write on. Ask Mother to write her letters in ink as they are so faint when I get them it is difficult to read. I know she thought if the ink got wet in transit that I couldn't read the letters at all. Thank all the dear ladies in her Red Cross circle that send us bandages etc.. Also, thank Dad for the metal instrument boxes he fabricated for me. A couple of days ago we moved back into tents. For the first time we have wooden floors and electric lights. It's really quite comfortable. I haven't had any spare time to spend there yet looking at the comforts. Was up all day before yesterday until 2:30 AM the next morning. I was so numb with fatigue that I couldn't sleep when I did get to my cot. Besides, the big guns were shaking the whole place; they make so much noise even a deaf person couldn't sleep. Since we have lights, I finally found my tiny mirror; it's a shock to look into it.
I salvaged a nearly new German inner spring mattress, and have permission to take it with me when we move. With the stove we should live the life of Riley. I've a mean cold that I caught when we lived in the last building. A few more days out in the fresh air and I'll be healthy again.
So you enjoy being a sophomore, I did too. Are you in a class play this year? Please send me a tiny vest-pocket size dictionary. Love, June

October 1944 Late this month, the mud was ankle deep in the area and the engineers built wooden floors for some platoons. Eight sections per ward tent and four sections per pyramidal.

10-31-44 France
Dear family,
The small wooden jewel box with the secret lock was the one I wanted you to send to Betty for her birthday. I mailed that package seven months ago. You can give it to her for Christmas.
We've been very busy this past week. This evening we watched our pilots strafe the Germans. The planes circle, go into a dive, and when they get near their target, those old guns spit fire. When it's dark it's really beauti-

ful. To add to the effect, the engine makes a blood curdling noise as it dives.
Love, June

11-1-44 *France*
Dear Betty:

     Remember the Halloween prank our GIs were going to pull on the Major? They checked it out with me to see if I thought it would fly. I would have done it if they didn't have the courage. At 4 AM one of the fellows went into the Major's tent with an ice cold urinal and stuck it in the Major's ribs. He was sound asleep. He must have thought a Kraut was attacking him. He was scared spitless in the dark. The soldier said "Major, the latest thing in curb service, Sir." The old buzzard, the GI's call him Prune Face-----USED THE URINAL. Better than wetting his jammies. His prostate isn't what it used to be. Ah well Archie, another nail in the coffin. Love, June

11-1-44 Today we were transferred from Natousa to Etousa

11-3-44 *France*
Dear family,

     The package with the jam and tinned mushrooms arrived in good condition. We're rushed to death with work. This is a terrific pace to keep up. Too bad the censor removed some of those negatives as there was nothing of military value on any of them. Perhaps a guy sees a negative he'd like for his collection and he just keeps it. Packages addressed to women didn't cross the ocean as safely as packages addressed to men. One way to insure getting your package was to have your parents use your initials instead of a first name.

     It's terribly cold all of the time. We don't have a damper on our stove, so one minute we roast and the next we freeze. The guns are farther away tonight; I can barely hear them. The other night, I only slept from 3 AM to 7 AM then worked straight through until after 10 PM. A bit worn out I was.
Love, June

11-6-44 *France*
Dear Family,

     Thanks for the Christmas package with the film, anchovies, candy and nuts. Work keeps piling up. Can't keep the shock ward empty. We have wooden slat floors in the hospital--over the mud. This morning, we had a bit of a break between surgical cases and I helped the fellows bleach the blood out of the floor boards around the operating tables. Also scrubbed all of the saw horses and litters and scoured all of the enamelware. I was hoping we wouldn't admit anymore, but the ambulances started to roll in and we're at it again. It'll last all night as usual. I'm so weary of war. Love, June

11-6-44 Denver, Colorado
Dear June,

Finally, I got your letter dated 9/26 and so here's the dope----had your last correct APO--wrote you in care of APO 464-- did you receive same?

Darling, I'm in the Fitzsimmons Hospital here in Denver awaiting retirement sometime this month. I think (and hope) it's back to civilian life for me--striped shirts, polka dot ties, plaid trousers--Whee!! Diagnosis was compound comminuted fracture complete of clavicle, scapula, glenoid fossa processes--outer third right. The ones in my left arm, right hip, knee and ankle don't count.

Gee, I miss you--come home, will you? I know just what you're doing over there and in lots of ways I'd like to be there. I'll try to have that sunken living room finished when you come by--what would you like for dinner?

Did I tell you I was fortunate enough to fly over Naples to Casablanca--Azores--Bermuda and Miami? Tell Nick if he'll write I'll answer. Give the other boys my regards.

I know how you'd like to be in the states, so I won't tell you how nice it is to be back. Is there anything you'd like from here? Nail polish, soap, shrimp, cheese or what?

Write please, I'm still remembering the fireplace--hamburgers--the ice cream--and the memories that go with them. Will I see you when you come back? As ever, Max

Undated note. France

Friends from VI Corps came to visit this evening and brought a huge frying pan and monstrous steaks from the General's larder. They even brought the wood for our pot-bellied stove. The fellows thought we were beginning to look undernourished. Every St. Patrick's Day from here to eternity I will think of them and bless their Irish ingenuity.

11-11-44 Somewhere in France
Dear Sawbones Saga,

The latest tissue issue tells me that Fred's hospital is on the French Riviera. What a spot to spend the winter! All rumors have me scheduled for November rotation. I'm so excited just thinking about it, I'm going in circles.

France's icy mountain blasts are bringing out more and more longjohns every day. Winter means more trench foot. The poor soldiers suffered last winter at Cassino from that. Strong men broke down and cried from their pain. Codeine couldn't hold them, and it was too early in the game to use morphine. We didn't see any gangrene because of it, but other hospitals did. At present we're sleeping comfortably on captured German inner spring mattresses. When orders come to leave here we'll have to leave them behind for the lucky PBS element that always brings up the rear. Everyone in camp tonight is slightly homesick from seeing Betty Grable in "Pin-up Girl".

Say a little prayer that I make that November convoy. Al, stop moving away to those God-forsaken spots in the Pacific. The field that we occupy now in France was forgotten too, except by the Boche. Two GIs out scrounging for wood stepped on a land mine in our area, one blew off his leg. His buddy suffered severe injuries to both his legs. It's snowing, sleeting, and raining alternately and the mud comes to the top of my combat boots. Despite all that, the wounded keep streaming in. This is Armistice Day, what an anniversary. Why Hitler doesn't throw in the towel and let all this murder cease--guess I'll never know. The Saga must not cease. That will go down in World War II history, along with the Roundup and Stars and Stripes. Love, June

11-11-44

Dearest family,

So my letter you gave to the paper caused repercussions from the safe, well-fed, stay-at-home contingent. Guess some people are alive enough to react. Every time someone new arrives from the States, we are told of the strikes and smugness existing on the home front. I know exactly what their sons are giving for $60 a month. We certainly had no part in creating this World War II. Talk to the wounded combat infantryman, he wasn't casting his ballot for FDR. "MAH friends, your sons will never fight on foreign soil", or some such tommy-rot. I can still hear that blathering old goat. My one wish was to live long enough to cast my vote against him. What can a million GIs do to counteract an overpowering civilian vote for this guy? Not much, but he can think, and he turns bitter -- just a bit more so than he already was. The overpaid war workers are lining their pockets with more money than they have sense to earn.

At present we are living in the mountains. It's brutally cold, the damp, penetrating variety that makes Wisconsin weather feel mild. The weather alternates between sleeting, raining and snowing. The mud comes to the top of my combat boots. But, mind you, the Army doesn't make provisions for coal or wood for our living quarters (tent). It isn't safe to scrounge for *wood here, the engineers haven't swept for mines--only on the roads and the actual area our tents set on. C'est la guerre! Then, there is the wounded civilian population. They come to us, so we care for them which means we have that much less time for our own wounded GIs. Confidentially, I didn't come overseas to live like an animal for the past two years in Africa, Sicily, Italy and France to care for the native, civilian population. Someone slipped up some place along the line. I can't figure out why the French can't care for their own civilians.*

What's the matter with Dad? Is there a paper shortage or did he lose his flat-sided pencil? He never writes. Love, June

11-14-44 Today, orders arrived relieving us from VI Corps and we reverted to Seventh Army control. We were assigned a sector in a combat zone to support the 100th and 3rd Divisions. Briefly we cared for the 2nd Armoured French Division during this month. My rotation to the states was cancelled. Invited to 45th Division dance at Bains les Bains. Wonderful music.

11-16-44 Invited to 3rd Division dance at Epinal. I went to the bar to ask for a drink of water and the Sgt. tending bar thought I was nuts. The place was loaded with liquor. They had to send out for water. My date thought it was quite amusing. He wasn't wearing his MD insignia, just his Captain's bars as he said he understood nurses hated MDs.

11-18-44 Was invited to the 57th Signal Corps dance. Hepatitis again, not feeling too sharp.

11-24-44 The week of November 24, 1944 seventeen members of the House Military Affairs Committee were preparing to tour European battlefronts. I never saw them going by my tent to the front. The Stars & Stripes said they were toting extra-warm clothes and veins full of shots. The War Department assigned a WAC Lieutenant to keep Mrs. Luce company. Glamor girl Mrs. Luce said her gear would include a brown hat and coat "for roughing" it and a pair of slacks. I would have been happy to lend her some worn out "roughing" clothes but she didn't stop. Perhaps she is still at headquarters in the rear, our privy without running water would have made her uncomfortable.

11-25-44 Somewhere in France
Dear Parents,

This week in UP FRONT, Willie and Joe are up in the mountains surrounded by rubble and weighed down with combat gear. Joe asks Willie "Do retreatin' blisters hurt as much as advancin' blisters?" Too rushed to write more. Love, June

11-25-44 We moved to Senones, France into a public building. It had five little dormer windows on each wing. The first night we had fish casserole and I thought I would share some of the leftovers with a very, very old widow lady I had met. Hanging on the wall of her kitchen was a New York newspaper she had brought home in 1937. It was her prized possession. She refused to eat the leftover fish because she had worked her whole life for a fish monger and could not stand the sight or smell of fish. She and the villagers existed on beets and potatoes. I wanted to take her picture as she was so beautiful. Her vanity wouldn't permit that but she did give me a treasured photograph of herself taken 20 years before. Every time I saw her, she would regale me with shocking hints of love and romance, French-style.

Her nephew lived in Indiana and she asked me to write to him because no mail was permitted between civilians in France and people in the States. I wrote to him. Months later he sent me $20 for his aunt. By then, I had moved many times. I gave the money to the Red Cross as I no longer had her nephew's address nor hers. The US government mail service did not serve the people of France.

French women who fraternized with the Krauts had their heads shaved.

11-25-44 Denver, Colorado
Dear June,

Greetings, Merry Xmas, and all that sort of thing. Today, my dear, I was retired from the Army, and Wednesday -- my birthday, of all days-- I'll receive my orders and can depart from this Army--to return no more--I hope! I'm very happy, as you well know, and only wish that you could be here--leaving at the same time, 'cause I know that you, too, would like to return to a normal life--No? I think I told you what my diagnosis was--if not, I'll repeat here--compound comminuted fracture of scapula and clavicle and destruction of glenoid fossa--multiple wounds on extremities. However, you wouldn't know, to look at me--that anything had ever happened, and I'm going back to take over my old civilian job. Please don't lose my permanent address.

After leaving here, I'll go to my parent's home for about ten days, then Mother and I will depart for Iowa, where we will visit for a few days prior to spending Xmas in St. Paul with the family (Dad will meet us there). Then to Chicago to see an old business connection, and back to Arizona, by way of California. What a lovely trip that would make for two--wanna come along?

I know that you are working hard over there and would like to be able to step in to say "Hello" or, perhaps, I could come in my little trailer and stick around for a while. Sorry (?) to hear that old sourpuss is down--but after I remember the way he made you cry one evening years ago, I could cheerfully sit und watch him pass away--the old devil! You may tell him I said so if you like! You can give George my regards--as well as all the others there--Nick--Amidi. And my very special regards to the little gal with the green eyes who used to enjoy hamburgers--ice- cream--and jeep rides with me. I'm looking forward to seeing her some of these days--s'pose I will?

Sorry, you weren't around when I left so that I could have left the little typewriter with you, so you could write me more and longer letters. As it was, I released it for a very nominal sum. I'd much rather you would have gotten it. However--such sentiments are a little belated, aren't they?

Darling, I feel like a 4 F....sitting here writing this letter to you. Me here, a civilian now, and you are still over there, plugging away. In lots of ways, I'd rather be back there than where I am. But I do prefer this to duty in the States, full or limited. Wish you were here, we should have pulled a "Gil" on them--then we could both be over here now, out of the army. Well, you can't say I didn't ask, can you??

Write----mmmmh? The address at Tucson will be the one. As soon as I get there, I'll simplify it by renting a box at the PO and will notify you of same. Then I'll put out the WELCOME mat and expect you to come along and brush your little tootsies on it--will you?

And please--don't be bashful in letting me know your wants-- I know that things come up that you'd like to have. I'll have access to PXs as well as civvie stores--be a good girl and let me know--will you? Nail polish, Kleenex--powders--lipsticks--you name it, I'll get it or die in the attempt-- and don't forget the guy that used to come around occasionally, will you? He isn't forgetting you--not by a darn sight--lots of love now, and I'll be looking for your letters--and praying that it'll be over sooner than either of us might suspect--and that you'll be one of the first to return. Love, Max

12-7-44 Moved to Brumath, relieved a hospital that had 23 filthy patients, guess they were too busy partying. We all cried. Jerry fighters over almost daily.

12-12-44 *Frigid France*
Dearest Mother and Dad,

The GIs are sitting here chatting foolishly, making me laugh. They call one of the nurses Meatless because she is so thin and another one Halftrack because she isn't. I have no idea what they call me, and I'm not going to lose any sleep over it. They are always up to some devilment. The youngest one is about 20 and he has a number of older sisters so he feels very comfortable with us.

There is an insane asylum near here, with a glassed crematorium in which they dispose of the deceased inmates. I'd never observed the procedure before.

Did your Red Cross ladies group finish the glove wrappers for the autoclave? Ours are wearing out rapidly. I'm going to try and borrow a sewing machine from the women in the village and make some myself. We are in a building at the moment and finally got the plumbing fixed, so that we can have a hot shower. It will be wonderful. I haven't had a bath in eons. In the last little village where we were set up, they had a large public bath house with separate cubicles for each shower. We used to walk over there and pay six francs to take a bath, that's 12 cents. The water is very soft, not like Africa, Sicily and Italy; here soap goes a long way. I'm still using soap I brought from the States over two years ago. In fact, I bought all the large 25 cent bars of Wrisley's pine that I could stash in my bed roll. I've slept on all those lumpy bars all of this time as well as the extra boots etc. that are in there. Some mattress. I was lucky I never had much time to sleep as my bony shoulders fought all night with boots, toothbrushes, soap, clothes pins, pup tent, and the pegs.

Brother will be home from CBI before you know it and no doubt discharged. I've never seen him in uniform. The Air Force seems more on the ball than the Army. Betty sent me some walnuts and fudge mix. I had no idea I had so many loving friends who wanted to help me eat it. One whiff of food cooking and it starts a stampede to my tent. Truly, I can put the proverbial Scotsman to shame, I can make a piece of candy last an hour in the eating. I doubt if too many of us learned to appreciate flavors before, or the abundance of tasty food. Love, June

12-16-44 I was sent to Forbach to assist in the shock ward of another surgical unit that was swamped. Shells landed a short distance behind our ambulance en route, close call. The litter bearers brought in a comatose GI patient with both legs blown off-they were attached only by two thin strips of tissue to his body. The surgeon kept ordering me to give more blood hoping that we could get some blood pressure reading. He had 12 pints of blood with no results before we gave up. Of the many gruesome days and nights I've experienced in this war, this one was the worst so far. I was so glad I had volunteered as a student to serve in the blood laboratory at Kahler hospital.

12-18-44 Went to Strasbourg with John Kearney from the *Stars & Stripes*.

12-22-44 France
Dearest Betty,
*   Things are going to be a bit rougher from here on. If you don't hear from me, it's because I'm too busy to write. You'll be reading the papers and you'll know where I am, our unit will be attached to the infantry clearing company. We were planning a grand Christmas here. Our plans never materialize, I don't know why we even bother making them anymore. One of our nurses got a wire saying her brother was killed. He was in the Navy. We've bumped into him in Africa, Sicily and Italy. He was a dear person and always brought us starving souls some good food he had baked himself. We will all miss him. There is so much sorrow over here. I hope that your husband comes to this theater, it would be nice to see him again. Love, June*

12-23-44 We moved from Stephansfeld to Sarralbe late in the day and set up a hospital in a bomb-riddled Solvay chemical plant to care for the 44th Division.

TWELVE

Retreat

12-24-44 Very late tonight, we were evacuated as the troops couldn't hold. In newspaper jargon, it's called a sudden change in sectors. When an Army retreats, so do all of the hospitals in the immediate vicinity. Destination unknown.

12-25-44 Somewhere in France, 9 AM, this epistle was done in many shifts from 12-24 through 12-25.
Dearest family,
    It shouldn't happen to a dog, the things that have happened to us since we left our nice home in the German hospital on the 23rd. We moved twice since then. I went to church Sunday in a tank. The quaint little old French church had felt the ravages of war. A chaplain from an AAA unit presided. We had communion. In church I met an old friend, a Captain in CIC, who invited me to dinner at his headquarters. They were interrogating a group of German men and women civilians that had just been captured. Many times the older German men are actually army officers who are in civilian clothes. The women were in peasant dresses. It was a somber scene in a dreary old building. The prisoners sat on wooden benches against the wall waiting for their turn.
    As soon as I had eaten, I was dashed back to our hole-y home to see

if any patients had been admitted. We were set up in a shell-riddled chemical factory. There weren't many windows left in the place. Large shell holes punctured most of the walls. I liberated some burlap bags from the cement works across the way and nailed double thicknesses of them over the window casings. Before we finished, we were nearly frozen stiff--as it was sub- zero weather. Most hadn't eaten all day as we'd been in convoy. The place was filthy so we scrubbed and nailed, until the place was fairly clean and less breezy so that we could set up our surgery. Then I re-autoclaved all of the surgical supplies. On the afternoon of the 24th, we had one bright spot, mail came by the bagful. The GI's found a tiny, scraggly, thigh-high tree, about the only living thing around outside, and I trimmed it. With my bandage scissors, I cut up the Christmas cards that we'd all received and hung them on the boughs. Then we took all of the bright strings and slivers of foil wrappings from our packages and scattered them over the tree like tinsel. So-very-shy Van made a beautiful star for the top out of cardboard, cotton, cellophane, and a tongue blade. The end result was astonishing. The cellophane came from a box of big fat 25 cent type cigars one of the fellows in the mess got as a gift. He insisted that I have a cigar. While all the cooks watched, I lit up this huge stogie and took a drag on it--it nearly killed me. The fellows thought it was very funny. They wanted me to lead them in singing Christmas carols in the entrance to the factory. Hurriedly they posted notices all over the place, giving the time etc. Everyone came.

We were startled by a pounding on the door and abruptly a field officer burst in. He said that our troops were not holding and that we should prepare to evacuate at once. We no longer had our own transportation so were at the mercy of finding a quarter master outfit to lend us trucks. Our CO and his driver took off at once to look for help. Everyone quietly started to repack the equipment for which they were responsible. The cooks had a half finished turkey dinner in the oven, which they turned off. We are efficient at packing but this time we broke all records. Hours passed. No sign of our CO. Every ear was tuned to the sounds outside.

We were prepared to move at the drop of a shell. More people checked to see that they were wearing their dog tags. The ranking officer left in charge, who had been a medic in the 3rd Division, decided to go and look for help too and disappeared into the darkness. The tension was pervasive. The smell of half-done roast turkey filled the building. God and goodwill seemed far away.

While we waited for emergency transportation to evacuate us, I thought we should sing carols until it came. I stood at the top of a large open stairway leading to the 2nd level and started to sing "Ave Maria" and was joined by one of the Auxiliary surgeons. Then the doctor and I sang "Oh Holy Night". We went from the sublime to the ridiculous from "The Rosary" to "Jingle Bells". I shall never forget all those tense, upturned faces at the foot of the stairs nor the brave music that poured with great fervor from every tired, frightened heart. The fellowship that was present in that group warmed our spirits and our bodies. The shabby, scrawny Christmas tree almost glowed.

Near midnight, we heard the rumble of trucks coming from the right--our rear--everyone shouted for joy. There were ten trucks and a couple of trailers. Christmas Eve was cold and dark and we were cold, hungry, and exhausted. We lumbered in blackout convoy, destination unknown, towards the rear. Eventually we stopped in a snowy field and unloaded our equipment. The ground was frozen so hard the men could not drive tent pegs into the earth in the dark. Some of us spent the rest of the night with some cows in a stable. During my fitful dozing, I heard the rumbling of tanks outside. When it was daylight, there were all these beautiful American tanks with that welcome white star on the turret right across the road from us. The first one was named Beautiful Bedilia. What a relief. A road sign pointed to Munster. The building on the corner was the GEMEINDE-SCHULE.

One of our delightful doctors had received a tin of Russian caviar and Ritz crackers from his wife for Christmas. Standing outside in the snow, he offered to share it with me for breakfast. With half-frozen fingers, he piled some caviar on a cracker and was guiding it toward my open mouth when he dropped it on the dirty frozen ground. We both shrieked. He bent down, scooped it up, and ate it. I reminded him of the spores that might be residing there dormant since the Middle Ages, just waiting for him to digest them and give them a warm home. Hope you had a peaceful Christmas, June

12-26-44 Today, one of our Auxiliary doctors discovered a lone chicken and asked me to help him catch it so we could eat it. We caught it after lots of running. For religious reasons, he said he had to slit its throat with a razor. His razor was so dull it wouldn't cut anything; I told Bill the chicken would die of fright. Poor chicken, wringing his neck was a blessing. The plucking, cleaning, and cooking wasn't worth the effort. We cooked it in the stable. We shared the tough old bird with another doctor who watched the whole operation...wailing and laughing like a banshee all the time.

12-27-44 A rash of combat troops got sick from eating the Christmas turkey...guess it was that stop and start cooking and other unsavory things on Christmas Eve in our bulging sector.

Moved from the field in Insviller to Vibersviller and established a hospital in the field, supporting the 44th Division. It's bitter cold. People are very unfriendly, Bertha tried to get us billeted in homes, but no one would take us. The propaganda was that we were vicious Airborne killers, and not nurses.

We have two southern nurses on detached service, when it snowed they ran out and started catching the snow in their helmets to make snow cream. The famous recipe follows. Take fresh snow, powdered eggs, powdered milk, crushed vanilla tablets, mix it rapidly in your mess kit and pour melted chocolate bars over it. Eat at once. Then smile.

12-28-44   As I sat outside my tent reading in the snow, someone snapped my picture. I didn't know until later that it was Bob Capa, LIFE war-photographer. We don't have windows in our tents nor electricity. Most of the time you feel like a mole.

12-31-44 Big offensive started at midnight.
Somewhere in France
Dear Betty,

Some of our surgical forceps don't approximate properly. Our other platoons have good ones. I complained to the Major but it didn't do any good. So I complained to some of the men. The next thing I knew they apparently used motor pool equipment to bend the tips so they were useless and I would have to get some new ones. I was thrilled until the Major harassed me for hours trying to find out who had done it. "Just tell me who did it and I won't do anything to him, I'm just curious." Phooey, he'd have their hide for a tent-top. I finally shut him up by telling him that I did it. He told me that I wasn't strong enough. I just laughed and walked away while he was blathering. He'll die without ever knowing my benefactor. I truly don't know which friend did it.

One of our happy wardmen was taking care of a German patient and was having trouble dressing him after his bed bath. I heard him say to the patient, "Sticken Sie armen in dis dad-blasted pajama toppen."

One of our nurses from another platoon said that they went through the village we had evacuated Christmas Eve and that the factory was just a pile of rubble. It was shelled apparently moments after we left. Love, June

By the end of 1944 we had earned Battle Stars for the Tunisian, Sicilian, Naples-Foggia, Rome-Arno and Southern France Campaigns.

Combat Stars
First, it was to Africa,
Guess I got there late.
Me down south, war up north,
Could find no fear or hate.

Then away to Sicily,
Got there late again.
Everything was movin' fast,
Gonna fight, but when?

Finally got to Italy,
Suited me just fine,
Great big fight at Anzio,
Wasn't there in time.

Once again across the sea,
Would get to fight at last,
Arrived in France D plus 2,
Everything had passed.

Guess I'll never see a fight
or win my battle bars.
Anyway, it could be worse,
I've got four combat stars.
        Pvt. J. H. Curtis: Stars and Stripes

1-7-45 France
Dearest folks,
        No mail for a week but plenty of excitement, which won't pass the censor. Early today the visiting chaplain came, this time he brought his portable organ. We met in a wall tent. One of our nurses plays by ear and really swings the "Old Rugged Cross" ...it's like old-fashioned Moody Bible Institute revival music. The organ just jumps with joy. Ordinarily, we sing acappella the few hymns we all know by heart, then he gives a wee sermonette. It's sad, there are never more than five of us. This preacher in a jeep doesn't come often.
        Yesterday afternoon, we had a bit of a break and three of us went for a walk to the village. Half of the town is pro-French and half is pro-German. Anyway, no one shot at us. The civilians at first think we are the officer's

mistresses, as all the German officers brought women with them and billeted them with the natives. They were surprised to meet nurses. One of the little German boys let me slide downhill with him on his homemade sled. It was fun, we sure whizzed around the curves. The perimeters of the houses and the pumps are banked with very unfragrant manure.

Admitted a 19 year old from Texas last night who had both legs blown off by a shell. He was unhappy because now he could never wear his nice cowboy boots. He died before he could be taken to surgery. The Germans have a potato masher grenade, the holes it makes look like bullet wounds, except these don't go all the way through a body. If the wound is jagged it is probably from a shell or a mortar fragment. Sudly, June

1-13-45 One thousand of our huge bombers went over us in a daylight raid, making magnificent vapor trails. Everyone took heart thinking the war was going our way faster. Special Service activities were at a minimum as all patients were too ill for entertainment of any kind and the hospital personnel was too tired.

1-15-45 Went to Epinal to the PX, there was nothing to buy for nurses.

1-19-45 France
Dear family,
When my next allotment arrives buy me another $100. bond. I'm enclosing two snapshots, the one where I'm sitting on a sled, see the home in the background with all the trash and the large manure pile. That's typical, manure included. Guess if you don't have a big pile out by your front door you're a social outcast. The odor in the wintertime is horrid, what must it be in the summer?

Yesterday, Floyd a friend from Italy, who recently arrived in France, flew over to see me on the way back from Army headquarters. His pilot landed the Piper Cub in the field next to us. Those planes are really marvelous, they can practically stop and start on a dime. Love, June

1-22-45 Attended a GI show at Sarralbe. Then I visited CIC headquarters and watched the seven agents interrogate the German prisoners. It was a real weird feeling; I felt like I was dreaming.

1-24-45 Somewhere in France
Part of a letter to Betty

Sometimes, we have chicken or hamburger -- even cake. Never any cookies or spice cake. That spiced fruit cake that Mom made was the best. Please send me some hooks and eyes. They finally issued us some real, long, cotton-and wool-hose. I'll snap them onto my mid-thigh cotton panties so that I don't have to wear a garter belt. I can't wear round garters on my game leg. It hasn't bothered me for a week, for which I am indeed grateful. Do you know what it is to dream night after night of the States and the comforts of home--to toss in fitful slumber, waking up every few hours from the cold or the dreams. In the morning my cot looks dilapidated, frayed, shabby, trashed! Disillusioned, June

1-25-45 Somewhere in France
Dearest family:

A peek out of the tent very, very early this morning sent me stumbling back to my cot to dream about "Snowbound". We have about two feet of snow. Every last ugly trace of tentage was covered with snow. All of the trees dripped icicles, while soft coverings of lacy snow crowned each branch. Over it all hung a whiteness -- not fog. Hoarfrost? It seemed that the very air had frozen into particles of white, and were suspended between heaven and earth on invisible strings. The stillness ate into one and brought a quiet peace.

War was far away. I found myself skating on the old pond at home. Some of the boys were shoveling the snow away to make room to play hockey. The tiny tots with their clamp-on skates were spending more time falling down than standing up. The teenage girls were trying to impress the older boys home on vacation. A few young couples -- hands crossed -- skated off down toward the river that fed the pond. There was the woody twang of the hockey stick against the puck --the scratch of skates on ice -- the thud of a fallen player. Some cold firebug tried to put his Boy Scout training into use, and soon a wet wood fire was smoking feebly. All that daydreaming and it didn't get me one mile closer to home.

Last night we had a return performance of "Tampico" with Edward G. Robinson. 'Twas of rather ancient vintage, and quite naturally a war picture. I do wish that the people back home would realize that we have war on four sides of us and that we don't care to see movies of it. Don't they make good comedies anymore? Porky the Pig or Popeye would be much more welcome. Just started "The Signpost" about a wounded RAF pilot on convalescent leave who inveigled his way into Ireland. On the fly leaf it says "To the good friends I am about to lose in Eire". It's the same here. Love, June

1-30-45 Somewhere in France
Dearest Betty,
Elmer is in the 7th Army, 103rd Division. He has an easy job, works in a message center. Phin sure gets the breaks. Imagine a seven-day furlough and he just got overseas. The war may be over before he gets back. We're both in the 7th Army. You could send him my address. My gut tells me he's not keen on a Lieutenant for a sister-in-law. Probably thinks I should not be seen and not heard. I'm glad you got Mom something so special for her birthday for me. Hope she doesn't tuck it in that huge blanket chest as something too nice to use now.

Yes, I imagine the income tax will really take a wedge out of our savings. Learn tax computation well. If and when I get home you can do mine. As for my salary at the moment...base pay $166.67, additional pay for foreign service $16.66, mess allowance $21.00, total of $204.33. Government insurance costs $6.60 per month. After 4 years of college and 4 years of working experience that's a disgusting salary. The crime is to tax this pittance for professional people. Brother gets $60. a month flying pay plus his regular salary. I think the combat soldiers now are getting fighting pay. Combat nurses should get frightening pay. Money doesn't mean much here. Most everything has lost its meaning. Sometimes I'm absolutely numb. Life here is so cheap.

Tonight I plowed through knee-deep snow over to the engineering camp to borrow some pickles in lieu of having a salad. I pretended I was back home, that I was just going to the neighbors with my begging bowl like Mr. Peterson. Remember, whenever he smelled mother's Parker House rolls baking, he'd come over with that little bowl and a napkin on top? The engineers didn't have any pickles. Everyday I live in eternal hope that something pleasant will happen to me. Letters from you have been arriving quite regularly -- that is always a happy occasion. Love, June

The month of January our platoons operated in direct support of the 70th, 44th and 103rd Divisions.

January 5th Five nurses were promoted to 1st Lieutenants. By now, I feel that promotions are coming with our K rations.

2-4-45 France
Dear Betty,
Send some 35 mm film and normal printing paper. I'm almost out. It has been raining for the past 24 hours...such mud, coal soot, and slush.

173

Marion wrote, told me all of her problems. Such a burdensome letter. She frequently asks me to purchase something for her, send it to her, and that she will reimburse me. I always send olive-wood boxes, coral, or whatever. She has never sent a dime in return, she even asks for my military script.
Got in a wounded German, the contents of his stomach had been blown into his lungs. He died last night.

I've often wondered what does Dad do all day long? Is he still putzing around, trying to work? Or is he being sensible at 74 and trying to enjoy life?

I dream many nights, and it is always about the States and home and the people I used to know. How funny it will be to walk down a paved street, meet well-dressed people who speak your language, and see miles of concrete highways. They just have old dirt roads overseas. To walk into a store and buy most anything you want -- oranges, bananas, fresh milk, ice cream, fresh rolls, whole wheat and rye bread, civilian clothes, beautiful lingerie, slippers with heels, and see houses with lawns and clean yards and clean smells ...instead of filthy ragged children and manure piles crammed in front of the shacks lining the road on both sides. And spotless homes with floors, tiled bathrooms, overstuffed furniture, writing desks...so you don't have to sit on the edge of an old army cot balancing a magazine on your knee trying to write by flashlight or candlelight. And furnaces and wood or coal stoves -- so you don't have to worry that the fuel will freeze in the rubber tube that feeds your stove. To eat from chinaware and use silverware and glasses, instead of a bare wooden plank with tin dishes and an occasional piece of a tin fork or a knife -- maybe even a spoon. I'll probably bite all of the glasses, drop all of the dishes, and spill everything on the tablecloth. And then a bed -- one with springs -- and it's big and wide, so you can roll over and over, and there are soft woolly comforters on it and crisp sheets and even a pillow made of eiderdown. And every time you want to go for a walk you don't have to wear a heavy steel helmet that nearly snaps your neck -- and carry a bulky old gas mask. And you don't have to wear any dog tag chains around your neck -- or carry your A.G.O. and Red Cross identification card -- just in case you get wounded or captured.

Those thousand planes going over night after night are friendly and they're not going on a bombing mission and you don't have to wonder how many of those young kids up there aren't going to come back. And you'll be judged by what you know and what you can do, instead of who you know and how much apple polishing you did. And you don't have to take a lot of demeaning abuse from some second class dim-bulbs who couldn't whip their way out of a wet paper bag in civilian life. And your mail isn't cen-

sored ...you can say what you think and why, and where you've been, where you're going, and where you are now and what you've done. And you don't have to look into a young kid's eyes...who is shot to shreds...and tell him he's going to live and go home on the little White Boat back to America -- when you know he'll go out on the operating table. And he believes you because he trusts doctors and nurses and he knows they'll do everything to pull him through. But he doesn't quite understand why he had to fight and why he had to see his buddies die on all sides of him. He's never even had a chance to vote yet, so how could he be responsible for the mess our politicians have succeeded in getting the world into. He's glad he could talk to you though -- the pain is terrible, but you're the first American girl he has spoken to in almost a year. It's good to be able to understand each other -- not to have to worry about your idioms being correct in Italian or French. Then, too, it is comforting and somewhat warmer, somewhat drier, and somewhat quieter inside the hospital tent. Every now and then the artillery breaks the silence. The lights are so warm and friendly and everyone is so kind to you -- trying to make you comfortable. Even the technicians treat you tenderly. Your tattered, blood and mud- soaked clothes were cut off from you so you wouldn't have to move. It hurts so much to move. That morphine given you is beginning to work. It sure helps to ease the pain.

I didn't realize I'd been rambling on like this, digressing. I'm just too tired. Love, June

2-12-45 Somewhere in France
Dearest Family,

When this war is over here, we are scheduled for CBI. It is impossible to win. There is absolutely nothing to write about that would pass the censor. "Hi, CENSOR what cutting remarks are you snipping out today?" It rains all of the time. The mud is too deep, the roof leaks, and the plaster falls in on you from every angle. The chow is corroding, sometimes we have one good tasty meal a day. The cook has never heard of herbs. A couple of countries ago one of our nurses got ill and our northern doctors couldn't diagnose her condition. They took her to a southern unit in the rear and when the doctor saw her he said "Why honey, you've got pellagra." Our Field Hospital TO didn't include niacin. There is no place to go, and nothing to see if you went, except the results of war. This afternoon, I am going to have my first shower in four months. I'll probably wash down through the drain boards on the ground and scare the living daylights out of the angleworm population.

The Baccarat crystal factory is right next to a church with a magnificent spire. The pilots use the spire as a point of reference. Much of the crystal *ware survived the latest bombing. Some of the most elegant and distinctive perfume bottles are not for sale as they are special orders for famous perfumes like Shocking de Schiaparelli. Has the crystal ware that I mailed home arrived yet? I sent two dozen little Baccarat wine glasses and one large decanter. Put the decanter and one dozen glasses in my cedar chest. The remainder of the glasses give to Betty for her anniversary.*

Plasma for the wounded men comes in those packing boxes, and the glass plasma bottle fits inside the metal can. We have used so much plasma on the wounded. Otherwise, we get fresh blood from the soldiers who volunteer to give a pint. Combat soldiers are a super special class and don't you ever forget it. Love, June

Unit in operation at Oermingen, France (Lorraine) Some of our Auxiliary surgeons discovered an abandoned French car. The Germans had stuffed the radiator with trash. After the doctors cleaned it out partially, they decided to take me for a ride. We didn't get too far--a little gadget on the dashboard kept calling for eau (water). The Krauts had also punctured the radiator enough for a slow leak.

2-14-45 I received a lovely 8 1/2" x 11" valentine from a friend in the 3rd Division Medical Corps. It's a pencil sketch of me sitting on my Army cot in shirt and pants wearing combat boots. I'm wide-eyed with long lashes, I'm licking my lips and there are three red hearts and other frills emanating from my head (like a halo). In my right hand, is a wooden lid with an assortment of food on it, a stack of sliced bread, a large round of Swiss cheese with a generous chunk removed, three open tin cans, one of sardines, the rest beans, and a single slice of bread. Behind the food--large red hearts and above the hearts the words "Here's food for thought, June." At my feet in large printed letters--Will YOU BE MY VALENTINE? Fred

CITATION For Award of The MERITORIOUS SERVICE UNIT PLAQUE ....Field Hospital is awarded the Meritorious Service Unit Plaque for outstanding devotion to duty in the performance of exceptionally difficult tasks for the period 16 August 1944 to 30 November 1944, in France. Working in conjunction with the Clearing Stations of the 3rd and 45th Infantry Divisions during the amphibious operations in Southern France and in a similar capacity with other divisions in the following land operations, personnel have shown an outstanding devotion to duty in treating sick and wounded troops entrusted to their care. Though called upon to move their hospital units as much as two and three times weekly, in order to keep up with the combat troops, all personnel were equal to the task and have managed to always be in position to receive casualties and give them immediate and proper care.

We received a medal to be worn on the shoulder strap of our dress uniform. The medal is about 1 1/8" each way, the back is a red cross, superimposed over it is a silver X. From the bottom tips of the X is a small banner saying "IN CRUCE VINCAM". Perhaps it means "In the cross we conquer". There is also a wreath of gold leaves on olive drab felt that is to be sewn on our right sleeve.

During February all three units cared for the 44th, 63rd and 70th Infantry divisions. Only my platoon spent almost the entire winter in tents.

2-24-45 I was sent to St. Avold to help out another platoon. We were shelled; one casualty from the medical battalion lost his legs.

2-26-45 My Paris leave starts. I took the train from Luneville at 8:30 PM and sat up all night in a wooden compartment.

3-2-45 France
Dearest Betty,
Just back from Paris. What a trip. Three hours by jeep over some of the roughest roads that exist anywhere..then we boarded the train at Luneville that night. There were six of us: four nurses and two GIs; we rode all night, sitting up in a wooden compartment on wooden seats. Some French soldiers kept trying to get into our quarters all night. It was annoying. We screamed at them in French to get out and stay out. They put their luggage in the narrow aisle in front of our door and sang songs at the top of their voices. We stopped at every cow pasture on the way. Consequently, I didn't get any sleep. We arrived at 7:30 AM and I didn't want to spend my 48-hour pass in Paris -- sleeping. I had breakfast at the hotel, crawled out of my combat clothes, BATHED IN RUNNING WATER, and put on my dress uniform. After lunch, there was a conducted tour of Paris and a high-fashion house. After dinner, they had a dance for us at the Hotel Normandy and I met a very gracious Lieutenant from the 26th Division. Later, we went dancing at the Washington Club. When I finally got to bed I passed out from exhaustion.
More sight-seeing the next morning and shopping via the elegant Metro. That afternoon, my new friend and I went to a musical at the Olympia.

177

That evening, we planned to go to the Folies-Bergère. As we were leaving the hotel for the Folies, six nurses asked me if I'd mind if they tagged along with us. I asked my escort if he'd mind. Being a true gentleman, he agreed immediately. Wow--did Gene get the kidding as he walked in with seven ladies into an all-male audience. The place exploded. All the fellows whistled, stood up, shouted, stomped their feet and groaned with envy. My date really blushed. He was such a good sport I hope he lived through the rest of the war. The show was shabbily nude, the fixtures frayed. On the way out the porno-postcard hawkers were in their element, making money.

The next morning, Lon and I went to the QM and the PX but couldn't find anything displayed that would fit us. We had problems getting assistance. The French clerks kept us cooling our heels while they fawned over the steady stream of incoming GIs. After about half-an-hour of this my regular Army, southern friend blew her stack with language that would make a longshoreman cringe. A deathly silence followed, then the soldier standing next to her said, "Please, Lieutenant, there are men present." Every night that dear soul spends at least an hour reading her well-notated Bible. I was only used to hearing her quote scripture. Now all I wanted the Lord to do was to help me go through the eye of a needle that was lying in a crack on the floor.

Spent the afternoon at a musical at the Empire. After supper, we dashed frantically for the train. This time I had a berth and slept all the way back. We got to the depot at 8 AM this morning. Then we sat for 3 1/2 hours waiting for someone to come and pick us up. Transfused, June

3-2-45 Was invited to dinner with the 45th MPs at a Red Cross Club.

3-13-45 We moved to Neufgrange and set up our hospital in a monastery. Whenever we got a march order and had patients that were non-transportable we formed a holding company of two nurses, a doctor and several enlisted men. This holding company would be left in a field by itself as the rest of the unit moved with the troops. The holding company had the barest of essentials, no transportation, no field phone.

3-14-45 Went to the 436th AAA formation and General Hibbs of the 63rd Division asked me to join him in the reviewing stand. 45th Division started a big push tonight.

3-15-45 Somewhere in France
Dearest Betty,

Yesterday I stood in the Division reviewing stand for a big formation on the banks of the Rhine river, dividing France from Germany. If the pictures the soldiers took turn out well I'll print and send them to you. We use x-ray developing solution and it isn't too good. Brother's letter yesterday said he was leaving India. I've never seen him in uniform.

We've had three whole days of sunshine. That's alright about forgetting to send the candy, I know a character from Waltham who gets Fanny Farmer packages. Last night, we went to see "Saratoga Trunk" -- a good picture compured to the ones we have been seeing lately. It was shown in a civilian theater; imagine having a back to lean against. I'd like to send you some good cognac for your hubby, but I'm sure it would pass the censor's lips. The bottle would be empty by the time it reached USA. Many things that you send to me disappear in the postal department. Finally figured out that they use my things for "trading material" with the local females. There is absolutely no place near us to spend any money, unless one drinks or gets one's laundry done by hand. I have always done my own laundry, that way I'm sure I have some clothes to wear. Otherwise there is so much attrition.

For Valentine's day could you please send me some little red cinnamon hearts?

Yes, your law experience will help no doubt but I don't think I would ever want a divorce. Why don't you wait until I get married or is this an ounce of prevention potion to be absorbed before you take the fatal swallow?

Recently, we received two fresh-from-the-states nurses on detached service. One day in the lull I took them for a short walk up the road. Posted all along the way were signs "MINES SWEPT TO THE DITCHES." Finally Lt. Georgia Peuch drawled, "Honey, why didn't they sweep them up completely?" Love, June

In some areas of France, the mud was so deep around our tents that when our hospital had to move to another area we had to have tanks come in and pull us out to the road. In late March my platoon supported the 45th and 3rd Division. Our units leap-frogged each other as the front line moved. The nurses were shifted to whatever area they were needed.

France

Last half of a letter to my sister with diagrams of the road and where our tents were and where the open-air-latrines were of the bivouacking combat troops mentioned in this story.

Dear Betty,

For some months we have had a tinned butter that is full of wax and it sticks to the roof of your mouth. Judging it on taste and texture it is unfit for human consumption. Troops in ETO abhorred it, complained about it. Nothing was done about it. Lend Lease shipped it to the Russians--FREE, gratis along with other war hardware. Russian troops although hungry, loathed it. Because the Russians complained about it, American scientists graciously rushed back to their laboratories to create an acceptable dairy product. Voilà. Now we have a soft, spreadable cheese butter that doesn't pull out your bridgework when you try to eat it.

The other day I ventured out of our new area for the first time. Four GIs were just getting up from the open-air latrine box; one was still concentrating. They were so embarrassed. I always salute them. Just trying to get even for the ragging we used to take in North Africa when caught in a ditch in a similar situation.

My new Georgia tentmate and I went to the movie "My Pal Wolf"- two nurses to about a thousand troops. Walking back in the pitch dark, we bumped into several men relieving themselves beside a truck. I got my boots urinated on as I rounded the truck so rapidly. Poor Georgia has only been overseas 45 days and she is still gasping for breath.

Were the folks happy about my promotion? They didn't mention it. When my creepy hospital CO notified me of the promotion he said he ought to rate a kiss for that. Old dead- eye, I hit him with a snowball instead and told him that he didn't pay my salary, that I wouldn't kiss anyone for a measly $18 a month salary increase. The audience guffawed. Besides, I knew that he had thrown out four prior recommendations. I loathe his ilk. If you didn't toady up to the toad he makes your life miserable. Survivor is my middle name. I had a lovely shower today and got to shampoo my hair; that's better than a promotion. Love, June

I had pneumonia and they gave me penicillin intravenously. The pharmacist told me that the men took my chest x-ray and hung it over one of their cots. That's real desperation.

Re: 25 Months Overseas

My eyes will never crowd with tears
If I don't ever see again Algiers.
And Tunis holds no special thrill
To make me cross old Neptune's swill.
I know I'll never want to be
Again in "sunny" Italy.
While even France, with all its "chic",
Will never bring a second peek.
Yes, any fool can write a poem,
But only God can send me home.
           S. Sgt. Robert A. Klein: Stars and Stripes

Sledding next to manure.

THIRTEEN

Sammy

3-19-45 At Bliesdalheim, we were the first 7th Army hospital to operate in Germany.

During the move to Herbitzheim, we observed strafings and dive bombings, which were too close for comfort. Bedraggled and dirty, we unpacked in a field, at the base of a small hill. A row of neat houses nestled on the crest. A German civilian appeared out of the woodwork and offered to let the nurses use his shower. He set the time we should come and pointed out his house. Fortunately, we were late for the appointment. As we started up the hill with our towels, there was a loud explosion and smoke poured out of the second story of his house. More 24-hour duty.

3-25-45 to 3-26-45 Moved to Kaiserslautern. We're in a large field next to a beautiful forest. I dug out my galvanized laundry pail and soaked and scrubbed many neglected garments. Throngs of refugees and German soldiers are walking to the rear.

3-25-45 *Somewhere in Germany*
Dearest Betty,

Today in convoy we saw only misery and destruction. To describe it adequately would require a hundred books. Tonight I am bitter. Because I am bitter, I probably won't do justice to what I have seen. Most every village and every sizable German city that we see is a mass of rubble. Hundreds of refugees are cluttering the pock-marked roadways, limping along, pushing a baby buggy with pitiful scraps of belongings, pulling a small wagon or cart piled high with threadbare essentials. Some had a skinny horse or two hitched to an old wagon, all were heading for the remnants of their homes. Utter dejection and defeat are written all over their faces. They're beaten and they know it...they all look so very stunned. The German propaganda must have been excellent to have kept them in such ignorance. They stare coldly at our continuous lines of supplies and troops that head for the front in waves. We are not allowed to speak to them. The fine is $64 if we violate that order. They're sullen, there are no smiles on any faces.

All along the way you meet unarmed Jerry soldiers limping to the rear, carrying a canteen. There are so many prisoners our troops can't handle them all...they disarm the stragglers and send them to the rear on foot.

Yesterday we saw some German soldiers along the way changing from their uniform into civvies. In the town we just left, most houses had German uniforms lying in them. Enclosed are eight pictures; give them to Mom to put with my things, except the one of me and the dog, keep it if you wish.

We moved into the most beautiful field tonight with a small stream. We're on the outskirts of a large city in shambles. It was just taken by our troops. The woods on either side are magnificent, healthy stands, look like the North woods in Wisconsin. Germany is the cleanest country we have been in. All of the houses that are left standing are very neat, all the same style. You can see that all individuality was sacrificed to the State of Germany. Why weren't they satisfied with the beautiful country they lived in?

Hope I'm not repeating myself, did I ever tell you that in either Italy or France we took over a German hospital that was a baby factory. Only the most studley SS troopers were mated with the most gorgeous German girls to produce the pure Master Race. As I walked in, a couple of German nurses came up the stairs with several babies stacked on their left arms like cordwood. They were taking them up to the mothers to be nursed.

Everyone is singing Lili Marlen. Here are the haunting words.

Outside the barracks by the corner light,
I'll always stand and wait for you at night.
We will create a world for two,
I'll wait for you the whole night through
For you Lili Marlen,
For you Lili Marlen.

Bugler tonight don't play the call to arms,
I want another evening with her charms.
When we must say goodbye and part,
I'll always keep you in my heart
With me, Lili Marlen
With me, Lili Marlen.

Give me a rose to show how much you care,
Tied to a stem or lock of golden hair.
Early tomorrow you'll feel blue,
But then will come a love that's new
For you, Lili Marlen
For you, Lili Marlen.

When we are marching in the mud and cold
And when my pack seems more than I can hold,
My love for you renews my might
I'm warm again and my pack is light
It's you, Lili Marlen
It's you, Lili Marlen.

Would you please send me eight small hair combs, about an inch long?
I'm going to wear my hair up soon, it is almost long enough. Love, June

3-26-45 Germany
Dear Ruthie,
Today, for the first time since November, we put up the shower. It has been too cold to operate it.
Every night the German planes come over so low that it seems if I stretched a bit I could almost touch them. You are sleeping quietly when all

of a sudden the stillness is broken by the unsynchronized noise of the Jerry planes in the distance. It keeps coming closer and lower every second. Then all Hell breaks loose as the antiaircraft guns send up a shower of tracer bullets directed at the planes. The planes bank and dive, circle around and come back again. Then you hear the loud boom of a bomb dropping close by and the ground underneath your cot shakes like it has the DTs. Occasionally, you hear a motor cough, miss a few beats, then whine as the plane falls to earth. You relax, breathe a silent "Thank God," roll over, and try to go back to sleep. Two hours later, you go through the same ritual, and once again, before dawn, they come sneaking out of the sky to rain death and destruction on our installations.

We went through the town where the 3rd and 7th Armies first met. We're like butterflies now, flitting here and there, not staying long in one spot, just going wherever and whenever the troops need us. Sometimes we travel by day, other times by night, grabbing snatches of sleep whenever we can.

The bright spots in my existence are a good meal, hours of sunshine, a letter from home, a hot bath, clean fatigues, or a chance to waterproof and shine my combat boots (my most prized possession outside of my helmet). Every time I do my boots I think of Dad preparing his Russell moccasin hunting boots for tramping in the wilderness.

I follow the Stars & Stripes and its accounting of the war with religious fervor. Get maps and hunt up villages and rivers and try to guess where I will cross the Rhine.

It doesn't pay to dwell on the present too much because it is all pain, hardship, sleepless nights, and lots of young men dying miserably, or fighting to keep from dying, hanging onto my hand until it hurts, as if I could keep them from slipping into that dark chasm. Love, June

3-27-45 Tonight, silent as a fish swimming in water, we crossed the Rhine river, ferried by the Baby Navy; it was the blackest night in memory. Deathly quiet, eerie, I was almost afraid to breathe. The Germans didn't know we were coming. The assault boats were overcrowded. We were told that a Chaplain fell in, didn't cry out, and drowned. When we clambered out of the boats and no one shot at us, I was relieved and could breathe again. Everything was unreal at that point. Some of the units crossed at different locations, different times, over narrow pontoon bridges, some crossings had a heavy smoke screen.

Moved to Burstadt, slept on litters, no time for tents. The 3rd Division has lost contact with the rapidly, retreating enemy.

In operation in the field south of Bensheim. We have been moving fast, trying to keep up with the infantry. We are exhausted and so are they. Just life-or-death materials are unpacked at each move. Trying to do our laundry was impossible, the results were pitiful. Most of our moves are at night, we set up and then immediately go on duty. I've lost track of time on this 24-hour on-call status in the operating tent. Despite our primitive, harried conditions, my faithful, indispensable men (Cotton, Van, Charlie) and I have kept the supplies sterile and adequate.

We've been working full tilt since late 1944 and I'm sure it will continue until we have beaten the Germans into the ground. Our being here, up front, has saved many lives. Artillery barrages, night bombings, and sniper fire keep me edgy. Howling wind and flapping tents sowed the seeds for many sleepless nights. Many times I wondered where my guardian angel was hovering. I seemed to be in a place that the civilized world had forgotten. Dawn was always a blessing.

One of my patients was a sixtyish, old Kraut in civilian clothes who was caught directing fire on our troops by three strapping infantrymen. It took all of them to wrestle him to the ground--even with a large belly wound--he fought like a tiger. He was actually a high ranking German Army officer. After surgery he had a stomach tube in place, and a blood transfusion in his right arm, plus other assorted paraphernalia. When I bent over to check the transfusion, he yanked out his stomach tube and transfusion tubing and spit in my face. The spittle slowly oozed over my eye and down my cheek. Inside I felt on fire. The wounded GI in the next cot tried to come to my assistance, but I shrieked at him not to pull out his own transfusion in the process. Blood is like gold, we can't afford to waste it. I clamped off the patient's transfusion and not saying a word restarted it with sterile equipment. Then I called the surgeon to replace the tube. He was furious. What a waste of his time and our limited supplies. Three times the Kraut repeated his performance. The Jewish doctor refused to replace the stomach tube for the third time, and no one blamed him. He told me to just let the patient lie there and when his belly started blowing up he would be begging for it. With my limited German, I finally figured out that the prisoner thought the tube was being used to poison him.

3-28-45 Germany

Dearest Betty,

    When I got off duty, I heard that our troops had liberated a POW hospital with hundreds of patients several miles from us, in a place called Heppenheim. Although it had started to rain and was getting dark and I was exhausted, I wanted to visit the prisoner-patients. Nobody wanted to risk hitchhiking with me, so dressed in my usual ill-fitting mannish garb, topped by my helmet and sloppy raincoat, with my pockets filled with my pitifully small supply of cigarettes and hard candy rations, I took off by myself through the mud...without permission.

    Carefully slipping out of my tent, I disappeared in the blackness. After walking about a mile and a half, I was thoroughly soaked when I heard a jeep creeping along behind me in the blackout. I was walking in the middle of the road as the mines are only swept to the ditches. To keep from being hit I shouted "How about a lift?"

    The jeep stopped. A very surprised Captain Engle, the lone occupant, from the 3rd Division was going to the hospital to assess and investigate conditions. He promised me a round-trip lift. He was fluent in German as he had been born here. We had casually met a month before at a party.

    Two hundred and ninety of the prisoners were scruffy, starving, wounded Americans. The prison population included Russians, French, Italians, Slavs and Moroccans. Some of our men had been there for seven months. Their smaller wounds were covered with toilet paper, their brutal amputations were covered with rags. The men had torn their field jackets in shreds to bind the primitive dressings. Their bodies were covered with scratches, inflicted when they clawed at their body lice.

    Breakfast was a piece of wormy, black bread about two by four inches -- a loaf of bread a day for eight to ten men. Lunch was a small bowl of potato-peeling soup with sometimes a little rice in it. If they didn't finish it for lunch a little water was added to it, and that was their supper. They were shaved sometimes once a month, rarely oftener. Once a month they got a clean sheet. Blankets were never changed nor laundered. If they vomited in bed, it just stayed there with them. Our men who could walk cared for those who couldn't get out of bed.

    In the push through the Ardennes last December the Germans captured two American doctors, who were sent to this hospital to take care of eight hundred patients with less than minimal equipment. One of the doctors I had met back in Sicily. There were no nurses, just two German x-ray technicians.

    Our soldiers were allowed to write one letter in their long imprison-

ment. They had never received any replies. Cigarettes were nonexistent. The Morrocans who could walk outside made cigarettes of dry weeds and wrapping paper and sold them to the GIs for exorbitant sums. The bed patients were covered with festering bed sores from lack of care. Morphine was the only medication available.

Our troops had by-passed this village, leaving behind one lone GI who had become separated from his company. From their window, some patients saw him crouching at the corner of their building, rifle in hand. They sneaked out, brought him in, and showed him their horrible conditions. Finally he slipped out, found his company, and returned with them to liberate the hospital.

As American rations poured in, the men cried. The corridors were slacked with cartons of inappropriate food for these starved men and their shrunken stomachs, but I guess that was all that we had to give at that time. All those that could eat, stuffed themselves so full of rations that most everyone became nauseated. The walkers would go outside and vomit and then gorge themselves and vomit again. It was just for the taste of the food going down, they didn't worry about the return trip.

When an American died, the Germans wouldn't touch him. They'd make the GIs who were able to walk carry him out and dispose of the body. If one of the men died before he could eat his ration of black bread and slop soup the remaining fellows would fight over it but end up by giving everyone a nibble.

You should have heard the joyous shrieks when the men saw me walk through those sad, louse-ridden wards. I went cot to cot. They had dozens of questions, everyone talked at once. Some talked to me until they were hoarse. Others just stared in disbelief, some touched my cheek, my hair, my hands. Still others touched my rough, wet fatigue sleeves like they were made of gold cloth and satin. Tears ran down our faces. Everyone wanted to share their recently acquired cigarette and C rations with me...or they'd say, "If you can just wait a minute, we'll make you some coffee." The lump in my throat nearly choked me. It was difficult being carefree and gay. But they wanted laughter, and female chatter....and I tried. Blarney comes in handy.

A priest in the village had a secret radio on which he'd listen to the American broadcasts. He'd relay any news to the American doctors who in turn would whisper progress-messages to the men at night, when they made their rounds.

Most people will never be privileged like I was tonight. Exhausted but exhilarated, June

Tenting in Germany was the usual UP today and DOWN in less than a week routine, as our troops moved rapidly and we followed caring for the nontransportables. The pace left us weak and weary and our tents limp. In the Rhine valley there were large truck-garden farms. At first we saw few civilians. Their villages were nearly all destroyed. Where we are now, the civilians are plentiful and the buildings are in better shape, except for total destruction of the industrial plants. The only happy Germans we have seen are the prisoners, who are overjoyed to be in American hands.

3-29-45 Germany
Dear Ones,

We're like nomads moving from here to there rapidly as the Jerries keep retreating. Some nights we have tents some nights we sleep on litters. We crossed ye olde Rhine a couple of nights ago. I've always wanted to see the ancient castles adorning it's banks but we didn't have time as we weren't on a sight-seeing tour. It rains most of the time, just a drizzle to keep the dust down on the roads. Part of the way, we came on the autobahn, Hilter's very clever, super highway, two lanes for coming and two lanes for going with a sodded area dividing the two roads. It should cut down the accident rate. We'll have to install them in USA. Such driving comfort we haven't had since we left home.

Occasionally, I mention going to a party. This is not a Webster's dictionary definition of party. Here, it just means a group of rumpled, tired troops who want to chat with some kindred soul about anything but the war, laugh a little, reminisce about happier times, share food, drink, and family snapshots. It means a lot to be with someone who understands how you feel and how you cope with your dismal, daily existence. Love, June

3-30-45 Moved to Worth -- on the road for 12 long hours. Attended a party at the 3rd Division Medical Clearing company. In operation at Lutzelbach.

3-31-45 Robot planes killed 667 civilians. This past month our platoon supported the 3rd and 45th Divisions.

4-1-45 In operation in a field near Eschau. We have a trout stream right behind the tents. German robot planes over again; fantastic to see-hear them.

It felt like we were in the midst of a maelstrom in this hectic drive over the Rhine and across Germany. Everyday was dangerous and difficult. We operated in direct support of Infantry Division Clearing Stations and accepted only severely wounded patients and those in shock. Many patients received hours of shock treatment before they could even be taken to surgery. Blood was drawn from volunteer infantrymen. After the donation, we gave them a shot of whiskey and a slip to present to their CO for payment. The soldier returned to the battlefield.

4-2-45 Germany
Dearest Snooks,

We moved again yesterday. You're going to begin to think all we do is move, but we get patients at each stop. In our last area the Germans tried to dive-bomb the bridge in the village below us. They killed several civilians and wounded two small children about four years old. The little boy's arm was blown off at the shoulder and the little girl lost her leg below the knee.

Today we saw some Jerry jet propelled planes for the second time. They certainly travel at a terrific speed.

Our carpenter went fishing in the tiny stream that runs by us and caught nine trout, using worms for bait. I fried them in some captured Jerry butter. They were delicious. Love, June

4-3-45 Germany
Dearest Parents,

Bless you Mother, the two quart pickle jar of morel mushrooms arrived safely. The mail clerk said the package sloshed a bit, friends were curious what it was this time. These city slickers from the East don't know what morels are and aren't about to taste them. They thought they looked inedible. The jar was sealed perfectly. I love the silver spoon you sent along as a joke.

All the while I cranked up my tank stove, melted the German butter in my mess kit and sauteed the mushrooms...the clutch of kibitzers watched. How heavenly mushrooms smell. My salivary glands worked overtime. While they watched, I started to eat, finally my Sgt. got the courage to taste them and he and I polished off the whole batch. Everyone sat around and watched us, waiting to see us die.

When we didn't even get ill, they were ticked off that they hadn't tasted them. To quote you Mom...I love you a bushel and a peck and a hug around your neck, June

4-4-45 Early today the platoon moved to Partenstein. Seventh Army had broken through the Siegfried defenses. The Siegfried Line is a series of concrete and stone fortresses, huge tank traps, pill boxes and land mines. Transportation was a nightmare. Supply lines became overextended, and we frequently had to split our unit into a holding company, which remained behind with the nontransportable patients. Our holding company this time consisted of a doctor, four enlisted men, another nurse, and I. We were left in the middle of an isolated field with few supplies, no transportation, and no field phone. It rained all the time. Supposedly, an ambulance would return the next day with more supplies. They didn't come. Our troops had the Germans on the run and moved much farther and faster than expected.

Days passed. We ran out of food. I pulled out my assortment of fish hooks and line, my Dad's survivor gift, cut a small branch for a pole, and using angleworms for bait managed to tempt some tasty trout. We ran out of fuel. Vehicular traffic was almost nonexistent, but when I heard a stray coming, I was prepared. Grabbing my empty gas can, I'd run to the road to beg for a gallon or whatever they could spare. The nights were frigid. We had no news of the war and no weapons with which to defend ourselves from rear-running German defectors.

4-6-45 Somewhere in Germany
Dearest family,

It's midnight and the church bell in the village is tolling; it sounds so mournful. At the moment, I'm sitting here alone with Sammy our only patient, who has been dying for days. It is only a matter of hours before he'll be free. Sammy is a young, handsome, black-haired, married, Italian-American enlisted infantryman who has an angelic singing voice. He said he had sung with a big name band before the war. In his lucid moments the past few days, he'd sing all of the favorites of the past and insist that Slim, the night wardman, march around his cot while he sang to us.

For light, I have two stubs of candles and I have my flimsy table pulled up close to the fire at the foot of his bed so I can keep warm and watch him too. It's terribly quiet, except for his rapid, moist breathing--the rales in his chest sound like someone constantly crinkling paper.

Occasionally, a German observation plane drones overhead and then fades away. Every now and then Sammy shouts out some incoherent phrase or part of a prayer, or calls for Mary his wife.

Some days he thinks I'm Mary and he croons to me, while I hold his good hand. Then I'd rub what was left of his back and try to make him

191

comfortable. His temperature has been between 104 and 106 degrees most of today. He was severely wounded by a German grenade--the only part of his body that it missed was his left arm. Sammy had a belly wound, a chest wound, shattered right arm and legs and part of his right frontal lobe was exposed. He had pieces of shrapnel in his skull and also a concussion. Tubes went in and out of him in all directions. Bandages were everywhere.

Last night he said to the wardman, "Say, Shorty (the fellow is six-foot-four) why don't you give me some clothes like you're wearing so I won't be indecent when I go to the latrine. You leave me lying here in bed naked, anemic and clothesless." When we had to take off his pajama bottoms as it was easier to care for him without them he said, "Shorty, when you do that you take away my jeans with all the nickels in the pocket. How can you expect me to buy you a cup of coffee?" Then he'd look at me and say, "Nurse, you have a smile like a whooooole field of sunflowers." He wasn't allowed any food by mouth 'cause he had a Wangensteen suction going. So he'd say "Now Shorty I'd like to have you rustle me up a small breakfast about eight peaches, some pancakes and lots of coffee."

Aiken is the wardman on days. The nurse introduced him to Sammy, "You know Aiken...like my aching back." From then on Sam called Aiken "I'm a hurtin'." Sammy was brimming over with wit.

Tonight I walked out to the road and hailed a truck and got ten gallons of gas to carry us through the night. In the morning we're hoping an ambulance will come from our headquarters.

I've slept very poorly the past few days. My dreams are always about the States; they're very realistic I wake up with a start, only to find that I'm still in Germany.

My leg has been aching a lot the last few days because of the cold dampness. When I get back to headquarters I'll ask about an orthopedic consultation. There must be somebody, someplace who can do something for me. Love, June

4-7-45 Germany
Dearest family,

Despite Sammy's desperate battle to live, he slipped away just as morning broke. It broke my heart. Desperately tired, hungry, and sick of the misery and futility of war, I wept uncontrollably, my tears falling on poor Sammy's bandaged remains. Later this morning, our long overdue ambulance came to retrieve us. I couldn't bear to leave Sammy; I sat on the ambulance floor next to his litter and held his corpse as we bounced over the pockmarked roads on his last trip to Graves Registration. When he died, part of me died *too. His magnificent singing voice was stilled forever, but 'til the end of my days, I will still hear him say, "Nurse, you have a smile like a whooooole field of sunflowers." So sadly, June*

On the way back from Graves Registration, we were following a GI truck and a huge box fell off...two strapping German men came running out of the woods and grabbed the box, just like it was a planned rendezvous. I ran after them and demanded they give the box to me. It was full of frozen steak for a General, no doubt. We kept it.

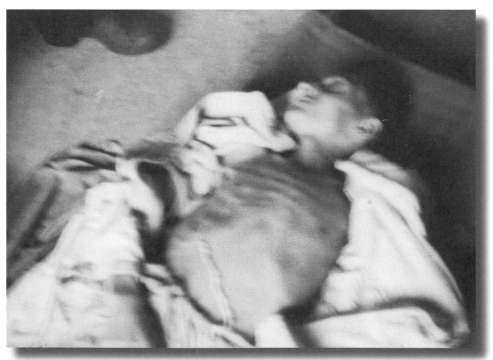

One of my Allach concentration camp patients, one of many who died.

FOURTEEN

Peace, Finally

Part of an undated letter to my parents from Germany.

If that is so, for God's sake, Mother, stay off your leg until it is healed this time. I'm back on night duty again. Everyone is ready to drop.

Our patients are mostly Germans now, all severely wounded. A recent patient was a very young German soldier who was in a concrete pillbox that had some gasoline stored there. One of our soldiers managed to throw a hand grenade into it. The patients burns were horrible, he spoke only a few words of garbled German before he expired.

It hurts me when these young men suffer so. I'm sure some of them must be unwilling draftees just like our men, taught to kill or be killed. Another six months of this and they can send me to a hospital too. They keep sending new hospitals over here, but they don't send them up front, nor send any of us home. You'll never know how tired I am of seeing people shot to shreds. Just had a young soldier on the operating table. We gave him transfusion after transfusion during his surgery. He was just riddled with holes. So happy brother got home safely.

Mother, for all those people back home who say they envy me so much because I am seeing the world please refer them to the nearest psychiatrist. I'd like to invite them to dinner and to spend the nights until the end of the war. What I sleep on I wouldn't dignify by calling it a bed. Breakfast today was insulting to the palate as usual...dog biscuits, tea, soybean cereal. Dinner...bread, lima beans, stewed canned tomatoes. Supper... bread, coffee, dehydrated potatoes, canned peas and some sort of bitter greens that were inedible. Our cook was a mortician in civilian life. He embalms all of our food. It is deadly. We do have a Chinese fellow in the motor pool who told me he was a California restaurateur. I'm making a big indentation in my vitamin supplies, thank you for sending them. Mother, even my fingers are getting skinny.

Please send me some small packages of cereal.

> *l. Bran-shreds*
> *2. Ralstons (baby)*
> *3. Dill pickles*
> *4. Cottage cheese, do you think it would keep--onions and all?*

The dairy industry should come out with a dried version for mailing. Love,
June

4-8-45 Left the holding company and joined my platoon in operation at Partenstein.. The area was strafed last night.

4-11-45 Moved to Bad Kissinger. I was taken by ambulance to an Evacuation hospital. The area was strafed again last night. My platoon is scheduled to move to Sendelbach early tomorrow and set up the hospital.

4-13-45 Germany
Dearest Betty,

Just a brief note to let you know that I'm in an Evacuation hospital with recurrent hepatitis. I'm supposed to be sent back to a General hospital for liver and gall bladder studies, but I don't know what they are going to do with me. If I go they will fly me either to Paris or England. Hopefully England, as I heard they had a Mayo unit there studying my problem and I'd be a willing guinea pig. I just hope I never get back to my own unit, but I'm not that lucky. Why don't they send me home so I can get a decent diet free from grease and fat foods? Ever since I had jaundice in Africa I've had difficulty finding food fit for me to eat. I'm enclosing a German Iron Cross for you. A GI gave it to me yesterday.

President Roosevelt's death was a shock to me I didn't know he was ill. When I was a student in Rochester he came to visit his son who was a patient. That's the first time I realized FDR was a cripple. The newspapers never had photographs of his disability. The railroad station was just a block from my dorm and I watched him pull himself along with his arms to get out of the train. Mrs. Roosevelt came to the station in a car; she didn't even speak to him. Strange couple.

Sometimes you see German slogans printed in white on buildings along the way. The only word I could recognize was Führer. Love, June

4-14-45 Germany
Dear parents,

While I was a patient in this Evacuation hospital waiting to be flown to a hospital in Paris I met a Red Cross worker who was also a patient. Her bed was at right angles to the foot of my cot. She had a large footlocker packed full of things she had looted from German homes and businesses. When she showed me the lovely things, I reminded her there was a very heavy fine imposed by the Army for looting. She laughed and said, "You nurses have to abide by their rules, but I don't. I enjoy all of the privileges of the Army, but none of their rules apply to me." She sickened me. I was glad when the C 47 came.

Another nurse and I were put on litters. We hadn't been airborne very long when the pilot had to feather one engine and the other started to sputter. The pilot asked us to get off our litters and help him look for a field on which to land. We both thought we were too young to die and frantically searched in that sea of lush forests for a level spot. We actually spied an air-strip. We landed safely in Luxembourg, thrilled to be alive. The Duchess of Luxembourg arrived at the same time, causing great excitement. We weren't important. Finally, someone noticed us and hustled us on another plane for Paris. Nothing like being swept under the rug.

First I was taken to the 108th Station hospital, but was transferred immediately to the 1st General hospital. One of our nurses was already there, covered with dermatitis, poor thing. What a beautiful place to work... or to be sick. The litter bearers were former SS troopers. After they put me in my assigned bed, feet dangling over the side, one of them knelt at my feet to take off my combat boots. I stared at the top of his head, thinking how the mighty had fallen...an SS trooper kneeling at my feet, taking off my boots. Love, June

4-19-45 The Yanks are outside Berlin. 1st Army crossed the Czecho-slovakian border. Former patients of mine from Ft. Custer are in Czechoslovakia with the 94th Division.

I received a letter from a sailor, in LCVP Boat Unit 2, who invaded

France with the English Rangers landing on Gold Beach. Operating there for 60 days they were frequently shelled and strafed by midnight Charlie. Sent back to England to rest, their stay was cut short by heavy casualties in France, and within 72 hours they were back on French soil. On the outskirts of Paris they joined Patton's 3rd Army. Their job was to ferry troops and materiel across the rivers. They thought of themselves as Patton's Baby Navy. After their successful crossing of the Rhine at Wiesbaden they joined the 19th Engineers and started sinking German boats up and down the river -- Martin was credited with 110-115 boats. By then only 45 of the original 115 men survived. On the day FDR died they turned over their boats to the Engineers and headed home, their lungs permanently damaged by underwater demolition.

4-20-45 We let the Russians enter Berlin's suburbs....a political move I'm sure we will live to regret.

The hospital recreation department took the semi-mobile patients to visit beautiful Versailles.

4-25-45 The 69th Division met the Russians at the Elbe River in Torgau.

4-27-45 Paris, France
Dearest Betty,
*   I've been here since the 14th and have this constant pain in my right side. No one will tell me what they are going to do with me. On nice days, when I feel good they give me a pass into the heart of Paris or to Versailles.*
*   The pilot from Louisiana, who flew me in from Germany, comes to see me everyday. He took me out to dinner at a posh restaurant. We had the toughest steak in the world--needed a two-man crosscut saw to cut it and they charged $20 per person. There was lots of atmosphere but no food. The waitress, who was thirtyish, fawned over my date, even Stan was uncomfortable. I was beginning to think she might poison my food. At this hospital they have a sergeant from Pennsylvania, who is in charge of the physical education department. He took me out to dinner in an intimate, little, family-owned restaurant. It was on the second floor, dimly lit, the rooms were small and had a few tables for two, the food was superb. Our teenage waitress hovered over my escort, touching him at every opportunity. The coup de grace was when she propositioned him mid-meal, telling him to return after he had taken me home. The manager, who I assumed was her father, heard it all and*

smiled benignly at me. As he didn't discipline her for her behavior, I thought he viewed the episode as his only chance to retire to America after the war.

The therapy I'm getting is strange, they send me off on trips etc. to stress and exhaust me. That's all I've been is stressed and exhausted for uncountable months. I'd like to hang up my helmet, put my feet up and have indoor plumbing.

I have a large cystic right ovary on top of the recurrent hepatitis. The doctor said I need surgery but as I will be going home soon I should have it done in the States. One of the nurses from my platoon is in the same huge ward. There's a very pregnant WAC here who can't recall who the father might be. She has decided not to return to her family when the war ends--just sort of disappear.

Dental care is mandatory here, the tooth-jerky who worked on me injected the novocaine into my bloodstream and half of my face swelled up. I was a mess. My doctor wants me to tour Paris tomorrow. Looking like a disaster in need of plastic surgery, I was furious with the dentist--he said he'd take the day off and go with me. Alone might be a better choice.

One field we occupied in France a long time ago, was next to a field of knee-high grain. We had a new volunteer nurse who had come from a large hospital in the rear. She was quite jumpy about our bleak, isolated surroundings. While we were outside of our tent brushing our teeth late in the day -- spitting with the wind....she noticed that the grain was making strange movements in spots. Thinking it might be a wild animal or a defecting Kraut, she fetched my field glasses and checked it out. It was none of the above, just a couple of very young lovers, experimenting.

In the HASH MARKS column of the Stars and Stripes M/Sgt. Samuel Dickie commented, "An ETO-happy GI never asks 'how long have you been over here?' It's always, 'How long did you live in the States?' " For me it's hard to remember living anyplace else. Here I only exist hour by hour. Love, June

4-29-45 Today, Sunday the Dachau Concentration Camp was liberated by one calm, American-Polish soldier from the 45th Division, pistol in hand. There were boxcars lined up, filled with dead and dying en route to the crematoriums.

4-30-45 Mussolini was hung in Milan by an Italian patriot execution squad. Benito was buried nude, in a plain wooden box lined with sawdust, in a potter's field grave at Milan. His brain was removed for study by criminologists.

Our entire hospital was constantly on the move during the month of April supporting XV Corps, which occupied the left flank of the 7th Army front. Places like Aschaffenberg, Lampertheim, Reichelsheim, Intzelbach, Eschau, Mernes, Partenstein, Fladungen, Schwurzelbach, Walfershausen, Massbuck, Nudlingen, Sendelbach, Prissendorf, Rentweinstadt, Ebermannstadt, Poxdof, Lauf, Uttenreuth, Schwabach (Danube crossing), Treuchtlingen, Gansheim (Danube crossing) Kaisheim (Danube crossing), Lamperthausen and Dachau became a blur.

5-1-45 German radio reported that Hitler is dead. The announcement was made after they played solemn Wagnerian music, including "Twilight of the Gods". Went to a GI-patient dance at the Red Cross, all they want to do is jitter-bug. All their stored up vinegar is coming out. Elements of the Seventh Army captured Munich.

5-2-45 HITLER DEAD.... Headlines in today's *Stars & Stripes*. Admiral Karl Doenitz is the new ruler of the Reich.

HUBERT a new cartoon by Sgt. Dick Wingert is in this Paris edition. Five helmeted, scruffy GIs loll in a building. One squints down the barrel of his rifle. Grenades encircle one's neck, his rifle resting on the windowsill. One is sleeping, one is reading, one is sitting in the hay paring his nails with a dagger. A box of grenades sits on the floor. The caption...."I see where the folks back home are startin' to wonder how we'll fit in the postwar world."

The Stars and Stripes published the following letter in their THE B BAG, BLOW IT OUT HERE column.

"The present policy of non-fraternization is agreed by practically all to be a wise one. It is, however, a two-way proposition. The American soldier, being by nature and teaching, quick to make friends, is finding it exceedingly difficult to refrain from engaging in conversation with German civilians.

Much of this difficulty is caused by the civilians attempting to induce the soldiers into conversation and into their homes. There are few who will deny that a smiling beautiful girl and a gleaming bottle of schnapps form a seductive combination for the individual soldier.

Why not punish the German civilian for fraternizing, too? Fraternization is a two-party proposition."

Capt. J. A. Witt, Engr. C Bn.

Some of the soldiers told me that they would be invited out

to eat by the mother, with the curvaceous daughter standing in the background. There was no father present and they learned the father was a Yank from WWI. After the meal was over, mother excused herself and said, "Schlaf gut." Who knows, you may be sleeping with your half-sister.

5-2-45 to 5-5-45 The German armies are surrendering all over from Italy, Austria, northwestern Germany, Holland and Denmark.
Today it snowed.

5-7-45 Today the unconditional German surrender was signed with 51 Parker pens at General Eisenhower's headquarters in Reims, France.

5-8-45 Stan and I were sent into the heart of Paris and we became part of the VE (Victory in Europe) celebration. First we watched from the rooftops. Then we decided to be part of the near hysterical crowd. French soldiers picked me up, hoisted me on their shoulders and carried me down les Champs Élysées shouting," Vive la France, Vive la America." It was very thrilling. I was kissed by innumerable, exuberant people. Everyone was out on the streets, planes zoomed overhead in huge formations, all the important brass was there...de Gaulle...and all, and I didn't have a movie camera.

Bless 'Em All
(Written in dedication to the fellows who go to the China-Burma and Indian theaters when the war is over, over here)
I.
There's a troopship that's bound for Bombay
That leaves from the port of Marseilles.
The Bluebirds are over
The White Cliffs of Dover,
So cheer up, my lads, bless 'em all.

Chorus
Bless 'em all, bless 'em all, bless 'em all,
A kiss for each cute, little doll,
Bless all our Allies who helped us to win,
Bless all the cognac with petrol mixed in.
Yes, we're saying goodbye to them all

As back to the troopship we crawl,
The battle's half won,
And there's still much more fun,
So cheer up, my lads, bless 'em all.

II.
There's a cargo that's crossing the sea,
There's no more in Europe to free,
We long for our home
But we've still got to roam,
So cheer up, my lads, bless 'em all.
Chorus
Bless 'em all, bless 'em all, bless 'em all,
Marseilles, Lyons, Epinal,
Bless Via Roma in Naples so fair
Bless battle stars which are not very rare.
Yes, we're saying goodbye to them all,
As back to the troopship we crawl
There'll still be rotations
And beaucoup pro stations
So cheer up, my lads, bless 'em all.

Pvt. Stanley Pasedernek: Stars & Stripes

Somewhere in Germany just where I'm not sure.
Dear June,
     We miss you, and hope you're getting better. Our platoon was hardly off the trucks today when the first group of German soldiers, about twenty, led by one carrying a white rag, came marching out of the hills and through the trees. They kept coming like that about every twenty or thirty minutes the rest of the afternoon and evening. Sorry you missed it June, you would have enjoyed the humiliation of their surrender. We contacted the 3rd Division and they came with trucks to pick them up. There were at least 200 that first day, as there were no towns nearby we had no idea where we were. We were almost as busy with surrendering soldiers as we were taking care of patients.
     One bunch decided to machine gun the hospital before the Infantry company rounded them up. No one was hurt. There is still some fighting going on, a bunch of young SS Troopers are holding out in a mountain. Hope nobody gets wounded in the roundup, as they have sent in some of the

divisions we have been following to get them out. Fondly, Bertha

5-10-45 Paris hospital
Dear Betty,

     Recently I was given permission to eat in the patient officer's mess as the food was tastier. I envisioned a large spacious dining hall, instead I faced a small, drab room with very small tables. Only pajama-clad men were eating there, all had their backs to the door.

     Gingerly I sat down at a table near the door, no one turned around to see who had come in. Except for eating clatter the silence was deafening I smacked the table with my fist and said, "I'm saving this place for the handsomest man in the whole room." Chairs scraped the floor, everyone turned around and smiled, and two of us let out a whoop of joy. There was my friend Woody, who had been shot down many months before and broken his back. The Germans had put a body cast on him, but had never changed it in all those months in the prison. The body lice loved his hairy chest and back and nearly drove him batty. The men had just been released. Woody's only possession, which he brought from captivity, was a wind instrument in a case that he salvaged from a Red Cross package. As soon as they could put on a new body cast he would be flying home.

     He invited me to attend his departure, and waved from his litter as they loaded him on the plane. I felt so tiny and alone as I stood on the steps and watched him fly home to recuperate and to finish medical school.

     Discharged from the hospital today. Irene and I flew from Paris to Munich on a Press plane (number on tail 223643 with a large A above) loaded with uncommunicative reporters. They were making the grand tour of all eight American posts in Germany. At one of the stops, I met a POW from the 34th Division who had been a prisoner for 27 months. He was so happy to be with friends.

     Irene and I were standing looking out across the fields surrounding one of the airports. In the great distance, I saw two specks frantically running towards us; they were GIs who had escaped from the Russians. A reporter on the plane was from the same town in Iowa as one of the returnees. In Munich we spent the night at 45th Division headquarters and General Frederick helped us track down the current location of our hospital. He gave me a pair of olive drab slacks one of our nurses had left with their tailor to have the front zipper taken out and put on the left side. Uniforms were a great problem for us. When our clothing wore out, we had to convert men's clothing to our use. Love, June

5-11-45 Bob Martin from the 45th Division MPs drove us back to our hospital at Feldweis. We met many unguarded German troops all day going to surrender.

5-14-45 Fred my medic friend from the 7th Infantry regiment took me to see Berchtesgaden, which was still smoking. We took turns standing in what was left of Hitler's favorite window and had our pictures taken. Later we toured Salzburg.

5-15-45 We were relieved from 6th Army group and assigned to 12th Army group and 7th Army until 6-9-45.

Our platoon took a ferry to an island in Lake Chiemsee to tour the palace of King Ludwig II. It was too beautiful to describe. The guide said it had never been lived in.

5-19-45 Austria
Dearest family,

This will be a diary for a few days. We came to Austria as the weekend guests of one of our favorite divisions, the 3rd. They called for us in Hermann Goering's specially built, ten-passenger, bullet-proof Mercedes Benz limousines. We were billeted in one of Hitler's gorgeous guest Doll Houses. The walls were covered with delicate, eggshell,silk moiré. The floors were marble and heavily carpeted. The linens, china, silver and crystalware were the finest in the Reich. We had a superb swimming pool in our yard and a four-piece band that played American swing music while we swam. We celebrated Lonnie's friend's birthday in extravagant, spectacular style. Finishing a toast some people smashed their lovely crystal glasses on the edge of the table. I couldn't destroy such beautiful things.

May 20 This morning we went sightseeing and toured the ancient walled city of Salzburg. It had been a medieval fortress. More swimming in the afternoon and then a party in one of the other mansions in which Hitler used to entertain all of the diplomats. A most magnificent setting. Then off to the General's dinner party and an evening of dancing to the best music this side of USA...a GI band. We danced until 4 AM trying to make up for lost years.

The young soldier who served dinner was so nervous he spilled soup down the back of my uniform, one of his many faux pas. I cringed at the desperate look on his face. I said, "You can't hurt my uniform or me; we have been through the war together."

Col. Hankus, my dinner partner, kept saying to me, "Smile, I'm tak-

ing your picture." I thought he was spoofing. He had a tiny camera the size of a small cigarette lighter; none of us had ever seen anything like it. They had liberated a cache of three hundred Minox spy-cameras. He gave me two, one to share with my tentmate. The instruction book was written in French, the camera was assembled in Riga, Latvia. The speed is up to a 1000th of a second, there are 50 pictures to a roll and it takes 8 mm film. I'll cherish it forever.

May 21 With snowcapped mountains for a backdrop, 3rd Division staged an impressive wild West rodeo in an arena on the outskirts of Salzburg. Hungarian cavalry officers also demonstrated their expert horsemanship. With the General as our escort, everyone had a wonderful time, but time was running out. After another delicious dinner, we started our long trip back. We piled into Goering's lovely limousines and were whisked off into the night to Berg, Germany. After a six-hour trip we found that our unit had moved again, this time to Wurmsee.

Now we're back to our old canvas city, ants, mosquitoes, tin dishes, crooked forks, helmets...our indispensable washbasin, and two-holers instead of tiled bathrooms, silk and satin, eiderdown pillows, china, sterling, roofs, flooring and plumbing. I'm enclosing a snapshot from Dachau Concentration camp. Exhausted but happy, June

5-22-45 45th Division's conducted tour route of Munich, Germany for our hospital.

City Hall, Munich Cathedral, Church of St Peter, Old City Hall , Asam church, Sendlinger Gate ,Surgical Clinic, Institute of Medicine, Theresien Field, Bavaria Hall of Fame, Church of St Paul, Post Office, Railroad Station, Telegraph Office, Palace of Justice, Old Botanical Garden, Nepturne Fountain, Karl Gate Bank of Germany, Residence of Max Herzog, Wittelsbacher Fountain, Park Hotel, Regina Palace Hotel Russian Campaign Monument, Brown House Royal Plaza, Führer Houses, Temples of Honor of the Party, National Gallery, Art Gallery, Arc of Triumph, Lenbach Gallery, Institute of Technology Old and New Pinakothek Gallery New Univerity, School of Fine Art, Victory Arc, Old University, Ludwig and Nornen Fountains, House of German Law, Institute of English Ladies, National Institute for the Blind, Ludwig Church, Central Ministry of War, Statue of King Ludwig I, Palace of Prince Rupprecht, Odeon Concert House, Feldherrn Hall, Royal Residence, Royal Grounds, Arcades, Monument of the Unknown Soldier, Army Museum, Court Church Palace of Prince

Karl, House of German Art, English Garden, National Museum, Air Ministry, Angel of Peace, Sports Stadium, Richard Wagner Memorial, Prince Regent Theater, Apartment of Adolph Hitler, Bavarian Military Academy, Maximilian Bridge, Bavarian Government Buildings, Old German Museum, Grand Theater, Hotel Four Seasons, Hofbrauhaus (Munich Beer Hall), court Theater, Residence Theater, Central Post Office, Monument of King Max Joseph, Marien Fountain, Holy Ghost church, Isar Gate, Ludwig Bridge, German Museum, Gartnerplatz Theater, The Munich Beer Hall is the CP for the 157 Infantry, 45th Division.

5-23-45 Germany
Dearest Ruth:
Yesterday we had a first-class personalized tour of Munich courtesy of the 45th Division. Much of Munich was bombed into rubble. We went in a big bus a civilian had hidden in the woods. He'd stacked huge trees all the way around it so that until you were within fifteen feet of it you would never notice it. That's his ingenious story, but I don't believe it. He's probably another Nazi, aren't they all? After the Americans took Munich, he came to A.M.G. headquarters and asked them if they wanted to use his bus. They picked it up for their use and are keeping him for the driver.

Last night for supper we had strawberry shortcake, I couldn't get my fill. That's the first I've tasted in years. One of our officers who speaks German got the huge berries. They were so sweet sugar wasn't necessary. Everyone else is living in a building except our unit.. Perhaps we will move soon. Hope I'll make it home for your birthday. Wouldn't that be fun? Love, June

5-24-45 Germany
Dearest family,
The ice cream mix arrived today. It is so cold at present in the old field that we are living in...hot chili mix would be more appropriate. Today I hit my thumb a good whack with a sledge hammer while trying to nail a package shut to send home. If I make too many typographical errors it is only because of my new injury. Did you have a nice Mother's Day?

My nursing school roommate is having her second baby in November, she wants me to hurry home and take care of her. I wish I could. Guess I'd rather be having one of my own babies; the war has hobbled and muddled my life plans. Marriage proposals are frequent. In this unstable environment, marriage would be a shaky affair. I'd prefer to know someone on their home turf first. One of the saddest marriage proposals I had was from an infantry officer in Italy, "Marry me today, I may not live out the week." He didn't.

My friend Fred was wounded again, not seriously, in the fighting around Berchtesgaden just before the end of the war. Fortunately, he was wearing a Luger in a shoulder holster; a bullet struck the holster and was stopped by the gun, saving his life. He has been in a battalion aid station ever since he came overseas, and the going has been rough. His Colonel told me that Fred would have been an excellent infantry officer.

Well, dears, I'd like to tell you that I will be seeing you soon, but I can't, so I'll only say that I'm praying that I'll see you all soon. My love, June

5-24-45 Starnberg, Germany

Someone finally got the courage to requisition a Nazi Baron's house and give it to the nurses. Our bedrooms were on the second floor. The basement was filled with chests of liberated finery from the countries the Germans had invaded and plundered. In the dining room there were locked china cabinets filled with exquisite porcelains. At odd times the Baron would come back and check the locks on the cabinets to be sure everything was still there.

A Jewish friend of mine was propositioned by a Rabbi. She was so discouraged and disillusioned and felt that life had betrayed her.

5-25-45 I hitchhiked 70 miles to Augsburg to visit my Bridge-playing friends.

5-27-45 Germany
Dearest family:

Today we got another commendation. This was from Major General Robert T. Frederick, headquarters 45th Infantry Division.

Elements of the -- Field Hospital supported this Division in its landing in Southern France, in the early part of the drive up the Rhone Valley, the assault on the Siegfried Line, the crossings of the Rhine, Main and Danube Rivers, and in the attacks on Nürnberg and Munich. Establishing in close proximity to the Division Clearing Station, the Field Hospital rendered valuable aid to the more seriously wounded at a time critical to saving life. The very nature of the cases handled called for the highest professional skill before, during, and after operations. The efficient manner in which the personnel of the -- Field Hospital accomplished arduous duties, often under the most adverse conditions, indicate a high degree of training and morale and resulted in the saving of many lives and the alleviation of much suffering among the wounded of this Division. Love, June

5-29-to 5-31-45 Old friends from 6th Corps invited us to Innsbruck for a few days of dancing and sight-seeing. The cable car trips up into the Alps were spectacular.

6-1-45 Went through the Brenner Pass into Italy.

FIFTEEN

Allach and Dachau

6-2-45 We were assigned to Camp Allach, a displaced person's hospital, five miles north of Munich. We relieved the 66th Field Hospital and inherited 400 patients. Many had tuberculosis, typhus, mental problems; all were starved. Patients confined to bed had huge bedsores. All had been punished or tortured. First, we had to clean the contaminated buildings and grounds and recruited 25 mobile, displaced persons to help. Every building was scrubbed and disinfected.

We all wore long-sleeved clothing that fastened tightly around our wrists and our trousers were tucked into our boots. Within a week we were able to transfer some of the patients to Dachau, just five miles away. Assorted VIPs from America and Russia are taking notes and pictures.

6-4-45 Allach, Germany
Dearest family,

I'm on night duty with a hundred corpse-like patients, wrecks of humanity...macerated skin drawn over their bones, eyes sunken in wide sockets, hair shaved off. Mostly Jewish, these tortured souls hardly resemble humans. Their bodies are riddled with diseases. Many have tuberculosis, typhus, enterocolitis (constant diarrhea) and huge bed sores.

Many cough all night long, as their lungs are in such terrible condition. They break out in great beads of perspiration. Then there is the roomful of those that are incontinent and irrational. It sounds like the construction crew for the tower of Babel...Poles, Czechs, Russians, Slavs, Bulgarians, Dutch, Hungarians, Germans. What makes it so difficult is that I understand only a few words. Their gratitude tears at my heart when I do something to make them more comfortable or give them a little food or smile at them.

One of the day nurses had a patient that kept leaving his cot and crawling under it to sleep on the bare wooden floor. She decided to put his mattress, sheets and pillow under there too as it seemed to be his favorite place.

The odor from the lack of sanitation over the years makes the whole place smell like rotten, rotten sewage. We wear masks constantly, though they don't keep out the stench. There are commodes in the middle of the room. Patients wear just pajama shirts as they can't get the bottoms down fast enough to use the commodes. God, where are you?

Making rounds by flashlight is an eerie sensation. I'll hear calloused footsteps shuffling behind me and turn in time to see four semi-nude skeletons gliding toward the commodes. God, where were you?

You have to gently shake some of the patients to see if they are still alive. Their breathing is so shallow, pulse debatable. Many die in their sleep. I carry their bodies back to a storage room, they are very light, just the weight of their demineralized bones. Each time, I breathe a wee prayer for them. God, are you there?

In the morning the strongest patients have latrine detail, it takes two of them to carry a commode pail and dump it. They also sweep the floors and carry out the trash. Many patients are only seventeen.

Our men sprayed the camp area to kill the insects that carried many of the diseases. We were told that the SS guards who controlled the camp used to bring a small pan of food into the ward and throw it on the floor. When the stronger patients scrambled for it, like starving beasts, they were lashed with a long whip. It's a corner of hell. Too shocked and tired to write anymore. Love, June

6-8-45 Dachau
Dearest family,

The odor of this place is improving a wee bit. It only smells like sewage in the fall instead of sewage in the hot summer. Or maybe the wind is stronger and blows the smell away faster.

It said in the Stars & Stripes today that 3500 nurses will be sent *home from here beginning in July. Do you suppose I'll make it this time? I'm saying my prayers. Phin said I should tell you he went to church last Sunday and that the chaplain apparently had not answered "the call" but had been drafted. No doubt he's right. The chaplains have their own little fiefdom, driver, jeep, TS cards, and answer only to God. There are exceptions. Love, June*

6-9-45 We were assigned to General Patton's 3rd Army. Each change of arm patches means more needlework for all of us.

6-10-45 *Allach, Germany*
Dear family,

Thanks for the box of 24 Hershey bars. I took it to work, broke it into tiny pieces, and offered each patient some. I warned them it might make them sick--so just to taste it and spit it out. Some did; others broke off a nibble and swallowed it. They were so excited and pleased, they'd just grab my hand and hold it. Wrapping the food we give them in toilet paper, they hide it under their sheets or mattress. The poor souls still can't believe that they will get more later.

If they are strong enough and can get ground transportation to their home country, they are shipped home as fast as possible.

I have a semi-private room with minimal space and a metal bed; to me that is luxury. Some of our friends are guarding a huge SS frozen food locker. They liberate a good selection of goodies and bring them to Lonnie and me every night as we are on night duty. The latest treat was frozen apricots and a cheddar, creamy cheese in a toothpaste-type tube. Love, June.

6-13-45 General Frederick hosted a dinner dance for our nurses.

6-16-45 Some of us commute to Dachau to work.

6-20-45 *Dachau*
Dear family,

A small group of Greek prisoners built a little wooden chapel, without any help from other inmates, as a memorial to the American soldiers who lost their lives liberating the camp. The Greeks were so friendly and appreciative compared to some of the other prisoners.

Many of the patients take 15 to 17 different medications. As they improve and their dosage is cut, some of them are furious with me--as they count their pills and they think I am trying to cheat them. One man spit in my face because I wouldn't give him what he had had in the past. Language is a big problem. Some of these people don't react to a smile. On liberation day there were 31,432 internees here. The OSS and CIC from Seventh Army gave us this list. 1173 German Nationals (including six women), 848 Belgians, 1 Dane, 8 British, 11 Estonians, 3918 French, 195 Greeks, 2184 Italians, 103 Croats, 79 Serbs, 2907 Slovenes, 27 Latvians, 39 Lithuanians, 36 Alsace-Lorraines, 133 Luxemburgers, 558 Dutch, 79 Norwegians, 9082 Polish (including 96 women), 50 Romanians, 4258 Russians (including 9 women), 44 Slovakians, 30 Albanians, 6 Americans, 1 Maltese, 1 Arabian, 2 Armenians, 1 Finn, 1 Iraqi, 1 Iranian, 3 Turks, 194 Spanish, 21 Exiles, 1632 Czechoslovakians, 670 Hungarians (including 34 women), 8 Bulgarians, 4 Portuguese, 2 Swiss, 253 Austrians, 2 Annex-Germans, 3 Sudetens, 2539 Jews (including 225 women).

Many of the young boys who were here and had been here for some years were still the same height as when they came, though now shrunken and shriveled in body tissue, with sad, haunted eyes. None of the horrible pictures of this place convey the stench of rotting flesh. Very sad, June

1945 Germany in June and June in France
Dear Betty,

Alphabetically I have always headed every work roster and ended every leave roster. It was with disbelief I heard my addled Chief nurse tell me I was scheduled for two weeks leave on the French Riviera. Her addition and mine never did match; I'll count the days. What a place for a birthday. From the depths of an underground tent to the finery of Juan Les Pines was mind boggling.

Before Chiefy could change her fickle mind, I packed my two musette bags, filled my canteen and, clutching my sealed leave papers, my tentmate and I hitchhiked to the Munich airport to ride in anything that could fly. It was a scalding hot day. We boarded a small plane that bounced like a yo-yo all the way to southern France. Everyone was sick in the community-bucket at the rear of the plane. We promised ourselves that we would walk back to Germany before we would fly again in a small plane.

After a four-hour flight, our plane bounced to a chattering stop. God finally smiled on these two tired, tattered waifs because another plane sashayed in at the same time and out popped two of our old combat friends. One officer's CO was scheduled for this Riviera vacation, but that very morning his orders came to return to USA.

We spent the long sun-filled days hiking, swimming, going on boat trips up the Riviera coast, sunning, exercising in a Pedalos (a small two-

person craft, you sat upright in it and pedaled all over the harbor), playing tennis, dining at Eden Roc, and acting like millionaires on Lieutenant's allowances. We saw Dorothy McGuire in "Dear Ruth", heard Grace Moore and Ninio Martini in concert. Went to Monte Carlo but were not permitted to enter the country. Instead, we stood up on the road and looked over the postage stamp principality. It looked like a tax gimmick for the wealthy from where we stood.

Grasse's perfumed countryside, all 62,000 acres beckoned us again on a guided tour. The fragrance of orange blossoms, roses, carnations, violets, tuberoses, mignonettes, jasmine and jonquils was such a relief from Allach and Dachau. We filled our lungs with fragrance and didn't want to leave.

Every major Riviera hotel was filled with officers on leave. Dance bands played "String of Pearls", "Begin the Beguine", "In the Mood" and all the marvelous danceable pieces. It was swig and sway time for many.

The night of my birthday we dined at one of the large hotels on their beautiful terrace. The trees, shrubs and bowers were illuminated with soft, seductive lights. I wore my slightly wrinkled, strapless formal. My friend had ordered a rose for my hair. But with the language problem, when it arrived it had blossomed into six huge, deep-red roses to be worn on my wrist. But who cared. The balmy ocean breezes blew quietly over us. The nightmare of the war seemed far away.

Suddenly loud squabbling broke out above us on one of the upper balconies. We glanced up to see a paratroop officer and French girl pushing each other and shrieking--he was saying "Kiss me" and she was saying "Non, non." Then he shouted ,"Kiss me or I'll jump". She refused. He shouted "Geronimo" and jumped. He landed on a table just a few feet away--one leg shoved up into his abdominal cavity. His alcohol content kept his pain hopefully to the minimum as he was dashed off to a local hospital--to recover and regret.

June 29th (I told you Chiefy couldn't add or read, the rest period was for seven days plus travel time) . We took a troop train headed for Nancy, France. The trip back to Germany from the Riviera was in wooden-seated coaches. We were packed in like sardines. Love, June

Everyone who holidayed at the Riviera received a 23-page book of recreational and amusement facilities in this section of France.

Officers were quartered in Cannes and enlisted personnel were stationed in the Nice area.

Caution: Pro Stations operated on a 24-hour basis as the V.D. rate is extremely high.

Caution: Swimming only in very restricted areas due to mines and pollution.

Caution: MPs are there to protect you as there are many enemy agents and questionable characters floating around.

7-1-45 Dachau, Germany
Dearest family,

As the weather was too rough for flying when our pass was over, we took the filthy old French train that just crawls. It took us thirty six hours to get to Nancy. Sitting up all that time with six to eight people in a wooden compartment was a nightmare. My bum leg was throbbing. The GIs zonked out, put their heads on our shoulders, and snored. I didn't think we looked that motherly. We kept pushing their heads off from our shoulders; they were just dead weight.

For toileting and feeding, we stopped twice a day at 4:30 AM and 5:30 PM at camps that the Army has set up along the railroad tracks. It was cold, damp and dark at 4:30 AM. In the dim light a long, neck-high (for me) watering trough greeted us with spigots that spouted or dripped ice water. You washed your face and drip-dried it, brushed your teeth, swallowed some water, gulped your non-gourmet food and clambered back on the wooden tortoise.

Arriving at Nancy, France at 12:30 AM we finally found an Army hospital stationed in a chateau. They gave us a cot for the night and a hot bath. I shampooed my hair five times before I finally got all of the coal soot out of it.

Shortly after we got off the train, a freight hit it and killed twelve GIs and injured twenty. At lunch today we both discovered former roommates we'd had in the States. This afternoon at 2 PM we got a plane from Nancy to Luxembourg, another plane to Manneheim. There we were stranded. I finally found a Piper Cub pilot who was going to Munich. I packed Lonnie in his plane and sent them off. A couple of hours later a General's plane came in and I talked the pilot into flying me back to Augsburg to 7th Army headquarters. Just as we arrived there I saw a Captain who used to be in Ed's outfit in Sicily, he offered to drive me in his liberated limousine back to Dachau. Here we are supervising German doctors and nurses in caring for the DPs, as well as working ourselves.

Lonnie's Piper Cub pilot landed his plane on the road in front of our CO's house. He had a bloody fit. Unfortunately these temper tantrums don't kill. While being shredded, the trick is to say nothing, shoulders back, chin up, smile faintly while staring straight into his hate-filled eyes.

This letter will have to suffice for the entire family in answer to their 25 letters I just received tonight when I arrived. Many letters were dated late March and early April. Betty the reason I never wrote to you was I didn't have your new address. The bathing suit and the other packages have never arrived. A belated thanks for your expensive efforts.

Ruth your requests for my formal arrived today, over three months late. The answer is no, anyway. It is too sophisticated for you; I'll buy you a demure one. Mom, please send the sun glasses. I'll need them if I ever break the sleazy ones I have now; we can't buy any here. Please send my birthday package.

The latest rumor is that it is six months to a year before we'll see USA. Because of that rumor, several of the girls are asking for CBI (China, Burma, India), so they'll at least get a furlough in USA. I'm undecided and disillusioned when I see people on all sides of us going home after only four and five months over here.

Aha, brother you're a civilian. Please save your uniform so I can see it. Happy to hear of your decision to go back to college, I like your choice of a major. Colorado is the better school, isn't it?

Yes, Mom, I got my bank analysis and I appreciate all of your book-keeping activity for me. No, I don't need to check your math, you're the mathematician. For years, one nurse I know sent her allotment home to be banked and just found out that her mother had spent every dime. How lucky I have you for parents.

It would be nice to win something. I've always liked to play with words, I needed the mental stimulation of writing the entry. They probably award prizes only to their relatives. Thanks to you, Betty and Ruth for all the letters I scooped up tonight. Brother sent one letter and Dad failed miserably. Over a month without mail from home was a difficult period. I tried mental telepathy to speed the mail service. Obviously I need more practice and faith. How's the leg Mom--better--I hope? My Love, June

7-4-45 Went horseback riding, played Bridge and Jack Benny is in Berlin.

7-5-45 So peaceful since last Russian DPs left for home.

7-10-45 1st Armored friends are at Schwabish Hall.

Old friends had liberated a gorgeous Mercedes and brought it over so we could try it out on the autobahn. The MPs were out in force. A smile cancelled the ticket the MP was going to write.

7-10-45 Dachau, Germany
Dearest Betty:

Ed just left for Southhampton, England this AM.

All the troops had the opportunity to apply for college at the Sorbonne in Paris or Shrivenham University in Swindon, England. There were a limited number of people who would be chosen. Lonnie and I applied and were accepted.

If things go as planned, we will fly to England July 30th. We will be there for two months. All the professors are from leading universities at home. If the hospital goes home in the meantime, I'll finish my courses and be sent to the Replacement Depot and eventually home as I have 97 points now. If the unit is still here, I will be returned to Germany.

We have an excellent soft ball team. Our men haven't lost a game this season. Tonight was the first night we haven't had a game. Saw a couple of cute movies "Three Men in White" and "Wilson"--all about the Wilson reign of error in the White House. Imagine they'll do one for FDR. I'd like to be in charge of titling the movie.

More old friends are turning up from 5th Army in Italy. Most of them are being sent to Germany for occupation duty. They keep dropping in day after day. It's fun, I never quite know whom to expect. Lonnie's cousin came to see her today. He's a Pfc. in the 20th Armored Division and is going home next week. He got here just as the war ended. When luck was being handed out, I was on duty. Is Phin home yet? Love, June

7-16-45 Dachau, Germany
Dearest family,

This watchful waiting is hard on me, my patience is wearing paper thin. They're singing "Were You There" on the radio. Yes, I was there and still am there! Soon we shall be moving to another area. We've been relieved of our Dachau assignment. If General Patton doesn't forget about us, maybe we'll catch the next ship home. I'm ready to try swimming to Wisconsin, think I'll come up the St. Lawrence.

They're making this concentration camp a POW camp just for SS troops, I think that is fitting. Every day they come in here by the hundreds. They'll all be investigated and tried. I only hope they get their just dues.

When the Nazi officers departed from Dachau, they left behind a stable of thoroughbred horses that we ride. I was barely in the saddle when a drunken doctor who had recently joined our unit slapped the horse's rump. It reared skyward and nearly dumped me. Terrified I tightened the reins and held on until the horse calmed down. The drunken idiot just stood there and *laughed; I was soaked in sweat.*

Your V-mail just arrived, but it was so stuck together the print came off. The mail plane crashed in the sea and all the mail got soaked and salted. What a disappointment to the troops that live from letter to letter. I hadn't had any mail for about five days and when I saw the V-mail lying on my cot I whistled a merry tune. At last, news from home, but I couldn't read it.

We don't do much of anything now except get on each other's nerves. I have some beautiful snapdragons and pink phlox in my room. The DPs (displace persons) here at Dachau have a greenhouse and they keep our quarters supplied with flowers. One of the DPs was a cobbler, and he made me a pair of boots for $ 3.

We also inherited the SS Troopers Officer's Club. When I'm in the club I think of those evil people sitting here planning the torture and death of the prisoners. Some Krauts are running the club for us. It's a place to go when you get tired of your own four walls. The men play a lot of softball, but the Colonel doesn't want to let me play. Maybe he's afraid I'll show the men up. Yesterday George, a Captain I knew back in Italy, came to see me (you may recall we flew in his jeep to Naples). He is assigned to be part of the occupation troops. There are only three fellows left in his regiment who came overseas together three years ago.

Enclosed are three picture postcards of prewar Munich. Love, June

7-17-45 Dachau, Germany
Dearest family,

Unhappy day, I woke up with a severe toothache, the left side of my face swollen. All of our dental equipment has been packed away. The Colonel told me that I would have to hitchhike to Munich to a hospital for dental care as he couldn't spare a vehicle and driver to take me. The insensitive clod suggested I might ask another nurse to hike with me in case I needed help. His constant belittlement gives me enough adrenalin to keep going. Donning my helmet and wearing the usual fatigues I started my long hike. Jeeps and trucks kept whizzing by and I wished that I'd worn a skirt. I'd walked a couple of kilometers when a jeep came to a skidding stop and backed up. "Want a lift, soldier?" the driver asked. I ran toward the jeep, and the GI took one surprised look at me and said, "Is your name June, maybe you know my mother, Doug Hunt's sister, she is head of the draft board at home?" He was just a little boy when I went away to college. Saved by a hometown boy. It was good to meet a pleasant person today.

My tooth was badly abscessed and the dentist almost had to put his foot on my chin to pry it out. He tossed me a bottle of pills--which I caught naturally. They wanted to sign me up for short stop. At Abscess Alley they didn't even ask me if I'd like to rest there awhile. One tooth--less, June

7-18-45 Dachau, Germany
Dearest Betty,

This letter-writing business is an effort when you never get any letters to answer. Lonnie and I played bridge for awhile this afternoon with a doctor from Baraboo, Wis. and a doctor from the Carolinas. We all went swimming in a tiny pool fifteen foot square. Great to cool off. The sun is scalding and beats down without mercy. Very peculiar weather.

One of our doctors was permitted to use the command car to visit his brother in Nürnberg and invited me along so I could visit your darling Phin. We had just been notified we could purchase a ration of British Scotch and a magnum of champagne for a few dollars. I decided to buy my ration this time and give it to Phineas...sorta greasing the skids. Bouncing along hour after hour, I held the bottles so they wouldn't explode. When I reached his camp, his officers insisted that I eat with them, but I chose the GI mess line. The GIs in Phin's outfit call him Pops. In the men's quarters was a large deep sink used for washing out mops etc.. The men decided to chill the champagne by setting it in the bottom of this sink and letting cold water trickle slowly over it. When the champagne had cooled a bit, the large brass handle on the faucet jiggled loose and hit the bottle and it shattered in all directions -- fortunately into the sink instead of into us. It was a sobering experience for all the waiting thirsty GIs. I could just hear Mother say, "Good, God knows what is best for you; His hand works in mysterious ways."

Did you know that Patton's Third Army had 105 Generals and one strategic planner? No wonder they made such progress across France into Germany....no committees to foul up the plans. Love, June

SIXTEEN

Off to School

7-19-45

When my tentmate and I got the following Army Special Order shorthand giving us permission to go by cattle car to school in England, we chose to fly. It was a short hitchhike to the Munich airport and a saving of four days travel time. We didn't want to carry four days of meat and beans anyplace but to the garbage dump.

Special Order
NUMBER 33

The following named officers are placed on DS with Army University Center at Shrivenham, England, for purpose of attending school. O will rpt to RTO, Munich, Germany, prior to 211430 July 1945 for transportation to a channel port. Upon completion of tour of duty will ret to parent unit. TDN. Travel by motor veh and/or rail is stazd. Four (4) days rations will be carried by each individual. Auth: Ltr Hq 3d U S Army, subject and file: "Quotas for Attendance at Army University Center # 1, AG 352-Gen-GNMCC, 3 July 1945", as amended, and Message No 1, Office of the Surgeon, Third US Army, 17 July 1945.

7-21-45 Munich, Germany

    Fog settled in shortly after our takeoff. Swooping down through the fog to find the white cliffs of Dover was exciting. Flying low over London, the view was sickening.

7-23-45 London, England
Dearest Betty,

    Since we landed we have been running full tilt: exploring, looking in, looking on, looking at Buckingham Palace, the Tower of London, Parliament buildings, Piccadilly Circus, the Haymarket and Petticoat Lane (the equivalent of Maxwell Street in Chicago), St. Paul's Cathedral and Westminster Abbey, Madame Tussaud's Wax Museum, and getting involved with the speakers in Hyde Park. By the time we finished our swivel vision tour our memory tablets were filled to overflowing. Chimney pots fascinated Lonnie; Louisiana doesn't have any. Her southern drawl intrigued a number of followers. She'd squeal with delight and ask questions about everything we saw and this string of characters trailed along behind us to explain everything. Of course, we had problems understanding their accent and explanations.

    Piccadilly Circus is full of prostitutes day and night. The fellows told us the females think if they have sex standing up they won't get pregnant.

    Some Brits really dislike the Americans. This is the most unfriendly country we have been in and they're our Allies. War makes strange bedfellows. It appears they only want our money, our materiel, our food, and our men to help fight their wars.

    Returning from the sight-seeing trip, we tried to contact Ed who was supposedly at Southampton. I couldn't get his unit but the officer in charge of the staging area said they definitely were there. Lonnie and I packed our overnight bags and grabbed a train for Southampton. We arrived there at 9:30 PM and called the number we had been given. It was not a Southampton number but a number for Tidworth, about fifty miles north of the harbor. We were stranded. With believable sincerity I told a fairy tale of woe to the transportation officer who immediately assigned us a recon vehicle plus a driver to go to Tidworth.

    At midnight we reached the restricted area where the unit was billeted. It was pitch dark, quiet, forbidding. Everyone was sound asleep, except the guard who materialized out of the blackness when we drove in. Ed was not with them. They had left him at Le Havre, France to bring the trucks over when there was enough shipping space. The helpful guard scrounged a few extra blankets for us. In full uniform we curled up on some dirty old straw bales and canvas in a storage shed and fell asleep completely worn out.

This morning the unit got march orders. They scooted us over to Andover, where we caught a train to London.

We arrived here in time for lunch. They have all sorts of food, plenty of ice cream and Cokes. What a chowhound's paradise, the one exception is the sausages, they are made of awful tasting cereal. Meals are quite expensive. After lunch we shopped at the PX and the QM, took a long hike, ate supper and went to see the stage play "Arsenic and Old Lace," starring Noel Coward. It has been playing continuously for over three years. It was the best comedy I'd ever seen. I'd like to play the part of one of the old ladies.

We changed all the rest of our marks to pounds. They have so many different coins and they all look alike, but their value is different. We'll catch on soon or be the poorer for it. Love, June

7-24-45 We live in Grosvenor Square.

7-25-45 Lonnie and I went to the Diamond Horseshoe with a Navy escort.

7-26-45 Joe, General Marshall's aide, escorted us around London.

7-27-45 Joe, and I went dancing at the Berkeley Hotel, Wilton Place, Knightsbridge, courtesy of the British War Department. I wore a formal and a corsage. We were the only Americans there, and the British brass snubbed us royally. A white hanky dangled from the cuff of the Brit's uniform. As no one spoke to us all evening, I couldn't ask the "why" of their quaint custom. Their wives were quite fat and elderly. We did enjoy the food and dancing.

7-29-45 Shrivenham University
Dearest family,

Ed didn't get over to England until the 27th. Lonnie and I stayed in London until he came for us. They're guarding POWs at a hospital in Cambridge. What a beautiful set up. The hospital has been in the same spot for the last two years. They have lawns and beautiful flower gardens. The hospital personnel there have no concept of the horrible life we led in the field.

The British charge the US Army 25 cents per head per day for each American in the camp. They have 3000 people there. All hospitals in England are run the same way--some even cost more we were told. Most of the hospitals are put up on some old waste land that isn't worth $5 an acre.

Watch, when we leave these areas all the fine equipment will be given to the British. It's cheaper than shipping it home and they have so little.

One day Lonnie and I visited the University at Cambridge, the architecture is very impressive. We made the trip in a jeep. Just the other side of Buckingham we had a flat tire. Army jeeps don't carry repair equipment, and our spare tire didn't have an inner tube. We were miles from nowhere and most Americans who were based here have gone home to ticker tape parades. Army traffic was nil. The driver was helpless, useless, unimaginative.

It was a very hot day, I suggested that he and Lonnie stay with the jeep in the shade. I started walking to find help. 'Twas better than a mile to the first farm house; they didn't have a phone. The lady thought that one of the farms miles down the road had one. Spying a bicycle I asked if I could borrow it to ride to these farms. Grudgingly she lent me the bike, and I gave her my name and serial number.

A few miles later I found a farm home that had a phone and asked if I could make a long distance call. Until I displayed some money she didn't answer. Their phone system isn't AT&T. After much difficulty I got through to the base, my friends weren't there but I left a message for them...send help.

Hot, hungry and exhausted I returned to the jeep. My glum companions were sitting on a blanket on the ground playing Hearts. In the middle of one game, Lonnie and I had to use a latrine...we waded through some tall grain and without looking I backhanded some tall weeds to make a cozy spot. In tune with the rest of our day, the weeds turned out to be nettles; my hand still tingles from the contact. Better the hand than the heinie.

In three hours no vehicles had passed. We contemplated sending up smoke signals but we had no matches...miraculously a jeep appeared. We borrowed his spare tire and arrived back at the base long after chow time. If you're not there on time you don't eat. Lonnie and I just finished a can of sardines we brought from Munich for a starved occasion such as this. For bread we had one doughnut-sized roll we got in London three days ago. Lonnie sliced it, topped it with sardines....voilà, appetizers. Aren't we the elegant ones?

There's a chapel on campus and we went to church, so refreshing to hear a good sermon. Oxford isn't far from here. Someday we might get a pass to go there and browse.

We live in duplexes that have small, wall-hanging, coin-operated gas heaters for water. The gadgets in the bedrooms don't work. There are more doors and hallways than room space. The architect must have been a student, *or it was a war project designed as a rat maze. Well, dears, I must go to bed; I've had a tiresome day and tomorrow holds so much that I must do correctly. I'll try and write frequently. It has been four years since I went to college and actually studied.*

There are 15 women students and 4500 male students. Love, June

7-30-45 Shrivenham
Dear Betty,

I wrote to a dear old former patient of mine, Miss Nellie Page from Canton, Missouri telling her I would be here at the University for two months and that President Truman was to give the opening address. Her father was very involved in Missouri politics, and Truman was one young man they had assisted over the years. She promptly notified Truman that I would be a student here and that he should look me up when he arrived. She has my picture in uniform on top of her piano between Harry's picture and his sister's picture.

Miss Nellie promised me that she wouldn't tell him that I'd been a rabid Republican since the age of eight and that I came from Bob LaFollette country. She thought it would be great sport to be a mouse in the house where we would meet on campus.

It was not to be. Truman didn't show and sent a General instead. My Journalism professor is from the University of Wisconsin; it feels just like home. Love, June

8-6-45 The first atomic bomb was dropped over Hiroshima, Japan, killing and injuring 160,000 people. At the time, I was in Journalism class in Swindon, England, and as this flash appeared on the teletype machine at my elbow, I read the message to the class. Everyone asked in unison, "What is an atomic bomb?"

Enola Gay was the name of the plane that dropped the bomb. We obviously received the message the same time as General Eisenhower and his staff.

8-12-45 Shrivenham American University, England
Dearest family,

Vas ist mit Die? No mail in weeks and I need some so badly. I fret and fume and worry and get all empty inside. Where is brother? How's my little lady, Snooks? Did Phin get home safely? How's your leg, Mom? Has Dad been behaving? Is Betty pregnant and if not--why not? Did my packages ever arrive safely? Did Dad pay my insurance? Is the evergreen sweet corn ripe yet? How's the bass fishing, or have I got my seasons mixed? Has rationing let up a bit and on what? Do you miss me? I've forgotten what you look like. I don't imagine I'd even recognize Snooks. Will she be a Junior this year? What classes will she be taking? This place is quite nice, but I want to go to America so badly. Love, June

8-17-45 Went to London for the weekend and saw "Blithe Spirit". The ushers charge for taking you to your seat. At intermission they hawked food up and down the aisles.

8-19-45 Visited the London zoo and all the animals looked very hungry. Their fur lacks luster. Poor beasts. We went walking along the Thames at night, and it started to rain. We couldn't get a cab, and were drenched to the skin, and chilled.

8-20-45 The soaking rain put me in the dispensary for two days.

8-22-45 Shrivenham
Dear Betty,
*   We study, play tennis, go to the gym and shoot baskets, ride bicycles to the neighboring villages and go dancing in the local gym. Practically everyone goes to church every time they have a service. We sing all the old familiar hymns. I'm taking French conversation, also voice lessons and have a private tutor.*
*   Some evenings we go to little village fairs or carnivals and knock down milk bottles with a hard ball. I won many homemade prizes. Pen holders and flower vases were popular items made from old glass bottles covered with wall paper or Christmas cards and sealed with shellac.*
One night I shared a cab with some soldiers to a nearby village. They had negotiated the cab fare in advance with the driver. When we got there he demanded double fare. The men picked up his cab and turned it completely over and spun the wheels on the cab, handed him the money they had agreed on and walked off. We had miles to walk back but it was worth it. I kept my cool and never said a word.
*   Could you send me some summer -weight lingerie, the kind human beings wear. I'm so tired of olive-drab Army-thickness. Choose a soft fabric any color but olive drab. Love, June*

9-8-45 Lonnie and I visited the place where the author was inspired to write the song Rock of Ages. Standing in the cleft of the rock, we sang the hymn with joyous abandon. We also visited Bath, Wells, Bristol and some interesting caves. The caves weren't as super as Carlsbad, New Mexico or Luray in the Blue Ridge Mountains.

9-12-45 Shrivenham University

We received the following orders, gathered our four student enlisted men and took a train to London. Spent the night at the Red Cross.

RESTRICTED
HEADQUARTERS SHRIVENHAM AMERICAN UNIVERSITY
APO 756   US ARMY
10 September 1945
SPECIAL ORDERS
NUMBER ...74
17. Fol named Off and EM (Stu) are reld fr further DS this University, fr SD w/Stu Co indicated and fr atchmt Shrivenham American University, WP ..... Field Hosp. APO 758, w/o delay, rptg upon arrival to the CO thereof for dy:

Travel by commercial, mil and /or naval acft, army T, rail and /or mtr T is auth. TCNT> TDN> 60-136 P 432-02 A 212/60425. PAC TWX ......Field Hosp. APO 758, 7 Sep 45.

My left knee locked and I had difficulty walking. Just before we left Shrivenham I was walking down the street when I met a GI riding a bicycle that had hand brakes. He saluted me, lost control of the bike and crashed into my left knee.

9-14-45 Schongau, Germany
Dearest Ruthie,

Yesterday morning I had breakfast in London, England; dinner in Paris, France; and supper in Frankfort, Germany. Lonnie and I and our four enlisted men received orders to leave the University and report back to our unit in Germany, which was leaving immediately for the States. We were raring to go.

Flying was the way to go if we could find someone to take us. I volunteered to get us back, by broomstick if necessary. The only thing I asked of my five cohorts was that they stay out of sight when we got to the airport but keep their eyes on me so I could wave to them to come out of hiding if I got a plane.

Checking out the various planes that could hold all of us, I approached a likely looking pilot and asked if he was planning to fly to Germany and, if so, would he take me along. He was only going to Paris but was delighted to befriend me and I sealed my deal with a handshake. While we were still holding hands, I casually mentioned that I had four GIs and another nurse with me. When I waved to them they came bounding happily around the corner. The flight to Paris was short and sensational. We were saving lots of time by flying and had time to goof off and look around.

At the Paris airport I used the London approach to get us a flight to Germany. Arriving in Frankfurt, I found a field phone and called Betty's old landlord, a regular Army officer from Oklahoma, who was stationed in Weisbaden. The friendly gentleman was happy to hear from me and invited me to spend the night at his villa. I accepted for the six of us. He was extremely gracious and sent transportation to pick us up, as he was preparing for his promotion party that evening.

We were met at the gate by his Sgt. who took care of our men for the night. Apparently the Colonel hadn't told the rest of his guests we were coming. An old WAC officer answered our knock. Cheerfully I said, "We've come to the party, sorry we're late, we're spending the night." If looks could kill we would both have perished on the spot. WAC..O (O for officer or whatever) left us standing at the door.

Lonnie and I are adept at ignoring rude behavior. We have an ingenious well inside of us that bubbles up joy juice. All we have to do is to look at each other and smile to rise above adversity. We've seen so many naked people and they're really funny--putting uniforms on them doesn't change their picture in our eyes. The party was great sport and the 'door opener' suddenly got a severe headache and left.

At 8:15 AM today we flew from Frankfurt to Nürnberg and then to Munich in time for lunch. There we phoned our hospital, and they sent transportation. Rotten roads made the trip exhausting. We reached Schongau in time for a supper of steak and ice cream. They have a German chef who is proud of his profession and does justice to the food.

After all that flitting I'm sleepy. Just finished my laundry and I'm eyeing that old cot with affection. See you soon, June

SEVENTEEN

Sailing to Sanity

9-17-45 Reims, France
Evening darlings,
Could be I'm finally coming home. I wanted to surprise you but I couldn't keep the secret any longer without bursting my seams. That's why I left England early, summer school wasn't finished until the end of September. They graded us anyway.

We had a mad dash by air from England to Germany and arrived just in time, as what was left of our unit was starting a long trek back across the continent by ambulance and truck. As Lonnie and I were the only two women, we had an ambulance and two drivers to ourselves. Leaving Schongau, Germany at midnight on the 15th we drove for eighteen hours arriving at Nancy, France the night of the 16th. We slept in a camp there and left this morning for Camp Philadelphia here at Reims.

When I'm actually coming I don't know, but I'll call you from the depot when I reach home plate. The reason I didn't tell you before is...I was afraid you wouldn't drive brother to college in Colorado if you knew. You'll enjoy the trip and the mountains. Don't tell anyone I'm coming home, as I don't want to see a lot of people...PLEASE. Love, June

9-19-45 Reims, France
Dearest family,

Sitting and waiting isn't fun. Yesterday we had influenza shots, most of the girls got sick. I'm still healthy and thankful for small mercies. Now that I have idle hands and idle time to write scintillating letters, I have nothing witty to tell. The censor has probably gone to his reward in Times Square, covered with combat ribbons filched from letters home.

Remember my roommate at the U of Chicago, she's in the Assembly area too, and going home with us. Only thirteen months overseas and she's sailing. You can see how badly our hospital was neglected after the cessation of hostilities.

Please find me a soapbox to use on landing. They can take General Patton and stuff him. Ever since we were transferred to 3rd Army they have shoved us around. They sent all of their high point units home months ago and completely forgot about us. Patton is probably out riding horses everyday or electioneering, instead of pushing the proper paperwork into the proper pigeon holes.

One of our irate enlisted men went to 3rd Army headquarters by himself and demanded to know why we were still over here, while units with half the points we have had gone home months ago to ticker tape parades in New York city. Two days after this brave soldier stood his ground, we received orders to return to USA. They had lost our paper trail after they dumped us in Dachau. How soon they forget. Love, June

9-25-45
Dear Mom,

No, I never save anyone's letters. We have to carry everything on our own backs, so I learned to travel light years ago.

Something is wrong with my left knee. The joint locks every now and then, it hurts to walk. I reported to the dispensary and they sent me to a General hospital in Mourmelon to have it x- rayed and have an orthopedic consultation. X-ray revealed I have a small chip of cartilage loose in my knee joint. Surgery, they say, is the only cure. Why do surgeons always say that? Immediately upon arrival in USA I should have this done. The doctor said I'd be hospitalized at least three weeks. A furlough at home now if I couldn't walk wouldn't give me much pleasure. As Dad would say, I'm about as low as a cricket's tit...I'd rather be fine as a frog's hair!

When we were in North Africa, in one of the Divisions we supported there was a Major Butcher. In civilian life he was Dr. Butcher. Every September 25th is trivia day and I get silly like this.

This copy is of my EMT (emergency medical tag).

189th General Hospital   1330 Hours
1st Lt ANC
Xray left knee
Orthopedic consultation
Line of duty: Yes

SUPPLEMENTAL RECORD
25 Sept 45
> *Small chip of cartilage off medial condyle--loose in knee joint. Moves easily. No interference with motion. Ace bandage & PT W?H? B. Brewster Capt. (He was not a Palmer Method graduate.)*
>
> *No interference with motion. (The man is daft, he about killed me when he manipulated it. I was ready to grab his knee and inject some gravel into his joint, but you just can't piddle with a Captain's patella.)*
>
> *Reminds me of a surgeon I worked for who spent his life doing sigmoidoscopic and pelvic exams on desperate people. He rammed the scope around like he was reaming out a sewer pipe. I prayed for the day he would need one himself. That prayer went straight to Heaven, my employer insisted I give him a grain of codeine before he went to be scoped. He had a personality change after that--strange--considering they were working on the opposite end of his anatomy. Dr. Ramrod became Dr. Gentle Correctum. Love, June*

9-26-45 Reims, France

We got orders last night to fly to USA today. All of our belongings were to be stored in our footlockers for shipment. As we were leaving for the airport, our flight was cancelled. I wonder what movie star and entourage, or non-combatant, globe-trotting congressman took our plane home.

9-29-45 Reims France,

Lonnie and her friend Walter and I went to the football game. The 101st Airborne was playing OISE base section, and the Reims Cathedral made a memorable background. I took colored photographs of the game.

Walt noticed that there wasn't anyone in the General's box and thought we might as well use it. He figured if the General came he wouldn't kick two nurses out.

10-3-45 Reims, France, 9:00 AM
Dearest family,
    No news in our case doesn't signify good news, but that is our plight at present. Keep writing to me, one never knows how long I'll be stuck here. There is absolutely nothing to do all day but feed ourselves and keep clean. We can't leave the area as orders may come at any time, and I wouldn't want to miss them. Idleness breeds discontent, and we have a great deal of both.
    FLASH !! 4 PM
    Orders just came for us to hurry and pack and clear the post as we would be leaving at 1 AM. We did as ordered, but as we finished packing, orders came ,"Nurses aren't going, only the male officers and enlisted men." Why? Because they won't let the nurses ride in 3rd class trains. It's funny, some of our nurses came all the way from Germany in a boxcar. We had the Colonel try again--told him we'd ride in anything. He called General Patton...the General said ,"NO! " Tonight our men leave without us. As to when we will catch up to them, we don't know.
    I was in Reims in the PX and saw a Captain I'd had for a patient at Ft. Custer in October 1942. He was going home, too, though he'd only been here with the 94th Division for 14 months. Enclosed are ten snapshots. Love, June

10-4-45 Mourmelon, France, 55th General Hospital
Dearest family,
    We were moved out of the assembly area this afternoon to make room for incoming nurses who have to be processed. After supper we were notified that the six remaining original nurses in our unit with their hundred points each were to report to the harbor at Le Havre. Now we will have to wait here until they send transportation for us.
    Lonnie was transferred out of the unit into the 178th General hospital because she is regular Army and has to stay over here in the Army of Occupation. The poor dear is heart broken. Though she doesn't cry, she just sits and stares around the room. She hasn't had a furlough in four years and then they gave her time off for her father's funeral. It's a bitter pill to swallow.
    I'll keep using my old address as a return until I get something different. Enclosed are eleven snapshots. Love, June

10-5-45 Camp Carlisle
    We were ordered back here today in one of those rush orders

to leave for Le Havre at 1 PM. We waited and waited, but transportation never came for us. Finally at five o'clock orders came that we should leave at 6:30 AM for Le Havre in buses.

Tonight they took all of our luggage away from us and sent it ahead. We are now supposed to go to Southampton, England and sail on the Queen Mary. Now I ask you, hasn't that been the most idiotic waste of time, money, patience and transportation for the past three weeks. I was in England only a short drive from Southampton last September when I was still in school. Will write again, if I can find some stationery and locate my printable, scattered thoughts.

None of us had enough script to buy anything, so I passed my cap and collected script scraps and hurried over to the PX to buy some souvenirs. One was a brass paper weight of a little Belgian prince urinating, the story was worth the price. I also purchased several small engravings of famous places. The shopping interlude was a welcome relief. Enclosed are eleven snapshots. Love, June

RESTRICTED

HEADQUARTERS CAMP CARLISLE
Oise Intermediate Section
APO 752   US Army

SPECIAL ORDER   5 October 1945
NUMBER   44
1. Fol O, ANC, org ind, are reld asgmt ind below and atchd unasgd to the 166th General Hospital, APO 562, Le Havre, France, WP o/a 5 Oct 45 by Govt trans to Le Havre, France to arrive by 6 Oct 45, reporting upon arrival to CO, Camp Phillip Morris.
BY ORDER OF LIEUTENANT COLONEL KOOPS, JR:
There were 56 high-point nurses on these orders. Four were Captains and all the rest were 1st Lieutenants, which shows how shabbily the nurses were treated in the promotion pursuit game.

10-6-45 Again we drove to Le Havre arriving at 6:30 AM. At 6 PM we returned to the Assembly area as there was no ship for us.

10-8-45 *Camp Phillip Morris, Le Havre, France*
Dear Betty,
I have had it! Methinks the officer in charge of this place is a graduate

of Mismanagement University. Welcome to snafu city Army-style. I've been shunted from the British Isles, regrouped in southern Germany, assembled, processed, staged and shafted in France...the gall of it all. Monthly I'm doing nothing but wasting government money, my life, and getting more impatient by the hour.

Did I hear you ask where is my Chief Nurse? She flew home eons ago. If you're in command, shouldn't you be the last to leave the sinking ship instead of the first? Before she left she used me for her tearful, daughter-confessor conference about the whole war, gave me her home address and begged me to write. Her hindsight was very revealing, little good it does me now; she hoped my scars would heal for the stacked deck I'd been dealt in the unit. The big shock to me was that I had been slated to be rotated to the States in Italy because I'd had severe jaundice and malaria a number of times. Instead at the last minute, she sent a slightly older nurse home who was buddy buddy with her and had had a session of diarrhea. Who didn't have diarrhea? Oh, if I could but count the times. Diarrhea was part of the Army diet, if you ate their food....you got it!

October 3rd our unit got orders to leave for Marseilles, but the men couldn't take us with them as they were going in 3rd class coaches. For the past 32 months in this hellish hole, we've been freezing or frying, starving and working days non-ending. In our frequent battle moves, we were hurled about and hauled about like cattle in a truck. Constantly thrown side to side and pitched end to end, we wrenched our backs. Now some DAMN General decides that we can't go with our men until they get 1st class coaches for us. What's a 1st class coach? Where have they been hiding them all these years?

The men had no choice but to leave us at Camp Carlisle. The next day we are moved two miles to the 55th General hospital, where we are told to await transportation to join our men in the south. That night orders came saying that we should report back to Carlisle at 11 AM to leave for Le Havre--as new orders have come in by cable direct from Washington, D.C. saying that there is a ship there waiting for 152 high-point nurses to go home immediately.

Next morning, we went back the two miles to Camp Carlisle with our trifling worldly possessions to get that transportation for Le Havre. We waited there all day and all night until the next morning at 6:30 AM.. We finally found ourselves on the way to Le Havre. After a twelve-hour ride, we bounced into Camp Phillip Morris. It's rumored we leave on one of the Queens from Southampton the 9th of October.

To waste more time and patience, they tell us we have to have another *physical. Two jokes in one week is too much. We just had one at Carlisle. There the physical consisted of the doctor looking in your mouth for about a second. I had just said the A of Ah when it was over. At this commercial cigarette camp, Doctor Caduceus barely touched our upper torso with his stethoscope. Obviously all those bare-breasted women frightened him.*

This morning THEY (the people who don't know what they are doing) called a meeting and told us THEY were sorry, but there wasn't any transportation for us to USA until later this month, possibly the 15th. If Hitler rose from the dead today, he could whip us all by himself.

In the meantime, our men are still waiting for us in Marseilles. October 11th is their sailing date. They'll beat us home. All of our records are with them and we can't get discharged from the Army until we get those back.

Worse than that, for so-called safe keeping, our MAC from Arizona took all of the nurse's German cameras and my Luger with the beautiful shoulder holster with the bullet hole in it. The Luger saved Fred's life and he gave it to me to keep forever. Yes, the MAC gave us a receipt for the goodies that he had coveted. Think we'll ever see them again?

It's too bad we got lost in the shuffle. At one point in this original lesson in stupidity, I was told that I was to be flown home, that I should ship my footlocker home by parcel post, and that it would get there in a matter of days. However, I would have to pay the postage myself--which was $5. Otherwise THEY said it would take six months for the footlocker to get home through the usual channels. My plane trip was cancelled, and I was left with the barest of essentials to wear. I'm weary with wandering and wondering and feign would lie down, June

10-9-45 Orders cancelled to sail....again.

10-15-45 Somewhere in France, I think.
Dearest family,
Have you noticed that my last few letters were edged in black? Very apropos. We board the West Point Tuesday at 7 AM for the trip home, provided they don't change those orders again.

There was a sign-up sheet for nurses willing to give flu shots to the 7000 GIs ready to sail home. Few volunteered, but I did. Now my right hand is swollen from the punishing exercise. It looks more like a catcher's mitt.

Two days ago they moved us over to the other side of Camp Phillip Morris. One day they moved us from one side of our quarters to the opposite side. I guess just so they could say that we weren't idle but had moved.

Visualize the headlines HIGH POINT NURSES HAVE MOVING EXPE-
RIENCE.

It's a bit better here, with only 16 nurses to a wooden barracks.
Over at Carlisle, 90 nurses "livid" in an elephant tent they had erected. No
self-respecting elephant herd would have lived there. It was very noisy and
crowded. I kept waiting for Ringling Brothers Barnum and Bailey clowns
and animals to appear and entertain us. Just the thought of roasted peanuts
kept me alive.

We played ping pong and croquet, and yesterday we pitched horse-
shoes. None of us have much ambition. Everyone is discouraged with our
Uncle Sam. Something is always wrong with the French plumbing; may be
the French plumber. Maybe he's like Lil Abner's girl friend--PLUM DUMB.
Because of the critical shortage of water, we can't get enough to take a bath,
and if there is water it is always ice cold. Cold showers for the troops must
have been part of the master plan.

We'll probably land in USA a bunch of dirty, tired and really worn-
out gals, with weather-beaten faces, lined with wrinkles, even grey hair.
Our clothes are in sad shape now, but we'll try not to embarrass the at-home
Americans too much. I think we dock at Hampton Roads, Virginia. That,
however, is only a rumor. This whole place is a rumor mill.

I have no idea how long it will take us to cross the Atlantic this time.
It's incredible that I should be coming home in one piece. Love, June

10-16-45 Aboard the West Point (a 1938 cruise ship that had been
converted to a troop transport in 1941)

Remembering the bloody seasickness of my last Atlantic crossing, I brought two sleeping pills. When the waves started going over
the smokestacks and visibility was zero, I took the pills but did not
retire to my bunk. That stormy evening they served pork chops, but
only a handful of us were well enough to eat. Those who thought
they were well enough to eat came to the mess, took one look at the
greasy meat and made a mess. There was no limit on seconds, thirds
and even fourths for the storm survivors.

After eating more than my quota of chops, I complimented
the cooks and asked about their ice cream supply -- my favorite
food. How I craved it. I swore I could eat a quart. They laughed and
promised that when the storm abated they would meet me by the first
smokestack with a quart of maple nut ice cream. If I consumed it all,
they would give me a gallon to take to my bunkmates. They doubted
my capacity and made bets that I couldn't eat a quart. However, two

people had to witness the event. After the storm passed, I went to the appointed spot. It was getting dark. Two characters, sporting a flashlight appeared with a biblical measure of ice cream....fully packed, mounded high and running over. I shivered while I ate in the windy spot they had chosen, collected my prize, and elated my friends.

The days rushed by as we swapped stories of the past few years, dissected our commanders, and shared dog-eared photos of our families. Shuffleboard, cards and conversation about our futures filled the spare moments. We were rag-tag strangers from all over America who had helped win the war, and it was sad parting. Our lives had been permanently altered; people who had stayed at home would never understand us. The West Point sidled into the near-deserted harbor in Newport News, Virginia. Home at last, five months late. We disembarked into a shabby dirty area -- no bands, no flags, no welcoming crowds. A few bums shuffled along the Southern Railroad tracks, two scrawny lonely dogs sniffing after them.

We boarded a filthy, vermin-infested troop train that smelled of stale tobacco, sweat and urine. Slumping into the hard, soiled seats, we stared at each other in disbelief....a coach load of high-point nurses home from the Big War. It was quiet; people immersed in their own thoughts.

We heard hurried steps and then sweet feminine voices chorused "Welcome Home". Several grey-haired Gray Ladies in uniform appeared, carrying trays of milk and cookies. They spoke to each of us. When it was my turn to be served a cardboard carton of milk, I choked because the lump in my throat was so big it hurt to swallow. Tears spilled down my face.

"All of this I saw, and part of it I was."
Herodotus, circa 400 B.C.

"And so say I."
June Wandrey, circa 1945 A.D.